SOGHOMON TEH

REMEMBRANCES

THE ASSASSINATION OF TALAAT PASHA

as told to

Vahan Minakhorian

translated into English by

Bedo Demirdjian

Gomidas Institute
London

Acknowledgments

Gomidas Institute acknowledges the Pomegranate Foundation's support for this book with donations from David and Margaret Mgrublian Endowment, Andrea Marootian Castello, Maggie Mangasarian Goschin, John Pridjian and the Ignatius Foundation. Also thank you to the ARF History Museum (Yerevan), the Armenian National Archives (Yerevan), the Armenian Genocide-Institute (Yerevan), Institute for Armenian Studies (YSU), the Mekhitarist Congregation (Vienna), Lepsiushaus (Potsdam), as well as Carla Garapedian, Gohar Khanumian, Vincent Lima, Pietro Shakarian and Gregory Topalian. A special thank you to Yervant Pamboukian (Beirut) for his path-breaking work over the years, and Bedo Demirdjian for the actual translation of this work and his ceaseless support to bring the project to fruition. Finally, we thank the ARF-Dashnkatsutiun, the original copyright holder of the Tehlirian memoir, for permitting us to publish this important work.

ISBN 978-1-909382-54-1   02 03 04 05

For further details and comment please contact:
Gomidas Institute
42 Blythe Rd.
London, W14 0HA
England
Email: *info@gomidas.org*

CONTENTS

Soghomon Tehlirian (cir. 1953).

Preface

As a grandchild of genocide survivors, I was always intrigued by the case of Soghomon Tehlirian.

I remember reading the first English translation of the trial transcript in *The Case of Soghomon Tehlirian* by Vartkes Yeghiayan. In that book's preface, Yeghiayan talks about meeting Tehlirian not long after he arrived in the United States, sometime around 1958. Vartkes' father was close to George Mardikian, a well-known businessman and restauranteur in the San Francisco Armenian community. Mardikian had employed Tehlirian as a bookkeeper.

One day, in Mardikian's office, Vartkes met Tehlirian. They struck up an acquaintance. Vartkes was the head of the newly-established Armenian Students Association at UC Berkeley. Over the next two years, Tehlirian would ask Vartkes if he might be interested in translating his memoir, which had been recently published in Armenian. Vartkes was humbled, but told Tehlirian he didn't think his Armenian was good enough to translate his memoir.

In April 1960, Tehlirian's son Zaven told Vartkes that his father was in the hospital. Vartkes visited him there. Tehlirian had suffered a stroke but he didn't want to talk about his health. He diverted the conversation to his memoir, asking Vartkes once again if he would translate it into English. Vartkes declined again. So Tehlirian took another tack – why not translate the German transcript of the trial?

Vartkes didn't know there was a German transcript available of the trial. Tehlirian asked his wife Anahid to go home and fetch a copy. "In a day or two you can come back and we will discuss it," Tehlirian told Vartkes. That never happened. Soghomon Tehlirian died before Vartkes could give him his answer. Vartkes would later publish the trial transcript in *The Case of Soghomon Tehlirian.*

What about Tehlirian's autobiography? It would be another 62 years before an English translation would be published.

That is this book.

I recount this story partly to put a marker down about the history of this translation. But I tell it also to bring Soghomon Tehlirian to life. What did *he* want? On his deathbed, he made his wish clear. He wanted his story to be told to an English-speaking audience. In 1960, Tehlirian couldn't know that English would become an international language that it is now. That said, as a new resident of the United States, he could see the importance of telling Americans his story.

Providing an English translation of Tehlirian's autobiography is a way of telling Tehlirian's story to the world. More than a half century has passed since he died, but his side of the story is now firmly on the record. That's important for anyone wanting to understand not only what happened during the Armenian Genocide, but also its aftermath – legally and historically.

—Carla Garapedian, May 2022

Introduction

About this Memoir[1]

"Soghomon Tehlirian's memoir does not present the entire story of Talaat's assassination... [T]his is not the time to relate the whole story to the public. ... However, Soghomon Tehlirian's memoir will always remain an essential part in that history."
  —Vahan Navasartian, 1953

The historiography surrounding the 1921 assassination of Talaat Pasha in Berlin is still hindered by a paucity of sources and subject to speculation.[2] Many accounts dwell on Talaat as the architect of the Armenian Genocide and the righteous nature of his assassination by an Armenian avenger. Other narratives valorize Talaat as a great Turkish patriot who was treacherously gunned down by an Armenian nationalist fanatic. Explanations for the killing range from an act of revenge to the more aspiring-to-be-sophisticated assertions involving broader, geopolitical considerations and foreign powers. Not all explanations are equally plausible, but all agree that the Armenian Revolutionary Federation (ARF) was the immediate organizer of the assassination and that Soghomon Tehlirian was the assassin. It is in this context that Tehlirian's memoir remains a critical reference in its own right. While Tehlirian was not privy to the political background behind Talaat's assassination, his account provides fascinating details about him as the man who was driven to kill Talaat, how he was recruited for that task by the ARF, and how he carried out the assassination. Furthermore, given that his memoir was published by and with the consent of the ARF, his work constitutes a semi-official statement by the ARF regarding its role in Talaat's demise.[3] To date, the ARF has not come forth with a clearer statement regarding its role behind the assassination of Talaat Pasha, and it may never do so.[4]

* * *

Soghomon Tehlirian's Remembrances: The Assassination of Talaat Pasha (Cairo: Housaper, 1953) was produced by three people in Belgrade, Yugoslavia (Serbia), in 1942-43, and went through two phases of preparation. The first was the collective exercise of writing the manuscript between 1942 and 1943; the second, the collective exercise of editing it for publication between 1951 and 1953. These phases involved different actors, but Tehlirian was central to both. The core content was initially provided by Tehlirian, the manuscript was written by Vahan Minakhorian, and a third collaborator was

Arshalouys Asdvadzadrian.[5] These three men worked closely together and cooperated to create a coherent work with some integrity.[6] Minakhorian wrote the account because, unlike Tehlirian, he was an accomplished writer.[7] He was also suited for the task because of his own experiences as a survivor of the Armenian Genocide.[8]

Politically, Tehlirian and Asdvadzadrian were members of the Armenian Revolutionary Federation (ARF), while Minakhorian was a former member of the Armenian Social Revolutionary party.[9] These differences gave them a certain critical edge when working together.[10] Furthermore, Tehlirian did not expect his memoir to be published during his lifetime and was not concerned about negative consequences following its release.[11] His work also benefitted from the use of published sources for important details and accuracy.[12]

While the memoir was finished in 1943, it was considered for publication circa 1949, and accepted to be published in 1951.[13] The lead editor was Simon Vratsian in Beirut, while Tehlirian, who was living in Casablanca at that time, dealt mainly with his editors at Housaper publishing house in Cairo – Vahan Navasartian, Kapriel Lazian and Yervant Khatanasian. It is important to note that at that time Vratsian was a veteran leader of the ARF and the other three editors were all members of the ARF Bureau. Moreover, Housaper publishing house, which printed the work, was an organ of the ARF. The Tehlirian memoir thus bore the stamp of the ARF and was probably the first authoritative, though indirect, disclosure concerning the organization's role in the assassination of Talaat Pasha.[14]

According to the correspondence records between Tehlirian and his editors, Tehlirian stood by the original text of his memoir and scrutinized the editorial process prior to publication.[15] For example, he accepted Vratsian's suggestion to obscure the names of a number of ARF operatives involved in Talaat's assassination to safeguard their well-being after the memoir was published. This task was accomplished by substituting coded names for the original ones appearing in the work.[16] Tehlirian also agreed to Vratsian obscuring the identity of another key operative in Talaat's assassination, Shahan Natali (Hagop Der Hagopian). In an exchange with Vahan Navasartian, Tehlirian provides us insights into the manner in which the memoir had been written and later edited. He explains that, while working with Minakhorian and Asdvadzadrian in Belgrade, he sought to give less prominence to Natali because the latter had been expelled from the ARF circa 1929 and had become an opposition figure. However, he was compelled by Minakhorian and Asdvadzadrian "not to deprive history of facts" and to give a full account.[17] When the Natali issue came up again during the editing process in the 1950s, Tehlirian allowed Vratsian to obscure Natali's name but not his role.[18] Vratsian proceeded to expunge Natali's name by taking out some passages in the memoir, paraphrasing others, and referring to Natali as "the representative" or "my comrade."[19]

In another interesting exchange, Tehlirian asked Navasartian for confirmation that the ARF had indeed taken a decision in 1919 to instigate an assassination campaign against Turkish leaders responsible for the Armenian Genocide.[20] Vratsian had indeed inserted this reference into the memoir and Tehlirian wanted confirmation when going over the proofs.[21] In the final analysis, Tehlirian credited Armen Garo and the Central Committee of the ARF in the United States for organizing Talaat's assassination.

While Tehlirian focused on the integrity of the original memoir, he allowed Vratsian to edit Minakhorian's introduction, which both men considered to be problematic.[22] Vratsian also added a new preface to the work to further qualify Minakhorian's introduction and reflect the ARF's position at that time.[23] The new introduction was written by Vahan Navasartian, who was one of Tehlirian's editors in Cairo. Neither of these introductory materials appear in this English translation of Tehlirian's memoir.[24]

* * *

As a rule, Tehlirian's memoir reads like a frank, chronological account of his road to Talaat Pasha's assassination. He maintains that he held Talaat responsible for atrocities against Armenians starting in May, 1915, when he first witnessed scenes of horrific murders and abuse committed by the Ottoman army.[25] He states that he heard similar accounts from other parts of the Ottoman Empire and began to worry about the fate of his own family in Yerznga, eventually reaching a point of physical and mental breakdown. He describes his first breakdown, which took place while listening to a survivor's account of a massacre in Jevizlik [Machka].

> "They first separated the men from the women and children," she said. "Then, they killed them with swords, knives, rifle butts, and in other ruthless ways. The screams of terror could be heard everywhere across the field. The soil and grass were soaked in blood. The wide-eyed little boys, seeing the horrors in front of them, were screaming. The

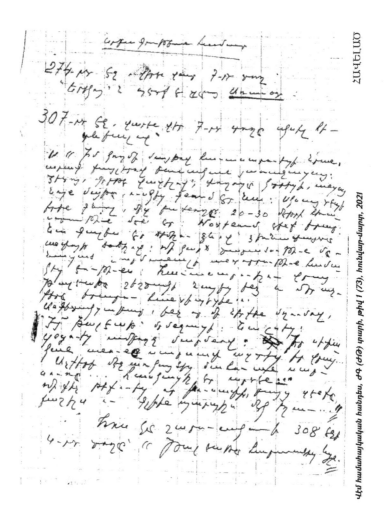

351

Tehlirian's hand written note concerning the moment of Talaat Pasha's assassination. This correction was sent to his editors but not entered into the Armenian edition of the memoir in 1953. The correction appears in this English translation. See Tehlirian to Lazian, Casablanca, 26 July 1953 in Yervant Pamboukian, "Soghomon Tehliriani Namagneru ir Houshakroutyan Arachin Dbakroutyan Artiv," *Vem Hamahaygagan Hantes* 13 (19) year, number 1(73), Jan-March, 2021, pp. 350-51.

women stretched out their arms, pleaded for their lives, and fell. The warm smell of blood was everywhere ...

Suddenly, I felt I was seeing all these scenes, hearing the screaming, the cries of horror and pain, desperate pleas, howls of madness and anguish. I was seeing the corpses exactly as I had seen in the village of Harissan. I sensed the warm smell of blood. Shocked, I got up to leave as I could not listen any longer, but my head was spinning, and I collapsed ...

When I came to, the woman was no longer there, and Hamo led me to my room. I could not close my eyes that night. As I dozed off, I would imagine horrible scenes, as if my mother was in the cave at the village of Sigounis [where Tehlirian had witnessed another atrocity]. It was as if all our children were around the tonir, screaming in unison, as if my brother, his head crushed, lay dead in the garden ... and every time I came to my senses, I could see Talaat's puffy, satisfied face in front of my eyes, an image I had seen for the first time in Van. I had visions of catching him, tying a noose around his neck, dragging him like a dog to the last of his slaughterhouses, and let him bleed in front of the dying victims .... From that day onwards, I began to be ill with periodic bouts of dizziness and fainting.[26]

For all the horrors of the Jevizlik massacre, Tehlirian states that he decided to kill Talaat in early 1916, when he had heard a devastating account of the destruction of Armenians in Der Zor and lost hope of finding his family members alive in Ottoman Turkey. The devastating information was relayed by Haig Toroian, who had passed through Der Zor and witnessed the appalling condition of Armenians who had survived the deportation process.[27]

My unfortunate compatriots deported to Mesopotamia consist mostly of women and girls. They can barely cover their nudity with rags and have nothing to protect themselves from the harsh weather. Some of them are sitting on the ground, under makeshift shelters put together from rags, but most of them are even deprived of such poor shelter. In the desert, everywhere, ferocious dogs roam around the sand dunes. Most of the corpses remain unburied. There are thousands of these skeletal people, with sunken cheeks, faded or very bright eyes, deprived of the ability to talk, deluded by their sufferings.

If I had had any hope that my relatives could survive the desert, even that hope was fading now. Only one thing remained for me to do: go to Constantinople and find Talaat. Only his death could soothe my grief. Like an unending nightmare, this thought would never leave me alone. Sometimes it would overwhelm me so much, that it would make me forget everything else.[28]

Tehlirian's resolve to kill Talaat was heightened further in 1916, when the Russian army occupied his hometown, Yerznga, and he returned to discover the ruined Armenian quarter of the city, and the absence of its Armenian inhabitants, including members of his own family. On this occasion, Tehlirian had haunting visions of his dead mother and brother, and passed out in the garden of his family home.[29] This theme of haunting visions, dizziness, and blackouts recurs many times in the memoir.[30]

* * *

Among the main turning points in Tehlirian's account of Talaat's assassination is his disclosure that he had also shot dead an 'Armenian traitor,' Haroutiun Mugrdichian, in Constantinople, 1919. As he explains, he took this step because Mugrdichian, who had collaborated with Turkish authorities in the persecution of Armenians during World War One, was living comfortably in Constantinople and not held accountable for his role in the deaths of hundreds of Armenians.[31] Although Tehlirian claims to have carried out the killing on his own initiative, his account clearly suggests the involvement of an enigmatic Hunchakian activist, Yeranouhi Tanielian.[32] Mugrdichian's killing reminds the reader of the gravitas of Tehlirian's account and his agency as a historical actor. Nevertheless, Tehlirian's efforts to find Talaat met one failure after another. By late 1919, he had exhausted all of his options and was working as a shoemaker in Paris. Every indication pointed to a hopeless, dead end, until he was approached, unexpectedly, by the Armenian Revolutionary Federation (ARF) and recruited to assassinate Talaat Pasha. This is a remarkable *deus ex machina* moment that marks a fundamental shift in Tehlirian's narrative. From this point onwards, Tehlirian becomes an operative of the ARF. He travels to the United States, where he is briefed on his mission and sent back to Europe to carry out the assassination. Making his way through Geneva, he goes to Berlin in the guise of a prospective engineering student, where he makes contact with his handler (Shahan Natali) and other operatives. Four months later, having tracked down their victim, Tehlirian assassinates Talaat in the Charlottenburg district of Berlin.

Regarding the aftermath of the killing, that is, Tehlirian's arrest, interrogation and trial in a German court, the memoir reflects his sense of uncertainty of what lay ahead, coupled with personal vignettes about his interrogation, prison life, and trial. However, at no point does he mention his actual brief regarding what he had to do after he had killed Talaat Pasha. He also does not comment on the arrangements for his defense in court, nor the strategy of his attorneys to highlight Talaat's guilt as a mass murderer and Tehlirian's innocence as a victim (even if Tehlirian admitted to killing Talaat). The trial transcripts, which are used extensively in this part of the memoir, show how several key witnesses testified about the extermination of Armenians in the Ottoman Empire during WWI.[33] As Tehlirian points out, their evidence was sensational, and he was presented as a living victim of the Armenian Genocide, a man who had been mentally disturbed by the loss of his family members in 1915. He had come to study in Berlin and chanced upon Talaat Pasha, eventually shooting him during a period of mental anguish and a moment of extreme psychosis. His attorneys argued, and several medical experts testified, that Tehlirian had not been responsible for what he had done at the moment of the killing, and the jury accepted the defense that was presented in court. Tehlirian was found not guilty and released.

However, much of Tehlirian's testimony during the trial was contrived to cover his tracks over the previous six years, including the involvement of the ARF in organizing Talaat's assassination. Tehlirian's own account of the road to the assassination was not told until the publication of his memoir in 1953. Until that point, the transcripts of his trial served as the basis of many people's understanding of the assassination. *Remembrances: The Assassination of Talaat Pasha* was thus a corrective, a cautious but accurate disclosure of Talaat's assassination from Tehlirian's perspective.

Remembrances: The Assassination of Talaat Pasha makes for riveting reading and is presented here as an important historical source regarding one of the great assassinations of the 20th century. It will undoubtedly feed into existing debates and discussions, as well as spawn new ones in years to come. Our purpose in producing it is scholarly.

This is a complete translation of Soghomon Tehlirian's memoir. The front materials and addendum appended to the original memoir, except for Tehlirian's biographical note and his note to his mother, are not included in this English translation. When working on the translation, we included the original names of individuals whose identities had been obscured (coded) in the Armenian edition of Tehlirian's work. We incorporated corrections Tehlirian had made on the proofs of the Armenian work but not incorporated into the Armenian volume. We also included all photographs used in the Armenian edition of Tehlirian's work. However, in some cases, we substituted better copies of the original or near-original photographs from elsewhere. Finally, we appended new maps, diagrams and photographs to this English translation.

—Ara Sarafian,
   Gomidas Institute, London,
   1 August, 2022

ENDNOTES

1. Soghomon Tehlirian (as told to Vahan Minakhorian), *Verhishoumner (Taleati Ahapegoumu)* [Վերյիշումներ (Թալէաթի Ահաբեկումը)], (Cairo: Housaper, 1953).

2. Among the more informed discussions of the assassination of Talaat Pasha, see Marian Mesrobian MacCurdy, *Sacred Justice: The Voices and Legacy of the Armenian Operation Nemesis*, (New Brunswick, NJ: Transaction Publishers, 2015), and Gohar Khanoumyan, "Soghomon Tehlirianu yev 'Nemesis' Gordzoghoutiunu," *Vem Hamahaygagan Hantes*, Oct-Dec, 2019, pp. 67-84.

3. Housaper was the Cairo-based publishing house of the ARF. The editors of the book were members of the party's top leadership tier.

4. The first formal acknowledgment of the ARF's role in Talaat Pasha's assassination was made on the occasion of the 60th anniversary of the killing with the publication of H. Kurkjian, *Tehlirian: Artarahadouytsu*, (Beirut: Hamazkayini Vahe Setian Dbaran, 1981). Even with this publication, the editor of the volume, H. Kurkjian, stated that *Tehlirian: Artarahadouytsu* does not claim to represent the whole history of "Hadoug Kordz" ["Special Mission"] to assassinate Talaat Pasha; but it brings together different materials related to the assassination.

5. We have two critical sources that provide invaluable insights into the Tehlirian memoir. The first is by Arshalouys Asdvadzadrian, who wrote a sympathetic commentary on the relationship between the three men and how they worked on Tehlirian's memoir in Belgrade.

See Arshalouys Asdvadzadrian, *"Sardarapati Patmashinoutiunu" yev Ayl Yerger,* comp., ed. and intro. by Vardan Grigoryan, (Yerevan: Hayakidag, 2007), pp. 752-97. A second source is the correspondence file Simon Vratsian kept when editing Tehlirian's work between 1951-53. This file contains correspondence among Soghomon Tehlirian, Simon Vratsian, and three editors at Housaper publishing house in Cairo during the final editing of Tehlirian's memoir. This invaluable correspondence record is produced in a meticulous study, Yervant Pamboukian, "Soghomon Tehliriani Namagneru ir Houshakroutyan Arachin Dbakroutyan Artiv," *Vem Hamahaygagan Hantes,* No. 1(73) Jan-March, 2021, pp. 313-65.

6. Asdvadzadrian states, "During those days, when Minakhorian was working on that project, we had many opportunities to talk about that work and related matters." See *"Sardarapati Patmashinoutiunu" yev Ayl Yerger,* p. 762. Tehlirian also mentions long, consultative meetings (*yergar-parag khorhrtagtsagan hantiboumner*) between the three men, when they had discussions and even intense debates about the memoir. Tehlirian mentions one instance when he was compelled to include certain details which he did not wish to include in the memoir. See Tehlirian to Navasartian, Casablanca, 31 Jan. 1952, *Vem,* pp. 322-23.

7. *"Sardarapati Patmashinoutiunu" yev Ayl Yerger,* p. 763. Also see further references to Minakhorian's superior writing in *Vem,* p. 323, 329, 331.

8. Much of the literary flair defining the memoir is due to Minakhorian's pen. Asdvadzadrian stresses that Minakhorian's personal suffering during the Armenian Genocide was also a critical factor in relating Tehlirian's story as only another survivor could. See *"Sardarapati Patmashinoutiunu" yev Ayl Yerger,* p. 763. For Minakhorian's account of his own terrible ordeal as a survivor of the Armenian Genocide, see Vahan Minakhorian, *1915 Tvaganu – Arhavirki Orer,* (Venice: St. Ghazar, 1949).

9. The different political backgrounds did not pose a problem to the three men. Asdvadzadrian speaks of Minakhorian in very respectful terms. Tehlirian, even when criticizing some aspects of Minakhorian's work a decade later, remained respectful to Minakhorian and his critical role in producing the memoir.

10. While a member of the Armenian Parliament in 1918-20, Minakhorian had been an outspoken critic of the ARF. See Richard Hovannisian, *The Republic of Armenia* (Berkeley and Los Angeles: University of California Press), vol. I (1971), p. 153, 418; vol II (1982), p. 283; vol. III (1996), p. 191, 214.

11. This state of affairs changed when the memoir was accepted for publication and Tehlirian was concerned about at least one of his revelations, that he had assassinated an Armenian collaborator (Haroutiun or Artin Mugrdichian) who had cooperated with Ottoman authorities in the persecution of Armenians during World War One. The assassination took place at the end of March, 1919. See Tehlirian to Vahan Navasartian, Casablanca, 29 Sept. 1951, *Vem*, p. 20.

12. For example, while Tehlirian does not cite any sources in his memoir, one can clearly see the use of the Armenian translation of the transcripts of his trial in Berlin. These transcripts provide much of the content in the last three chapters of his memoir. See *Tadavaroutiun Taleat Pashayi: Sghakragan Zegoutsoum*, (Vienna: Mkhitarian Press, 1921). Other sources mentioned in the memoir include Armenian translations from the foreign press, such as US Consul Leslie A. Davis's report of the abuse of Armenians in Kharpert (Harput) in 1915. See *Remembrances*, pp. 37-8. For the full copy of the original report and others like it, see Ara Sarafian (ed.), *United States Official Records on the Armenian Genocide, 1915-17*, (London: Gomidas Institute, 2004), pp. 172-76.

    Even when working on the final editing of his memoir a decade later, Tehlirian still asked his editor in Cairo to check specific details because Minakhorian had not had the relevant materials to check them earlier, see Tehlirian to Lazian, Casablanca, 3 April 1953, *Vem*, p. 334.

13. Tehlirian to Navasartian, Casablanca, 31 Jan. 1952, *Vem*, pp. 324-25; Tehlirian to Navasartian, Casablanca, 11 March, 1952, *Vem*, pp. 326-27.

14. Prior to the actual publication of the memoir, the "Housaper" editorial board formalized its work and passed a resolution consisting of 21 points regarding the new work. The seventh point of their resolution stated, "To note where appropriate, the decision of the 9th General Congress of the ARF to punish the executioners (*tahijner*) [of the Armenian Genocide.]" This resolution also included the title of the memoir, "Verhishoumner: Taleati Ahapegoumu," (literally, "Remembrances: The Assassination of Talaat.") For the 'Decisions of Housaper Editorial Board on the Occasion of the Publication of Soghomon's Memoir' with the participation of 'Yervant, Kapriel and Vahan,' dated 5 May, 1953, see *Vem*, p. 338.

15. While the original work was typed up in several copies, we do not have access to any of the original materials for purposes of comparison today. Tehlirian provided a typed copy of the memoir to his editors with some of his own hand-written corrections. He also acknowledged that there would have to be some basic editing and fact checking (i.e. chronological references). Tehlirian's correspondence

with his editors suggest that he remained faithful to the original draft of his memoir and was reluctant to make changes unless necessary. During the editorial process, Tehlirian also scrutinized and corrected the proofs of his book prior to publication. See Tehlirian's exchanges with Navasartian in *Vem*, especially pp. 226, 343, and 350, where he provided additional information about the actual assassination itself. While the original text of the memoir may not be available to us today, there was a requirement by the Housaper editorial board that all materials related to Tehlirian's memoir were to be deposited in the archives of the ARF. See Memorandum of Housaper's editorial board on the occasion of the publication of Soghomon Tehlirian's memoir dated 5 May 1953, Article 20, in *Vem*, p. 339.

16. See Vratsian to Navasartian, Beirut, 1 May 1952, *Vem*, p. 329. We have reversed these codes to the actual names of the individuals concerned in this English translation of *Remembrances*.

17. See Tehlirian to Navasartian, Casablanca, 31 Jan. 1952, *Vem*, p. 323.

18. *Ibid*, pp. 322-3.

19. Vratsian to Navasartian, Beirut, 25 April, 1952, *Vem*, p. 327; Vratsian to Navasartiain, Beirut, 1 May, 1952, *Vem*, p. 329.

20. In a letter to Navasartian, he stated, "... the decisions of the 9th General Congress [of the ARF] are unfamiliar to me. If such a decision was taken, we should certainly note it.... [However], it is more appropriate to credit the initiative to Armen Karo and the [ARF] Central Committee of the United States, as that was also the case in reality." Tehlirian to Navasartian, Casablanca, 31 Jan. 1952, *Vem*, p. 323. The reference to the ARF's 1919 decision appears in *Remembrances*, p. 136.

21. See footnote number 14.

22. Writing to Navasartian about Minakhorian's original introduction to the memoir, Vratsian states,"If it were possible, I would not include Vahan's introduction. In some places, he seems to be writing under the influence of Marx, Stalinism, but we should include it out of respect for his wishes. However, it would be well if the biographical introduction you are writing addresses his lapses." See Vratsian to Navasartian, Beirut, 1 May, 1952, *Vem*, p. 329. Tehlirian also agreed with Vratsian's sentiment, stating that Minakhorian's introduction "smelt terribly of Marxism" in some places, that Minakhorian had been too respectful towards the Turkish people, the masses, and that he [Tehlirian] had left the matter rest there because of Minakhorian's sensibilities. Tehlirian then added, "In my opinion, if we have to include the introduction, we must edit or remove those points which only honor the Turkish intelligentsia and ordinary people." Tehlirian

to Navasartian, Casablanca, 20 May, 1952, *Vem*, p. 330; also see Tehlirian to Lazian, Casablanca, 3 April, 1953, *Vem*, p. 335.

23. Vratsian to Navasartian, Beirut, 1 May 1952, *Vem*, p. 329; Tehlirian to Navasartian, Casablanca, 20 May 1952, *Vem*, p. 330.

24. None of the front materials and addendum in Tehlirian's work are included in this English translation, except for the biographical information and Tehlirian's note to his mother. The excluded materials are outside the remit of the memoir as a primary source.

25. Tehlirian mentions the massacre of Armenians in the Aghpag and Nordouz regions of Van, with specific descriptions of atrocities at Harisan and Sigounis villages. See *Remembrances*, pp. 26-30. For the massacre of Armenians in Van province and the resistance that followed, see A-Do (transl. by Ara Sarafian) *Van 1915: The Great Events of Vasbouragan*, (London: Gomidas Institute, 2017).

26. *Remembrances*, pp. 36-37. The massacre scene at Jevizlik can be compared to a similar account by a child-survivor, Onnig Siurmelian, who witnessed the abuse of Armenians near Jevizlik from the Greek Orthodox monastery of Vazelon where he was in hiding. Writing many years later, he stated, "We could clearly see everything from the high terrace of the monastery, and the image cannot be erased from my memory until today... Sometimes, at night, when we sat on the terrace of the monastery, the wind carried the sound of gunfire, the cries and screams of women..." His account includes a description given by another survivor who escaped to the monastery after he had witnessed the abuse of Armenian women and children and himself survived execution-killings in a valley nearby. See Onnig Siurmelian (ed. Antranig Dakesian), *Gyankis Koubaru Choutagis Hed*, (Beirut: n.d., 1988), pp. 25-28.

27. Toroian was a soldier in the Ottoman army and crossed Der Zor with a German officer on their way to Baghdad and Kermanshah (Persia). They were in Der Zor between November 24th to December 2nd and Toroian managed to escape to the Caucasus while in Kermanshah in December 1915. Toroian's testimony was eventually written down and published in the Armenian press in the Caucasus. See Hayg Toroian (as told to Zabel Yesaian), "Zhoghovourti Mu Hokevarku (Aksoryan Hayer Michakedki Mech)," *Gorts* (Baku, 1917), No. 2 and 3.

28. *Remembrances*, p. 39. This imagery of people dying in the deserts of Der Zor becomes a theme in Tehlirian's memoir, even in his opening note to his mother at the beginning of his work. In all likelihood, Tehlirian's family members were killed in the Yerznga region or along deportation routes and never got as far as Der Zor. According to Talaat Pasha's personal report on the Armenian Genocide, based on a special survey conducted in February 1917, practically no Armenians

from the whole of Erzeroum province, which included Yerznga, could be found alive in Der Zor. See Ara Sarafian (comp. and intro), *Talaat Pasha's Report on the Armenian Genocide, 1917*, (London: Gomidas Institute, 2011), pp. 59, 66.

29. *Remembrances*, pp. 48-49.

30. *Ibid.* pp. 48-9, 94-5, 124-5, 156, 178-9, 213, 238-9.

31. See *Remembrances*, pp. 110-116. Regarding Mugrdichian's activities during World War One, see Yervant Pamboukian, *Medz Yegherni Arachin Vaverakroghu: Shavarsh Misakian*, (Antelias: Armenian Catholicosate of Cilicia, 2017), pp. 347-50, 390, 429-32.

32. Tehlirian was particularly concerned not to expose Tanielian to potentially criminal liability by his revelations, and he raised the issue with his editor, suggesting that her name should be obscured in his memoir for her own safety. See Tehlirian to Navasartian, Casablanca, 31 Jan. 1952, p. 324. Interestingly, Tanielian also played a crucial role in the ARF's approach to Tehlirian at the end of September 1919 for the assassination of Talaat Pasha. See *Remembrances*, pp. 131-2.

33. The most powerful witnesses were Mrs Christine Terzibashian, who related her experiences of deportations and massacres, and Krikoris Balakian, who gave a lengthy account of what he had witnessed during his own arrest, deportation and escape. Of the two expert witnesses, Johannes Lepsius gave a comprehensive, devastating account of the genocidal process, while Liman Von Sanders attempted to exonerated Talaat Pasha of responsibility for the mass killings that had taken place. See Armenian transcripts of Tehlirian's trial, *Tadavaroutiun Taleat Pashayi*, pp. 84-112.

REMEMBRANCES

THE ASSASSINATION OF
TALAAT PASHA

TO MY MOTHER[*]

Terrified by the thought of losing you to obscurity, I wandered from country to country, desert to desert. I passed through the unfortunate, ruined towns and villages of our homeland, mountains and valleys …

All my efforts to find you were in vain. Everywhere in front of me was the terrifying panorama of desolation. No longer was there a vision of life, the hustle and bustle in the fields, the bubbling streams, the happy songs of the birds …

All, all had been destroyed to satiate the bestial desire of the bloody, wild hyena.

Our homeland was now ruled by a kingdom of owls …

Desolation, desolation …

The Euphrates was angry and raging as it changed its ancient course because of your tortured bodies … One could only hear the roar of its protest and disapproval in its rising waves. It too lamented its past.

Its clear and pure waters were colored by the innocent blood of Armenian mothers, children, young and old … Its spirit was disturbed as it witnessed the terrible tragedy of the Armenian people.

The far away, the unknown deserts were cruel and silent, as if they had been satiated by the skeletons scattered on scorching sands …

I lamented bitterly as I witnessed the vilest horrors in human history. I wavered with thoughts that took me to the dark edges of hopelessness, but the anguish, the terrible scenes of the tragedy

---

[*] This is a free translation of Tehlirian's note addressed to his mother. It was submitted for inclusion with his memoir on 28 Nov, 1952. See Yervant Pamboukian, "Սողոմոն Թեհլիրեանի նամակները իր յուշագրութեան առաջին տպագրութեան արխիվ" [Soghomon Tehliriani Namagneru ir Houshakroutyan Arachin Dbakroutyan Artiv], in *Vem Hamahaygagan Hantes*, Jan.-Mar., 2021, p. 331.

shook my soul, and strength and vigor pushed me to take stock, compelling me to live on. Perhaps this was a signal to me, an Armenian child, to carry out my basic responsibility to you and countless other Armenian mothers, who were crucified in the Armenian Golgotha ... to commit the memory of the rivers of blood that were spilled to eternity ...

You, my mother, who gave me life, kissed me with your tearful eyes and bitter feeling, that we would not see each other again. You were right. You were also correct, when you exclaimed, "As soon as I raised you, you took wings and flew away from me." Yes, I did, not ever to see you again. But the milk you gave me and your unlimited motherly care left such long roots in the depths of my soul, that it was impossible to forget everything and remain indifferent to what happened, especially your infinitely tragic *yegheragan* death.

Today, like a faithful mystic, I want to build "a grave of the unknown mother" in my soul and pray piously in front of it as an altar ... I want the thoughts of my pagan prayers, mixed with the sweet aroma of frankincense, to rise and reach the heavens, as my heartfelt offering to your unforgettable memory, oh mother, as well as the thousands upon thousands of those who were sacrificed, *voghchagizvadz*, martyred in our nation's struggle for freedom, all disappearing forever without graves or tombstones ...

—Soghomon

SOGHOMON TEHLIRIAN

(Autobiographical Notes) [*]

Soghomon Tehlirian was born on April 15th, 1896 in Vari Pakarij village, in the Taranaghyats (Gamakh) region of historical Armenia.

His father was Khachadour, and his mother Hnazant, Haroutiun Der Katrjian's daughter. They had five sons. Their second child died at the age of three or four, leaving Misak, Setrak, Avedis and Soghomon. By 1915, Misak and Setrak were already married with three and two children respectively.

The villagers in the Gamakh region could not make an adequate living because of a lack of land to cultivate. Consequently, the men went abroad as migrant workers (*bantoukhd*s), especially to the Balkans, where they worked for several years and returned with their savings.

In 1898, Soghomon's father left for Serbia for the second or third time, where he ran a business with his brother. His brother returned to Vari Pakarij first, and Soghomon's father came, in his turn, in 1905.

The return of such workers were major occasions in the village. They paid more attention to the reception of such travelers (*silaji*s) and the formal opening of their saddlebags (panniers) than to weddings. The returning men would bring gifts for everyone.

Soghomon's father had been due to arrive for Easter, 1905. However, on the eve of Easter's Holy Week (*Avak Shapat*), a muleteer delivered two boxes to their home but there was no sign of Soghomon's father. They soon found out that the Turkish

---

[*] For the original, longer biographical note submitted by Tehlirian to his editors, see *Vem Hamahaygagan Hantes*, pp. 316-19.

Yerznga, 1910. Front row (left to right) Soghomon's brother Misak's wife, Hripsime (martyred); their daughter Armenouhi (survived deportation); Soghomon's mother, Hnazant (martyred); his brother Misak and Soghomon Tehlirian. Back row: Soghomon's uncle's daughter, Persape, and brother Avedis (both martyred).

authorities had imprisoned him when he had disembarked at Trabizon. The celebration turned into mourning. Six months later, Khachadour Agha[*] was released and sent to Serbia.

However, prior to leaving for the Balkans, Khachadour was able to see a compatriot, Misak Boloian, and arranged for the family to move to Yerznga. They later learned that Khachadour had been arrested and imprisoned because he had boarded a Russian ship when he had left for the Balkans in 1898. He was classed as a revolutionary and arrested when he returned in 1905.

In the winter of 1905-06, Soghomon attended the Protestant school in Yerznga. The following year, he went to Yeznigian School, until 1911. Then, for his last year, most of the students in

---

* *Agha* is an honorific title usually given to landowners.

his class went to Getronagan School because of a shortage of teachers.

With the declaration of the Balkan War (1912-13), some teachers were conscripted into the army, and the school trustees arranged for Soghomon to teach the first-year students at the primary school.

In 1913, at the age of 17, Soghomon finally saw his father. Although Khachadour could have returned after the 1908 constitutional revolution, he had to delay his return for five years because of work commitments.

In the fall of 1913, Soghomon left Yerznga for Serbia, where he wanted to prepare himself to study in Germany the following year. However, the First World War turned everything upside down and scuppered his plans.

Until the horrific days of 1915, the Tehlirian family had 85 members in Yerznga and Pakarij, not counting those who were abroad with work.

Of those 85 people, only Soghomon's elder brother Misak's daughter survived. The 12-year-old was found with a Kurd after the Russians occupied Yerznga.

Soghomon's mother, the wives of his two elder brothers and their children, as well as his brother Avedis (who had studied medicine at the American university in Beirut and returned to Yerznga) were killed in 1915.

In the spring of 1914, Soghomon's father and brother Setrak had left Yerznga and gone to Serbia to attend to the family business. They were thus saved from certain death.

Soghomon's father died in Serbia during the Second World War, at the age of 84. His brothers, Misak and Setrak, are living in Yugoslavia. They have remarried and have children, even grandchildren.

Soghomon was married to Nshan Tatigian's daughter, Anahid. The Tatigians were originally from Yerznga but later settled in Tbilisi. Nshan Tatigian had been a close collaborator with the Armenian revolutionary, Keri (Shishmanian). However, when Nshan faced serious dangers in Yerznga, he escaped to the

Caucasus, around 1895, and settled in Tbilisi. He later married Hagop Shavarsh's daughter.

Hagop Shavarsh was one of the founders of *Miatsyal* organization.

Soghomon and Anahid have two sons.

CHAPTER ONE

From Serbia to Vasbouragan[*]

I had just arrived in the Serbian provincial town of Valjevo from Yerznga [Erzinjan] when everything turned upside down. A Serbian student had assassinated Franz Ferdinand, the Austrian heir to the throne, in Sarajevo. Everyone presumed that there would be war. Then, events followed each other at a dizzying speed. At the end of July, Russia mobilized its naval and land forces. On August 1st [1914], Germany took the initiative and declared war on Russia. France stood by her ally, Russia, as the first shots were fired on Belgium, providing the perfect opportunity for Great Britain to declare war on Germany. Thus began the first mass slaughter in history.

The Serbian people embraced the gun to attain their national aspirations. The time had now come to achieve their national goals. The people of Valjevo, who had become indolent eating and drinking in their eastern ways, had awoken. There were many gatherings and lively demonstrations. The leaders invoked the times of Stefan Nemanja and Dušan Silni, calling on the people to be inspired by the martyred heroes of Kosovo in the Valley of Marica.

The flames of war reached the borders of Serbia in mid-August, when the Austrians invaded the country with two armies to put an end to the boastful Serbians with a single blow. However, after four days of heavy fighting, the Austrians were forced to retreat. The setback was so unexpected that the Austrians only repeated their attack four months later, when the Turks had also joined the war.

It was not clear what was happening outside Valjevo. The town's six or seven other Armenians visited us almost every day. It was as if the entire weight of the war had fallen on their shoulders.

---

[*] Vasbouragan is the ancient Armenian region to the south of Lake Van.

Everyone had a family back in the homeland [in the Ottoman Empire] and were anxious about their loved ones. My father and brothers were more anxious than the others. Their worries were incomprehensible to me. What could happen to women and children when the Hamidian regime had already been overthrown and the just government of the Young Turks was in power? It is true, that the Adana massacres of 1909 had taken place under their watch; but who didn't know that those killings had been the last tribute of the Turkish counter-revolution that Armenians had to pay as the main cause of the Turkish revolution a year earlier? Or were those massacres the first expressions of what was to come?

I therefore tried to offer hope and encouragement with my latest impressions from our homeland. My words were of some comfort, except for my father, who listened with his head slightly bent, his chin resting on his cane, and his glass-like eyes fixed on me. That gaze always confused me.

At the end of the year, my father received a letter from Sofia. It was from his longtime friend, Ghougas Agha, who for many years had been involved in community and revolutionary work in Bulgaria. Ghougas Agha wrote that the time had come for the final liberation of the Armenian people from the Turkish yoke. He added that Armenians in Bulgaria were forming volunteer groups to join the Armenian liberation movement in the Caucasus. If his age had permitted, he would also have joined these groups to fight against the centuries-old enemy. Attached to the letter was an appeal to all Armenians capable of carrying arms to volunteer.

I was barely 18 years old and the letter stirred me with its rousing content. However, contrary to my expectations, these developments had a deadening effect on our people.

"It's all over," said my father, completely depressed. "We must think about getting our family out of that hell."

I didn't care about that. I was totally obsessed with the idea of going to Bulgaria, which would have been very difficult in those days without my father's consent and a passport. The excitement of the Serbs in the town had reached its peak. The Austrians had suffered a crushing defeat in the Ratekh region and retreated in disarray. The Allies, according to reports, were victorious

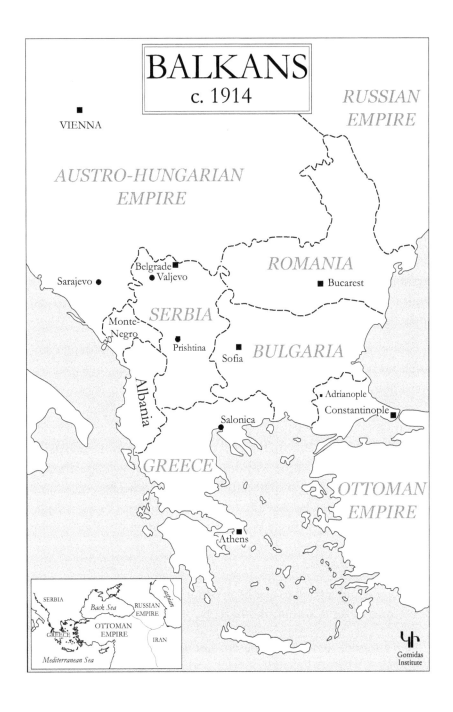

BALKANS
c. 1914

VIENNA ■

RUSSIAN EMPIRE

AUSTRO-HUNGARIAN EMPIRE

Sarajevo ●   Belgrade ■
● Valjevo

ROMANIA

■ Bucarest

SERBIA

Monte-
Negro

● Prishtina

■
Sofia

BULGARIA

Albania

■ Adrianople
Constantinople ● ■

● Salonica

GREECE

OTTOMAN EMPIRE

■ Athens

SERBIA   *Caspian*
Back Sea   RUSSIAN
EMPIRE
GREECE   OTTOMAN
EMPIRE   IRAN
Mediterranean Sea

Gomidas
Institute

everywhere, even though, with the exception of the Russian front, the fighting was taking place on their own territories. The Russians had entered Silesia and Poznan, and were supposed to soon descend from the Carpathian mountains. The days of Vienna, Budapest, and even Berlin were numbered.

At the end of November [1914], I was arrested on the Serbian-Bulgarian border as a spy but managed to explain the misunderstanding and entered Bulgaria. In those days, there was no difference in the disposition of the two Slavic peoples. Ordinary Bulgarians were also on the side of the allies. They had no grudges against their former enemy, the Serbs.[*] But attitudes in official circles were different. The partition of Macedonia and the loss of the Bulgarian part of Dobruja were still very fresh in their memory. Bulgaria was neutral, but it was already clear that its neutrality was meant to gain them time until there was an opportune moment to seek revenge.

There was extraordinary commotion among the Armenians of Sofia, with meetings, gatherings, and brilliant plans everywhere. Mardigian's "Shesti September" café was full of party activists.[†] They argued over possible developments. Ghougas Agha, a stocky man of medium-height, solid as an old oak, was also there. He refused to include me in the list of volunteer groups when he found out that I had come without my father's knowledge, though some others were in a similar situation. Those who had registered a week earlier were also not allowed to leave so that Ghougas Agha was surrounded by furious Western Armenian youngsters asking him questions, "Why? ... Until when? ... What are the reasons for these delays?"

Ghougas Agha tried to establish order through evasive answers, sometimes sweetly, sometimes harshly.

---

[*] The reference here is to the Second Balkan War (1913), when Bulgaria lost territory to Serbia, Greece, and Romania.
[†] These activists were probably members of the Armenian Revolutionary Federation (ARF) or the Social Democratic Hunchagian Party.

"You have to wait. It has been arranged for the movement of volunteers to be temporarily halted. What should we do? We must obey the orders coming from higher authorities!"

However, no one was willing to obey the instructions of that unknown body. The liberation of the nation had begun, and everyone felt a strong desire to participate in that sacred struggle as soon as possible.

I managed to go to Romania with a group of volunteers. In Bucharest, I discovered that my father had sent a telegram demanding my return. It was already too late. I left that same night for Rostov [on Don] with some friends, thanks to the assistance of the Russian Embassy.

The commotion at the station was extraordinary. Trains were leaving loaded with artillery, ammunition, soldiers, and horses. Occasionally, there were farewell gatherings for those leaving for the front. They were sent off by waving of handkerchiefs as the trains left the station. Afterwards, only the elderly, young women, and girls remained on the platforms, weeping quietly into the same handkerchiefs they had been happily waving a few moments earlier.

***

I was soon in Tbilisi and registered as a *gamavor* [volunteer].[*] Together with my friends and other volunteers, we were quartered in a large national property [belonging to the Armenian community] at the end of Velyaminovskaya Street. It was one of several dormitories for the volunteers. This property was adjacent to the Botanical Gardens, where we conducted military exercises. Although a week had passed, I was only now getting used to the diverse city of Tbilisi, which fascinated me right from the beginning. In the evenings, I usually went down Velyaminovskaya Street, all the way to the pharmacy at the corner of the city's municipal hall.

---

[*] Gamavor: volunteer. The Armenian term used to describe Armenians who volunteered to form separate battalions to fight on the Russian side against the Ottoman Empire in World War One. There were also Armenian volunteers in French and British armies.

In February [1915], our mountains and valleys back home in Yerznga were still covered in snow whereas, here, the beautiful Yerevan Square [Freedom Square in Tbilisi today] was shining in the warm rays of the sun. This large square, paved with small cobble stones, seemed to represent the city of Tbilisi in miniature, surrounded by hotels, merchant houses, shops, underground taverns, and the extensive caravanserai of Tamamshev, which occupied an entire side of the square with its hundreds of kiosks facing the municipal hall.

In those days, Yerevan Square was the center of Armenian political life. There were three places where Armenian national, public, and revolutionary figures usually gathered. The first, opposite the pharmacy, under bare trees and not far from a corner of the square, was "Anatolia" restaurant, which was operated by an Armenian from Erzeroum. Here, you could see many leaders, soldiers, and volunteers in Tbilisi sitting around tables, arguing or laughing with each other. The second, at the other corner of the square, under Tamamshev's caravanserai, was the famous "Tilipuchuri,"[*] a first-class underground tavern known for its fine meat and the best Gakheti wine. It belonged to an Armenian from Tbilisi. Among those gathered there were rich Georgian and Russian-speaking Armenians of Tbilisi, whose sense of being Armenian had been suddenly heightened by the latest developments in the region. There were also other Armenian public figures who came to Tbilisi from different parts of the Transcaucasus, as well as Armenians dedicated to the national cause. The third place was "Sakayan's Kanditerski," a European-style café which was on a steep street off Yerevan Square, on the corner of Sololak quarter. Actors, writers, revolutionary party activists, teachers, students, and all kinds of Armenian intellectuals gathered here.

Life was in full swing at these meeting places. People's spirits were raised by debates covering Armenians and Armenia, the

---

[*] Tilipuchuri tavern was a well-known location in Tbilisi. It was taken over by Bolshevik revolutionaries in 1907 to prepare for a bank robbery. The robbery resulted in the deaths of 40 people. Stalin was one of attackers.

Armenian Question,[*] the world war, the relative strength of fighting forces, and the situation on various fronts. The Armenians of the Caucasus were living through an unprecedented period of hope and emotions as they sensed the realization of national dreams that had been cherished for generations.

I spent almost all of my free time with my only compatriot, Yanikian, who had a modest dairy house under Severniye Nomera Hotel. However, at the end of the month [February 1915], I found out by chance that the Tatigians were also in Tbilisi. Of the two brothers, I only knew Mr. Khachadour, who had left Yerznga only three or four years earlier. My longing for my birthplace was so great that I searched for his address and went to see him.

Mr. Khachadour's modest grocery store was on Mikayelian Street, which stretched parallel to the riverbank from Vorontsov bridge to the garden of Moushdayed.

When he saw me, he immediately recognized me and jumped up from his seat in a manner that occasioned the laughter of the young girl standing nearby. He then asked so many questions that I didn't know which one to answer. I was also confused by the young girl, who was now staring at me with her serious, large, dark eyes. It was as if I had seen her before or dreamt of someone like her.

"Well, where are your folks?" continued Mr. Khachadour.

"My father and my two brothers are in Serbia. The rest are in Yerznga."

"And what are you doing here?"

"I am a volunteer and will be going to the front soon," I said very cheerfully in the presence of the girl.

"Does your father know?"

"I wrote to him the day before yesterday."

"From here?"

"Yes."

"What about before leaving Serbia?"

---

[*] The Armenian Question was linked to Article 61 of the Treaty of Berlin (1878) regarding reforms addressing the condition of Armenians in the Ottoman Empire.

Soghomon, Samuel and Hovsep Tehlirian (paternal-cousins).

"He knew, he knew ..."

"Well, let me introduce you, this is my brother's daughter, our Anahid."

The girl looked at me, boldly.

"How was our family the last time you saw them?" asked Mr. Khachadour.

"They were well."

"What will happen to our Shahen now? He was going to graduate from the [Ottoman] military academy this year. So, it will be brother against brother, one a volunteer, the other a reluctant participant."

"Yes, what a burden. He must fulfill his civic duty, though I doubt they would send new graduates to the front."

"May God hear your words. We are going to suffer until this war ends. Last time he wrote, he said that Roupen Efendi would come and tell us everything, but he never came. How were they?"

"Who?" I asked.

"The Momjians."

"Their business was doing well, they were fine."

"Anyway, you have to meet my brother. Naturally, he also wants to have more news."

"Yes, my father will be glad to see you, sir," said the girl in a modest tone.

I left, promising to visit them at the first opportunity. As I left, I was shocked at myself. My soul was swinging like a pendulum, up and down under a torrent of unfamiliar emotions. I could neither see, hear, or feel my surroundings. Arriving at the dormitory, I sat on the bench at the end of the courtyard. It was as if I were drunk; I had no clear thought in my head. The twilight was fading. The birds in the trees in the nearby garden strained themselves with their shrill and passionate calls. Some flew about with fine straws in their beaks. The spring scent of tepid soil, new leaves, and blossoming trees wafted through the air. It was dark by the time I began to understand what was happening to me. Was it possible that a stranger could overwhelm someone at their first meeting, as had just happened to me? Such feelings digressed from the mission I had set for myself.

Having sobered up, I went straight into the dormitory. It was noisy as usual. The topic of the day was the battle of Diuz-Dagh in the region of Khoy [Persia], during which there had been a misunderstanding between the Armenian volunteers and the commanders of the Russian military unit. Colonel Nalgiev had instructed the volunteers to capture Diuz-Dagh. He knew that this was impossible and his main purpose for the attack was to engage the opposition at that front so that he could maneuver around the mountain with his forces and destroy the enemy. However, the Armenians had apparently managed to capture Diuz-Dagh and the enemy had retreated to the open plains before the arrival of the colonel. Thus, instead of being annihilated, the enemy had inflicted several dozen casualties on the Armenians and fled.

***

Two weeks went by. We were now well into spring. According to the decision of the National Bureau's organizational body,* we were to leave for the front. Contrary to my promise, I did not go to the Tatigians before I left. I thought it was better not to see the schoolgirl who had given me so much to think about. However, on the eve of my departure, wherever I went in the city, it was as if her face was in front of me. I had decided to leave her to chance because I first had to fulfill my national duty. In the future, if I remained alive and if luck would have it, she could be mine. I knew I should not have pursued her then. I had a strange sense that my feelings were dangerous, but I still had a strong desire to see her again before my departure.

Idle people like me were strolling on Vorontsov bridge. A poor man was standing on a corner of the bridge playing the pipes. A ten-year-old boy with tired eyes was standing near him and

---

* National Bureau (*Azkayin Buro*), based in Tbilisi, was the Armenian national body responsible for the political and military affairs of Russian Armenians. It was initially a quasi-governmental organization, supported by the Russian government. It was later renamed National Council (*Azkayin Khorhourt*), which declared the independence of Armenia on May 28th, 1918. The Organizational Body (*Garkatritch Marmin*) was responsible for recruiting Armenian volunteer fighters for the Russian army.

Tamamshev caravanserai, Tbilisi.

watching people walking past. The father and son probably had to provide their large family with daily bread. Everything depended on their luck, whether the passers-by would notice them. The boy suddenly looked at me and I gave him all of my change. He was shocked and his father stopped playing.

The Kur river had flooded and was running wild. It was carrying away pieces of wood, bushes, and tree trunks it had dislodged from its banks. However, it became calmer as it passed under a bridge. On the other side, the water level rose against the walls of a tavern, a meter below its windows. People were leaning on the metal railings of the bridge and watching the wall. There was a cat looking out of a tall, narrow window. Its head was outside and its body inside the building. It was terrified of the rushing water and could not walk backwards. It was trying to turn around carefully with its whole body, but the window was too narrow, and its efforts made matters worse. It was now meowing from fright and seeking help from the people on the bridge. A Russian woman rushed down to the tavern to help. A few moments later, the cat jumped into the torrents of the river and disappeared. Only then did a wooden pole with a hook attached to it appear from the wall.

It was evening. Soldiers were walking with young women and eating sunflower seeds in the lower part of Alexander Park. Further up, sparrows chirruped on the branches of newly planted trees. I walked onto Golovin Avenue [Rustaveli Street today]. On the opposite sidewalk, a little further down, was Nshan Tatigian's store. I could visit him there without going against my decision not to see his daughter. Mr. Nshan was a tall, young man, with a kind face. He looked at me quizzically until I revealed my identity. In those days, being from the same region of the homeland was the same as being related, and he accepted me accordingly. After about an hour of questioning, he led me through a side entrance to an apartment on the third floor of the same building. Anahid was there. When she saw me, she was surprised, but greeted me cordially and disappeared immediately. Then, somewhere inside, perhaps in the kitchen, I heard laughter. I was confused.

Although I had left our homeland a year and a half earlier [in 1913] and the news I had was dated, the same detailed interest was shown in what I had to say by his wife, and even their daughters, for whom Yerznga was simply a name. They probably knew that their father had been a revolutionary during the old regime and played a modest role as a comrade to Roupen Shishmanian (Keri of Dersim). That generation consisted of good people and good Armenians. As for Mr. Nshan, one could say that he was a broadminded man of the world before he was an Armenian. Back in the 1890s, he had held the view that the well-being and freedom of Western Armenians depended on cooperation with their immediate neighbors, especially the Kurds. He spared no effort in that direction with Kalousd Arkhanian and Shishmanian, until the latter's arrest, when he escaped to the Caucasus. But then again, he did not abandon that idea. He knew that Shishmanian's successors had tried to establish cooperation with Ibrahim Pasha in Diyarbekir, as well as the powerful Kurdish tribes of Silvan, who had a strong influence among the Kurdish tribes living on the Armenian Highlands. He knew the sad ending of the Armenian-Kurdish agreement established with Ghasem Bey, the failure of the negotiations with the Kurds of Demlig, the tragic death of the tribal leader Zeynal in Bingeol, and so on.

TO THE FRONT
Feb.-March 1915

RUSSIAN
EMPIRE

Batum

Trabizon

Erzeroum

Kars

Tbilisi

Alaverdi

Karakilise

Alexandropol

Elizavetpol

Echmiadzin

Yerevan

L. Sevan

OTTOMAN
EMPIRE

Bayazid

Maku

Nakhichevan

Pergri

Julfa

L. Van

Aghtamar

Van

Kotur

Khoy

Bitlis

St. Bartholomew

Salmast

IRAN

Tabriz

KEY

- - - - - - - International Frontiers
——————— Railroads (South-Caucasus)
————▶ Tehlirian's route

Ourmie

L. Ourmie

Gomidas
Institute

Mr. Nshan knew all this, but he was now concerned with family worries, raising his children with an Armenian spirit, fighting against the threat of assimilation into the Russian way of life. In his rich library he had Abovian's book, "Wounds of Armenia" [the first Armenian novel published in the eastern Armenian dialect] and many other Armenian books. There was a strict rule to only speak Armenian at their home. Mr. Nshan was also aware of current affairs. He knew that the time of freedom for the Armenian people had come, that Armenia would flourish and develop, and he would finally have a place with his children in it.

He gradually felt happier during dinner, glass after glass, offering and drinking toasts, becoming excited and hopeful for the near future. And suddenly, he started singing:

"Kind, beautiful, virtuous friend, who brightens the image of a man like the sun ...

"Anyone having such a faithful friend, passes the dark night as if in daylight."[*]

Suddenly his daughter started laughing. Her father smiled and turned to her:

"My daughter, that laughter of yours is Russian! Armenian girls don't laugh like that."

And turning to me, he said:

"I have nothing to complain about. My children are good, but again, they are not what I wanted them to be. Anyway, let us drink to the success of the 'sacred duty.'"

It was midnight when Mr. Nshan allowed me to leave. Anahid led me to the outside door of their yard.

"Now we are friends, I hope you will visit us again."

"I would gladly come, Miss, but I have to leave tomorrow."

"Where?" she said, in a surprised tone, making it obvious that my departure meant something to her.

"To the front, Miss."

---

[*] A few lines from the Armenian ashough-singer Jivani (Serob Stepani Levonian).

"Oh, like that," she said, almost talking to herself, and continuing in an offhand manner.

"When you return, don't forget us."

"And if I don't, I hope you sometimes remember me as a friend."

"Of course," she said, immediately talking about something insignificant.

Sebouh

***

On March 28 [1915], our group of about two hundred volunteers left for the train station and settled in our carriages. The cries of joy from the crowd of thousands could still be heard a great distance from the station. The enthusiasm of the Armenian people was boundless, and the scene was touching, as if we were the embodiment of the national aspirations of many generations. There was great upheaval inside me as I contrasted our festive departure with memories of Yerznga during the Hamidian days, my uncle's arrest, underground revolutionary activities, the constant fear of massacres, and the martyrdom of many Armenian freedom fighters while crossing the border from the Caucasus.

The train departed Tbilisi and soon took the Alexandropol [Gyumri]-Yerevan-Julfa line. The ground was running backwards. Around me sat famous *haytougs*,* young and old, cheerful and thoughtful. Passing through the Georgian regions, the train entered a very winding section. We crossed the Lori

---

* Haytoug (hajduk): term to describe guerrilla fighters, especially in the Balkans.

Gorge at dawn, almost touching the edge of that river. Exhausted, the train stopped on a steep mountain slope. It was the Sanahin Bridge. The lush greenery was just waking up.

Hanging from the abyss, the train moved like a hedgehog, as it climbed the bridge, shaking. It then began to slow down.

"Karakilise! [Vanadzor]" they shouted inside the train.

"Hurrah!" the crowd roared on the platform of the station.

Around us were children with bouquets of flowers, peasants with farm produce, and a crowd of scattered people looking at each other with dazed eyes. More people gathered around and shouted, "Hurrah ..."

From here we crossed bare mountains over snakelike tracks, on the slopes of which the sun shone brightly. Then we entered a wide gorge and there seemed to be no way out. On the slope of the mountain, I noticed a black dot that swelled up and turned into a tube. Suddenly, with an indescribable tremor, we were covered in darkness. It was the Jajour tunnel. The six to seven minutes it took to pass through it seemed like an eternity. Then the darkness began to fade away and we returned to daylight, and later, we arrived at Alexandropol's white-painted station. Here, brightly dressed people danced on the sidewalks accompanied by the music of the davoul and doudoug.*

In April [1915] we were in Salmast. There was a lot of excitement among Persian-Armenians. They took the volunteers into their homes. A few days later, we were sent to the village of Vartanlou to bolster Sebouh's platoon in Antranig's battalion.†

This battalion consisted of 250 soldiers and included people from different places. The Battle of Dilman [c. April 19th] had just ended and the soldiers in Vartanlou were talking about it. Among the soldiers were two compatriots of mine, Kevork Hovhannesian,

---

* *Davoul* and *doudoug*: traditional drum and reed folk instruments.
† Sebouh (Arshag Nersesian, 1872-1940) was a renowned Armenian guerrilla fighter and military commander. He figures prominently in Tehlirian's memoir as the author's immediate superior officer in cir. April-May 1915. Antranig (Ozanian, 1865-1927) was a renowned Armenian guerrilla fighter and military commander. He was Tehlirian's battalion commander in 1915.

who was still well-known in Kamakh as an experienced revolutionary activist, and a younger man, Kerovpe Yeretsian. After target practice, I spent my free time with them. Kerovpe had a reputation as a brave and daring soldier, but when it came to telling stories, he somewhat exaggerated, and Kevork often had to intervene!

On the Persian front, apart from Antranig, were the rest of the former revolutionary leaders: Sebouh, Avo from Gumushkhane, and Smpad. Antranig was a central figure, as the commander of the 1st battalion of Armenian volunteers. The latter two, Avo and Smpad, were still renowned for their courage, modesty, and self-sacrifice. I only knew Avo, whose wife was from Yerznga, and their son, Nshan, who was my classmate. I had seen Sebouh seven years earlier, during the "revolutionary honeymoon,"[*] when he had visited Yerznga with Mourad.[†]

On May 2nd, our platoon moved to Araoul where Khalil Pasha's forces had retreated after their defeat in Dilman a week earlier. We were accompanied by a detachment of Cossacks, consisting of 400 men. When we reached the top of Souk-Boulak, it turned out that the enemy was preparing to fight at Araoul. This was the mountain near Khanasor, where Armenian haytougs had initiated their attack on the tents of the Kurdish Mazrik tribe [in 1896].[‡]

A Cossack company of a hundred soldiers and Avo's cavalry received orders to approach the mountain. We then started

---

[*] This was the term used to describe the period immediately after the Ottoman Constitutional Revolution of 1908, when Armenian revolutionary organizations in the Ottoman Empire put their arms down and became legal political parties. This period fizzled out after the Committee of Union and Progress' coup d'état in 1913.

[†] Mourad Khrimian of Sepasdia (Sivas) or Sepasdatsi Mourad (1874-1918) was a famous Armenian guerrilla fighter and later regional commander in Yerznga.

[‡] This was a punitive Armenian attack on the Mazrik tribe which had supported the massacre of Armenians during the Hamidian massacres a year earlier, in 1896. The Armenian attack on the Mazrik tribe was organized by a coalition of Armenian revolutionaries, led by the Armenian Revolutionary Federation.

Sepasdatsi Mourad.

climbing from different sides. The fight gradually intensified. Bullets were raining down and cannons were thundering on all sides. As we reached the top of a hill below the mountain, Simon from Vozm, one of the volunteers in the cavalry unit, suddenly fell to the ground at my feet. During that chaos, I barely took a step and also fell down.

"Oh no," I said to myself, "I have been shot without doing anything!" I was in shock. Then, someone picked up Simon on his shoulder and took him away.

"Hey, why don't you get up?" shouted a giant of a man. I jumped up and touched myself. I was not hurt. Nothing had happened to me. I felt so humiliated that I stormed to the front line in rage.

I could hear shouts of "hurrah" from behind. Simon's fall on the field had angered everyone. In the true sense of the word, the volunteers performed miracles against the seemingly overwhelming numbers of the enemy. In the evening, the Turks fled from the heights of Araoul and began to retreat to Peleri. As darkness fell, the battle gradually subsided. We were ordered to take up positions, guard against the enemy vigilantly, and wait for dawn. In the distance, the star-studded darkness burst into flames like scattered candles. The calm of night was disturbed by fires lit by the enemy. It was very cold. We also lit fires. After midnight, it was my turn for guard duty. Standing far away from the campfire, I just stared into the distance. The cold on the mountain was deadly. Smoking was forbidden. The unfamiliar work and the impact of the day had so overwhelmed me that I seemed to be asleep on my feet. I was trying hard to keep my eyes open, to look around me, but in vain. My eyelids were closing. We were not allowed to move back and forth, though standing on the same spot was boring. Squeezed into my fur-lined coat, I sat down under a rock that sheltered me from the icy wind blowing from the front. The starlit sky overlooked the mountain. I carefully watched the candle-shaped fires in the open plain below. But my need for sleep was pressing. If only I could have slept for just five minutes, I could guard for five hours!

"Hey, to whom the security of the group has been entrusted!" I thought to myself and stood up. "I must get used to this.

Weakness is betrayal. I have to fulfill my duty conscientiously. Only in that way can I become a sergeant, then a lieutenant, and finally, a captain."

A stray bullet whistled past me. A shiver shook my soul. I sat down. "Our Father who art in heaven," I murmured. And silence fell again. "And why only a captain?" I thought. "Who knows what bright future awaits me. Why can't I climb to the highest ranks? What ranks were Loris-Melikov and [Valerian] Madatov before they achieved fame?"

And I began imagining myself in a general's bright uniform in Tbilisi. A tall building in front of Alexander Park had been provided for my use. There was a guard in front of the house. On the second floor was an extraordinary event, where I received citizens. The doorman was wearing a gold-threaded uniform. People had gathered in the corridor, and those sitting stood up immediately and greeted me. Then, a large reception hall opened in front of me, where clerks and assistants were on their feet. Off the hall was a velvet room where my personal secretary, Anahid, was sitting. Finally, my private office opened up. I buried myself in an armchair and, after a while, I picked up the small silver bell from my desk and rang it. Anahid entered, stopping at the threshold.

"Start receiving," I said, as I lit my cigar.

"There's a girl here who claims to know you from Bulgaria. She wants to see you."

"Ah, the girl with the abundant hair," I said suddenly, remembering Ghougas Agha's daughter.

"No, her hair is fake, I saw it," exclaimed Anahid.

"It's all the same, let her come in."

"So, you want to see that girl?" asked Anahid, not very pleased.

Surprised, I shrugged my shoulders and looked at her. She left my office a second later and came back with an old woman who was barely able to walk and held a paper in her trembling hand. I looked at Anahid.

"This is the girl's mother," she said.

"What does she want?" I asked.

"She wants you to free her son from the army, that is, release him," said Anahid, taking the paper from the old woman's hand and putting it in front of me.

"Release him," I wrote on a piece of paper and signed it in a zigzag scrawl ...

Whoosh ... a bullet again whistled by. "Jesus Christ!" I murmured and jumped up like a spring. No, it was nothing. But, what if suddenly I was hit and fell to the ground like Simon? ... I sat down again ...

Remembering my fall and "dying" during the day, my heart was filled with relief because, while others had died, I had survived. Of course, the incident was not very pleasant. But in the heat of the moment, anyone could slip and fall. I was just thinking that the imaginary death had lasted a little too long, until someone shouted, "Hey, why are you lying down? Why don't you get up?"

I thought, anyway, one day the war would end, and I would return to my homeland and tell my stories, from beginning to end, to my mother, brothers, sisters-in-law, and neighbors. Then, suddenly, I remembered the horrible stories of Ashod, who had just escaped from Alashgerd. "Men, women, elderly, children are being slaughtered mercilessly," he had said. What if the massacres had reached Yerznga? I then felt someone moving towards me and started trembling.

"Who is it?" I shouted, but my voice did not rise with the required boldness ...

It was Bolsetsi Levon. He had come to replace me.

The stars were falling. The fire that had been lit in the cave had changed its color to copper. Kevork spoke about the Khanasor expedition. Whatever I heard vanished in my head, only some names remained: Sako, Khecho, Garo, Bidza, Touman, Sarkis, Vartan, Der Krikor from Daralagyaz ...

"It was revenge for all the massacres [Armenians had suffered] in Aghpag and a revolutionary trial and judgment," said Kevork ...

We listened to him while kneeling or sitting around the fire.

"The first army consisted of 250 fighters. It was dark when they moved towards Sharaf Bey's 250 tents, right there in the plain, extending in the hundreds," Kevork told us, freezing in the cold.

"We were very close when the Kurdish guard in the semi-darkness started shouting."

"Lo, lo ... houn chi maripn?"

And then the guns thundered. The remaining 3,750 fighters encircled the plain from the following directions ... only the names of Sipan, Ardos Varak, Arnos, Gortvats mountains, St. Bartholomew remain in my head ...[*]

The flames of the fire lit up the faces of the boys listening and threw strange shadows under their *papakh*s [lambskin caps]. I wondered who would survive and who would die ...

***

Before dawn, it turned out that the enemy had retreated. We descended unobstructed to the plain of Khanasor and set up camp near St. Bartholomew's Monastery. Here, we saw the first scenes of massacres, about which I had heard when in Tbilisi. The retreating enemy had put the inhabitants of Harisan village to the sword. There were women, children, and old men, sometimes clustered together, sometimes separated, near smashed doors, inside huts, under walls, in barns, on roofs, under trees ... They were lying everywhere in twisted positions, with pain on their cold faces. Off the road, near some rubble, were the corpses of about twenty girls lying with their clothes torn, their eyes glazed in horror, looking up to the blue sky ...

On May 4th, our detachment left for Choukhagedoug [Choukour Gedig]. Captain Avo had left with his cavalrymen. There was something magical about this silent and brave man. He was everywhere on the front lines during the battles, but no one would see him afterwards. He was either asleep or sitting alone.

By the time we reached Choukhagedoug, Avo's cavalry had already taken up strong positions. The fighting was intense. The carnage we had seen at Harisan had had its effect on everyone. The enemy was also furious, and the retreating Turkish army had apparently decided to wage a decisive battle here. According to

---

[*] This paragraph is somewhat confused and at odds with what we know about the Khanasor expedition. The number of Armenian fighters was also in the hundreds, not thousands.

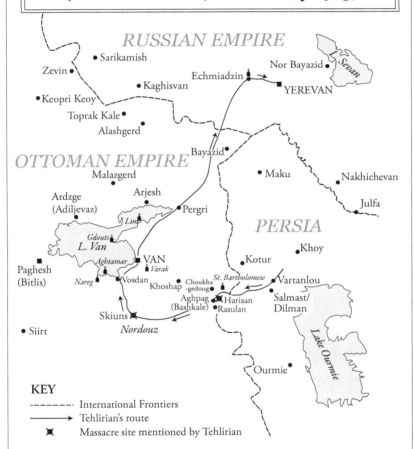

RUSSIAN CAMPAIGN
(advance on Van, March-July 1915)

RUSSIAN EMPIRE

● Sarikamish

Zevin ●

Echmiadzin

Nor Bayazid ●

L. Sevan

● Kaghisvan

● YEREVAN

●Keopri Keoy

Toprak Kale ●

Alashgerd ●

Bayazid ●

OTTOMAN EMPIRE

Malazgerd ●

● Maku

Nakhichevan ■

Ardzge (Adiljevaz) ●

Arjesh ●

● Pergri

Julfa ●

Lin

PERSIA

Gdouts

L. Van

● Khoy

Paghesh (Bitlis) ■

Aghtamar

VAN ■
Varak

Nareg ■

Vosdan ●

Khoshap ●

Choukha -gedoug ●

St. Bartholomew

Kotur ●

Vartanlou

Salmast/ Dilman

Aghpag (Bashkale) ●

Harisan

Rasulan ●

Skiuns ■

Nordouz

● Siirt

Lake Ourmie

Ourmie ●

KEY

-------- International Frontiers

⟶ Tehlirian's route

✖ Massacre site mentioned by Tehlirian

Map shows Tehlirian's movements from Persia to Van (April-May 1915) and Van to Echmiadzin (July 1915). Tehlirian does not provide any details of his movements between the end of May and the end of July.

Gomidas Institute

ARF General Congress, Garin [1914]. *(Front, left to right)* Arshag Vramian and Roupen Der Minasian. *(Back, left to right)* Vahan Minakhkorian and Simon Vratsian.

our information, the enemy had received auxiliary forces from Van and was successfully resisting our onslaught. After a while, when our artillery arrived, the situation changed. The ground shook under the bombardment from both sides, as well as twenty to thirty thousand rifles firing away everywhere. The smoke and dust sometimes brought visibility to zero. After noon, the enemy's left flank weakened, but they resisted stubbornly in the center. The two cavalry and infantry forces were at each other and deadly bullets were flying in all directions.

The volunteers were charging forward, falling, rolling over, getting up, and roaring for vengeance. People were filled with anger and had only one thought in their minds. In the evening, the enemy's left flank gave way. Avo's cavalry chased them, but our infantry was delayed, and the remnants of Khalil Pasha's army managed to escape once again, massacring the unarmed Armenians on its way.

The Russian troops fighting with us did not lack courage and were far superior in their discipline and fighting skills than the volunteers. But, as far as I could see in Araoul and here, at decisive moments, the fate of battles was decided by the volunteers.

On May 5th, we began to pursue the retreating enemy. We were after them until the evening. However, Khalil Pasha headed to Van [*sic*, Sghert or Siirt], spreading death along the way. On the same day, we captured Bashkale. The Turkish population had fled and the Armenians had been massacred to the last person. During the next two days we pursued them non-stop. We entered three or four deserted villages. Avo's cavalrymen rescued several Armenian girls who had been abducted by the Kurds and had them sent to Salmast. During that long pursuit, the Armenian cavalrymen led the way, followed by our troops. Then came the Cossacks' cavalry, followed by the Russian infantry. Then the artillery, and again the Russian infantry. In the rear was the supply column.

On May 15th, we left Razan and reached the mountains of Eomerzade late in the evening. We had a skirmish with the enemy's rearguard, but it soon became dark and the fighting stopped. I could not close my eyes that night. I was concerned about the effectiveness of what we were doing. The enemy was

Autographed copy of General Antranig's photograph addressed to Soghomon Tehlirian on December 8th, 1921.

retreating and massacring Armenians. We were capturing abandoned, deserted villages ...

At the end of the day, an unusual scene appeared in front of me. It was close to sunset. The rays of the sun were fanning out and, in the haze of semi-darkness, the rows of bone-colored rocks of Eomerzade appeared like a pile of skeletons in the distance. There was a deafening roar in the air. The horizon flared behind the rocks, the blaze spreading like a lake of fire. Shadows arose from the hollows and trembled away.

In the morning, we were ordered to continue the pursuit and force the enemy into battle. But the Turks continued to retreat and entered the vast gorges of Eomerzade. We pursued them, sparing no effort, but the enemy no longer cared about us. Undisturbed, they retreated to Sghert and Bitlis, spreading death around them. On the morning of May 18th, we had closed in upon the enemy and were preparing to fight. But, as the sun rose, it became clear that they had fled, and no trace of them could be seen.

Now, we were moving forward along the bare, gray mountain paths of Nordouz. We were tired and broken, but the condition of the cavalry was worse. The mountains and valleys were filled with sheep, and boundless treasures were dumped everywhere along the way. Expensive carpets, various household items, food, etc.

We descended from the mountains to the Armenian village of Sigounis, where a couple of deranged old women appeared from caves. Their village had been destroyed. The Turkish troops who had destroyed it had now crossed the Tigris river and headed for the Jarjalan Mountains.

At the end of the month, we entered the Vasbouragan region and reached Van, which had been liberated thanks to its heroic resistance with the help of outside volunteer groups, particularly the efforts of its fearless leader, Aram [Manougian]. This was the only consolation in the otherwise widespread misery. Our battalion was temporarily dispersed here. The Russian command had postponed the decision to seize the practically abandoned city of Bitlis. One of our local comrades, Krikor, hosted me and Sahag from Giurin. For two days, we inspected the ruins following the glorious resistance. Even in a half-ruined state, Van looked magnificent. Looking from Zimzim Maghara, the endless mountain ranges of Arnos, Ardos and Krkour filled the horizon. The majestic, snow-covered Mount Sipan was lost in the clouds. From these mountainous heights, the wind gently descended into the great plain below, where the pristine Lake Van lay asleep. Beneath the blue sky shone a vast valley at the foothills of Mount Varak, where shadows and lights played in multicolored shades, and the sun shone on the grass with a glow of gold and coral. The rocks of Semiramis' ancient fortress rose at the edge of the valley, which then extended to the village of Ardamed and the port of Avants. During the fighting, the Turks had fired 16,000 artillery shells on the city of Van.

We descended from Zimzim Maghara along the Armenian fortifications and trenches, where immortal heroes had defended the city. In those days, there were probably no fewer than 80,000 inhabitants in Van because of the influx of refugees from neighboring villages. Despite the devastation and the increase in the number of inhabitants, Van was experiencing unprecedented days of enthusiasm and reconstruction. All night long, we were listening to Kevork's stories about Van's resistance, which was a major boost in morale and to our lost souls. But this atmosphere did not last long. The general retreat of the Russian army in this region began in the first days of June [1915].[*] It was a situation which no one comprehended. The defeated enemy was retreating on all fronts; the victorious Russian army was also retreating; and we volunteers were retreating, too. Behind us, we left abandoned people to an enraged enemy, from whom no one could be saved ...

---

[*] The retreat of the Russian army in July 1915 meant that the Armenian population of the province also had to leave in a mass exodus.

CHAPTER TWO

The Great Catastrophe
– Medz Yeghern[*]

With the retreat of June [*sic*, July-August], 1915,[†] around 250,000 people were displaced from Turkish-Armenia.[‡] Around 20,000 people from the region of Pergri should be excluded from this figure because they were unable to join the main movement of refugees and were exterminated. The rest, 207,000 people, moved to the Russian Empire through Kars, Igdir, and Julfa. The balance [around 23,000 people] perished during the retreat. The majority of those arriving in the Caucasus were women and children. Barely 10 percent were men – mostly elderly.

The main flow of the displaced, 170,000 people, was in the direction of Igdir. I was among them. Behind us were those who had fled from much further away. The end of those lines of refugees was lost in clouds of dust. Special horsemen were stationed at the Turkish border crossings to search for lost children and the sick. From these points all the way to Igdir, the refugees were scattered over vast expanses of fields, pastures, and orchards. 20,000 people were crowded into the city of Igdir. There were 45,000 people in Echmiadzin alone. A large current of refugees moved towards Yerevan, like a swarm of locusts, mowing all edible plants and gnawing the roots of vines on their way. In the first two days, the horsemen guarding the crossings gathered

---

* "Medz Yeghern," literally "Great Cataclysm," is the Armenian term that encapsulates the Armenian Genocide of 1915.

† This would be the great retreat or exodus of June 1915.

‡ "Trkahayasdan," literally "Turkish Armenia," refers to those parts of the Armenian Highlands located in the Ottoman Empire. Similarly, "Rousahayasdan" refers to those parts of the Armenian Highlands in the Russian Empire.

about 500 abandoned or missing children. On our first day in Echmiadzin we buried 103 refugees, and 80 more the next day.

The sudden retreat had made it impossible to prepare for the needs of such a mass of people. There was no space for them. Nor was there enough bread or hot food. Medical care was also scarce, even though most refugees were sick.

The hospitals in Yerevan and Echmiadzin were barely able to accommodate 1,500 people. In Echmiadzin,[*] most of the sick were spread out around Nersisian Lake, under the trees and walls of the monastery. The number of sick children was very high. In Echmiadzin Seminary were 3,500 children whose parents were missing. On the evening of the third day, I counted 110 children lying on the wooden floor of the Great Hall. They were practically naked. Some were asleep, but most of them were just crying.

The relief work was very difficult due to a lack of organization. Someone would become an organizer, and everyone would follow their orders until someone else appeared. I was involved in that work as a self-appointed guardian of orphans and children. But this did not last long. The crowds began to disperse when the National Committees of Tbilisi and Moscow and the aid agencies of the Union of Towns (*Kaghakneri Mioutiun*) arrived with their numerous chapters.

The Union of Towns' Yerevan branch appointed me as an "orphan gatherer," a task I was already doing. This work was not as simple as people might think. One had to check whether particular children already had relatives with whom they could stay temporarily, until the establishment of new orphanages and the improvement of existing ones. There was another problem. After a day or two, the older orphans would run away, preferring to beg on the streets. These children could only be caught at dawn, when they were sheltering in front of shop entrances, under trees, street corners, or sleeping in the ruins of buildings. Once they woke up, we couldn't get hold of them. However, as the

---

[*] Echmiadzin is the location of the first cathedral that was built after Armenia adopted Christianity as a state religion in 301 AD. It remains the seat of the Armenian Catholicos, the supreme head of the Armenian Apostolic Church.

conditions of orphanages improved, the number of refugees [in the streets] decreased. Instead, a new problem arose with the daily arrival of "fake" orphans. Displaced parents in difficulties, unable to provide for their families, would bring their children from the farthest villages to the city and abandon them. These "fake" orphans were mostly housed with Armenian families who determined the names of the orphans' parents; that is, if the children could be understood at all.

The most troubled group consisted of those who had been orphaned before the mass exodus of refugees from Van. These, with few exceptions, consisted of children between the ages of eight to twelve, rarely up to 14. During the massacres, these children had fled from Kurds and returned to their abandoned villages, somehow surviving until the general retreat. They had then joined this or that volunteer group and traveled with them. One 14-year-old orphan had not only managed to escape from the Kurds but had also carried his five-year-old sister all the way to the Caucasus. These children were daring, smart, and resilient. They did not like to talk. When asked about their parents, they replied with a stock answer, "They were killed."

They did not seem to be in pain. Only one wept and said that they had been hiding in the *tonir* (clay-oven) and got burned. Almost all of them had their stories. Among the orphans, girls were more talkative than boys. They were also more friendly towards their male guardians than female ones. It seemed that such guardians were able to fill the void left by their fathers, uncles, or brothers, but never the void left by their mothers.

What were the military reasons for the retreat of June 2nd* and what was the relationship between that retreat and the terrible massacres that broke out in Turkey? I do not know. However, this is how events unfolded after the retreat. The 150,000 Armenians of Bitlis, Moush and Sassoun were deported. On June 7th, the 20,000 Armenians of Yerznga were sent away. On June 16th, the 18,000 Armenians of Erzeroum, on June 28th, the 14,000 Armenians of Trabizon, and on June 29th, the Armenians of Papert, Sivas [Svaz], and Kharpert were forced out of their homes.

---

* The actual exodus took place around August 2nd, 1915.

By the end of the month, from Sivas to Kharpert, about half a million people were already marching to their graves.

The Armenians in Yerevan were in mourning. The retreat had turned life upside down and created an atmosphere of indignation. A rift had opened between the Armenian people and the previously "friendly" Russian government. Everyone saw the evil purposes of the retreat. The reason for this judgment was the well-known thesis of "Armenia without Armenians." Everyone was talking about the massacres. The Armenian newspapers in Tbilisi, which until then had written about events taking place in Van, the retreat, the exile of Armenian intellectuals in Constantinople, and news of sporadic massacres, were now sounding the alarm about the wholesale destruction of Western Armenians.* A number of survivors from the furthermost corners of Turkey were still arriving in the Caucasus, bringing with them terrible stories of violence, death, and slaughter ...

Hamazasp Paraghamian, a humble young man from Divrig, lived near the orphanage in the Kond district of Yerevan. Previously, he did organizational work among the volunteers. After the retreat, he went to Tbilisi. He now returned to Yerevan as a correspondent of *Horizon* newspaper and would interview the refugees all day long, gathering information about different events.

He was a well-known figure among the deportees, who called him "journalist Hamo," and every newcomer would see him at the first opportunity. I used to spend all my free time with him, hoping to obtain information about the deportees from Yerznga. There was information from everywhere, except Yerznga. Although I was prepared for the worst regarding the fate of my relatives, the uncertainty overwhelmed and wore me out, making me physically ill. At the beginning of August, I saw a young woman who had recently escaped from Trabizon, telling her story to Hamo. She explained, in a monotonous voice, how about 500 Armenian intellectuals, who had been arrested and supposedly exiled to Samsoun, only to be drowned at sea. The woman's descriptions were so heartbreaking that they were very difficult to

---

* Western or Ottoman Armenians.

listen to. Hamo, with an investigator's indifference, took notes on long sheets of paper, as he asked questions. When the woman began to describe the massacre of Jevizlik [Machka], I forced myself to listen:

"They first separated the men from the women and children," she said. "Then, they killed them with swords, knives, rifle butts, and in other ruthless ways. The screams of terror could be heard everywhere across the field. The soil and grass were soaked in blood. The wide-eyed little boys, seeing the horrors in front of them, were screaming. The women stretched out their arms, pleaded for their lives, and fell. The warm smell of blood was everywhere ..."

Suddenly, I felt I was seeing all these scenes, hearing the screaming, the cries of horror and pain, desperate pleas, howls of madness and anguish. I was seeing the corpses exactly as I had seen in the village of Harissan. I sensed the warm smell of blood. Shocked, I got up to leave as I could not listen any longer, but my head was spinning, and I collapsed ...

When I came to, the woman was no longer there, and Hamo led me to my room. I could not close my eyes that night. As I dozed off, I would imagine horrible scenes, as if my mother was in the cave at the village of Sigounis. It was as if all our children were around the *tonir*, screaming in unison, as if my brother, his head crushed, lay dead in the garden ... and every time I came to my senses, I could see Talaat's puffy, satisfied face in front of my eyes, an image I had seen for the first time in Van. I had visions of catching him, tying a noose around his neck, dragging him like a dog to the last of his slaughterhouses, and let him bleed in front of the dying victims .... From that day onwards, I began to be ill with periodic bouts of dizziness and fainting.

In mid-September, I read in one of Tbilisi's Armenian newspapers, a translation of an official report dated July 11th [1915], written by the United States representative in Kharpert:

"During the first days of July, caravans of sick, starving Armenians, clad in rags, reached Kharpert from Garin and Yerznga. They had spent nearly two months on the roads with almost no food or water. Mothers were willingly giving their children to anyone who wished to take them. Young girls were subjected to medical examinations by rich Turks, and the prettiest were taken away for their harems. According to these unfortunates, most of them had suffered extortion or been killed by the Kurds, who had constantly attacked the caravans.

"Many have died on the road due to starvation and exhaustion. Two days later, new caravans arrived. Among the deportees were three sisters who spoke English. Eleven of their 25 family members had already been killed on the road and the only surviving male was eight years old. When they first left, they had horses, money, and bags, but on the road, everything was stolen, even their clothes, and one of the girls was completely naked. In Kharpert the deportation order was preceded by the arrest of thousands of men. At night, they took them to the nearby mountains, and no one returned. Among them were the Prelate of the Armenian church, the teachers of the American College and the city's leaders. Also, all the soldiers and all the youth of military age, who had paid the "bedel."* On June 5th, eight hundred more men were arrested. The next day, they were taken to deserted parts of the mountains, tied in groups of 14, since their ropes could not bound more than 14 persons, and were gunned down. In the neighboring villages other groups of Armenians were arrested. After three days without food or water, they were taken to nearby rocks and shot. Whoever was still breathing was killed with swords and knives. On July 10th, new massacres of thousands of Armenians took place two hours from the city. The same killings took place in all the surrounding villages."

In late November, Sepasdatsi Mourad arrived in Tbilisi. After ten months of fighting in the mountains, he had managed to escape with 13 of his comrades to Samsoun, where they seized a sailing boat and successfully reached Batumi. *Horizon* published the story of that legendary escape, "The Odyssey of Mourad," allowing readers to have an idea of the mass deportations and massacres between Sivas and Samsoun.

Soon began the publication of shocking reports of various missionaries and Italian diplomats, revealing that these Armenian

---

* The *bedel* was a military exemption tax which Armenians were allowed to pay, at least temporarily, in lieu of military service.

massacres had surpassed all other massacres in history in their scope and organization ...

At the end of the year, we read in newspapers about a number of uprisings in Shabin Karahisar, Ourfa, Ayntab, Zeitoun, and the Armenians of the mountains of Jebel Mousa [Mousa Dagh] ...

It was now clear that the Armenian massacres would only end when the general war ended. But Lord Kitchener, Secretary of State for War, said Great Britain could only take an active part in the war two years later, and the situation on the two main fronts was not comforting. Although the Germans had already deployed a large part of their forces to the eastern front, all the efforts of the British and French to break through the German lines around the Somme had been in vain. The Western Front had turned into "trench warfare," thus giving Germany the opportunity to hold their lines with the minimum of forces and continue fighting the Russians on the Eastern Front.

At the Straits, after the disaster of March 18th [1915], when the Allies lost four large naval ships, the Franco-British fleet did not attempt to force the Dardanelles again. Hamilton's army, which was on the outskirts of Gallipoli, remained unsuccessful all year long.

In the Balkans, during October–December [1915], the heroic resistance of Serbia was crushed by the simultaneous attacks of superior German-Austrian-Bulgarian forces from the north and east under the general command of Von Mackensen.

The situation on the Russian front was even worse. In May [1915], the German forces around Krakow forced the Russians to retreat to the left bank of the Vistula river. Shortly afterwards, the Russians left Przemysl and Lvov, and by the end of the summer, all of Galicia. In the fall, the Germans captured, one after the other, Kovno, Grodno and Brest-Litovsk. Thereafter, the Russians began to retreat on all fronts, putting up limited resistance at a few fortified positions.

***

At the beginning of 1916, our despair peaked when we learned that Hamilton's army had withdrawn from Gallipoli. All hopes of saving the lives of the remnants of our people vanished.

In Yerevan and elsewhere, sharp thinkers interpreted these developments in terms of Anglo-Russian rivalry. Great Britain could have seized control of the Straits had it decided to do so, but in that case, it would have had to surrender Constantinople to the Russians. It therefore delayed matters for a year and withdrew ...

Doctor [Hayg] Toroian, who had fled Mesopotamia, arrived in Tbilisi in those days and reported on the fate of remaining deportees.

"My unfortunate compatriots deported to Mesopotamia consist mostly of women and girls. They can barely cover their nudity with rags and have nothing to protect themselves from the harsh weather. Some of them are sitting on the ground, under makeshift shelters put together from rags, but most of them are even deprived of such poor shelter. In the desert, everywhere, ferocious dogs roam around the sand dunes. Most of the corpses remain unburied. There are thousands of these skeletal people, with sunken cheeks, faded or very bright eyes, deprived of the ability to talk, deluded by their sufferings."

If I had had any hope that my relatives could survive the desert, even that hope was fading now. Only one thing remained for me to do: go to Constantinople and find Talaat. Only his death could soothe my grief. Like an unending nightmare, this thought would never leave me alone. Sometimes it would overwhelm me so much, that it would make me forget everything else. I still had my position at the "Union of Towns," but I wasn't doing anything.

Shortly afterwards, the Russians captured Erzeroum [February, 1916]. That news exploded like a bombshell in Yerevan, where nobody had any confidence in the effectiveness of the Russian army in the Caucasus. It was already well known that the best units of that army had been transferred to the Russian-Romanian front, and the rest did not have the required weapons to attack.

Now, a new cycle of hope emerged. People livened up once again. All was not yet lost. Had any nation been liberated from the Turkish yoke without being subjected to mass murder? Why should we have expected to be the exception to this rule? In what condition was the population of Bulgaria when it was liberated [in 1878]? Such was the mood during those days. And a new movement began towards the front. That same day Hamo came to say goodbye, packing his loads of paper. He was going as a journalist to report the latest news. Afterwards, all my friends who were in the volunteer groups in Yerevan departed. However, this time, the volunteer groups were scattered, as they had fulfilled their supposed mission when they first enrolled. The newly formed groups, as well as the remnants of the former volunteers, were transformed into Armenian rifle battalions under the supervision of regular officers and integrated into the Russian army.

At the end of March [1916], I also left, having barely recovered from my illness. I was going forth on behalf of the "Union of Cities." I was warmly received by two Russian Army artillery officers from Sarighamish [Sarikamish], Der Agopov and Der Bedrosov, who were transporting field communications' equipment to the Erzeroum front.

This was the first time I was entering the homeland by this route. Mountains and valleys testified to historical sites and more recent, bloody events. In the evening we reached Karaourgan. My pleasant, polite friends, seeing that I had just recovered from illness, offered me care and attention. The next day, we passed through Zivin and moved towards Keopriu-Keoy. Zivin, which was hardly noticeable just before sunrise, reminded me of the martyrdom of the Vagharshag-Gaydzag group of fighters, about whom I had read or heard many years before. We did not stop at our ancient city of Vagharshavan. In the evening, we reached Hasan-Kale, where Vahan Mamigonian and his brave men had found refuge from Persian armies 1,400 years earlier. We left at dawn. The road was difficult, but the weather was good. It was sunset when we reached Garin [Erzeroum]. The last rays of the sun played on the delicate and sharp tips of the minarets.

At every step in the city, we saw officers, soldiers, loaded carts and camel caravans. Suddenly, I saw Sahag from Giurin, with whom I had taken care of the orphans in Echmiadzin. He took me in his care. He was staying near Sanasarian College and led me there. There were no volunteers from the United States in Erzeroum with him. He was planning to go to Van and Bitlis, which had been recaptured by the Russians.

Garin (Erzeroum).

Of 18,000 Armenians in Erzeroum, only 120 remained, six of whom were men, the rest, women and children. All the Armenians in the villages of the region had been annihilated.

In the morning, I introduced myself to Dikran Aghamalian, who was in charge of the "Union of Cities" in that area. He was tall and pale with big, melancholic eyes, and much absorbed in his work. Dozens of orphans from the nearby areas had already been taken to Alexandropol. However, there was still a lot of work to be done, as far as Khnous.

Shortly afterwards, I was with Hamo. I had read his terrifying reports in Yerevan of the massacres organized by members of the Ottoman Parliament, Seyfullah and Ingliz Ahmet Bey, Commander Kouzi Bey, Behaeddin Shakir and Haji Bey. Hamo was still engaged in the same type of work. His life had no ups and downs, and his morale was intact. He explained the situation to me in a few words. Whatever had happened, had happened; now was the time to think about the future.

He was in a hurry to report on a certain memorial. He picked up a handful of long sheets of paper from the table and stood up.

"By the way, you could be helpful to me here. Let's go, we will talk on the way."

The "memorial" was an unfinished building site located just below the Armenian cemetery, on a hilly plain. It was supposed to be the Unionists' biggest club, with gambling halls, sport sections, lakes, footpaths, etc. It had been left unfinished due to the Russian occupation of the city. The two-meter walls of the building had been constructed from tombstones brought from the Armenian cemetery. Apparently, the location was chosen to be close to buildings and not the beautiful fields of flowers further away. Paraghamian now made me sit on the stones not far from the center of construction so that I could take notes.

"Write," he shouted. "East wall, from left to right, first row, here lies ..."

"What?"

"'Here lies Kevork, church clerk, the son of Nakhran, from the house of Hagop of Khnous, who with a bitter death, ceased to live in 1845.' Write the next one.

"'This is the grave of the daughter of Nouri Khatun, who died during her first childbirth bearing twins, went to Christ with her children, and was the wife of silk merchant Hovhannes Chelebian, nicknamed Chukhur.' Write the third.

"'Here rests Moughdousi Madteos, who switched worlds after his heart attack. When you see him, recite the Lord's Prayer and ask for mercy.' Second row, write.

"'Under this tomb rests Haygaz from Erzeroum, surname Avakian, from our nation of Haygazoun, who wished for his tomb to be dedicated to Apostle Saint Peter.' Alas! Write the other one.

"'This is the tomb of Srpouhi, daughter of Mahdesi Hagop from Erzeroum, who died prematurely in the year 1889.' Write under it.

"'When you meet this ark, do not give blessings, because this world is only a transitory ground for us to roam.'"

My heart was pounding, I was getting hot. Hamo entered the building and was shouting, "Here rests," "here rests," ...

"Write, 'Tomb of Minas Agha, kehripar merchant, husband of Hanum ...'"

"That's enough," I shouted.

45

"Write, write, the last of this series. 'Here rests Tateos Agha, son of Arakel Amira Chutchutian, imperial gunpowder chief.' Underneath it, write 'Passersby of my life journey, welcome to the sight of my soul ...'"

***

In April [1916], the Russians captured Trabizon, and in mid-July, Yerznga. Petrified, savage children appeared everywhere in the Erzeroum plain, most of whom had survived in the ruins of Armenian villages. Those who fell into our arms were trembling like autumn leaves. We had to make great effort to make it clear to them that they were no longer in danger. They had forgotten their language, Armenian identity, and humanity. About two hundred of them were gathered in Khnous. The work with orphans was of paramount importance everywhere. Every single orphan was a new brick to rebuild the nation. I was trying to finish my work as soon as possible, so that I could go to Yerznga. In late August, we saw Hovnan, who had escaped to the Caucasus with Mourad. He had returned via Batumi-Tbilisi-Kars and was going to join him [in Yerznga]. Sahag and I left with him.

The road was lined with countless ox carts carrying food and ammunition, accompanied by Russian soldiers. We were going in a two-wheeled cart belonging to the "Union of Cities." It would return from Yerznga with orphans. The coachman, Karekin, was more interested in listening to Hovnan's story of escape with Mourad than driving the cart. We soon found ourselves stuck on the tails of loaded horses. Every time Hovnan talked about the difficulties of their long road from Sivas to Samsoun, Karekin would whisper, "Hey, Msho Soultan Sourp Garabed" or murmur, "Yaa, yaa!" Indeed, some parts of Hovnan's story were very moving. For example, when he described how Mourad and his friends had hidden in a cave and helplessly watched the deportation of their relatives – mothers, sisters, brothers and children – unable to fire a single bullet. "What could we have done? We could have killed five or ten of them, and they would have killed everyone."

Avedis Tehlirian. Soghomon's older brother, who was a medical student at the American University of Beirut. He was one of the victims of the Armenian Genocide in 1915.

Or the time when they reached Douzasar and Mourad received a letter from his wife, stating, "Do not worry about me. I will kill myself. Please write to the pharmacist to give me some poison."

We reached Mamakhatoun. There were great changes there. Huge wooden boarding houses, dormitories, and warehouses had been built. The square was occupied by oxen, horse-drawn carriages, soldiers, and ammunition. We barely stayed there for an hour. The Euphrates crossing was near Kotour-Keopri. As we got closer to familiar places, I was overwhelmed more and more with emotions.

The next day, we saw the barracks at the junction of the roads leading to Trabizon and Garin [Erzeroum], both cities now under the Russian flag. From the heights above Yerznga, I saw the sharp peak of Yeni Jami. A little further on, I could see the sun shining on the domes of Sourp Nshan and Sourp Prgich churches.

It was evening when we entered Yerznga. In the foreground to the Turkish neighborhood, Turkish boys, holding their trousers in one hand, were running in the thick dust and trying to catch up with our cart. Squatting in the shadow, under the walls, were older Turks who looked rather worried. Turkish women remained on the sidewalks, carefully covering themselves.

We entered the neighborhood's central square. Facing each other, all under Russian flags, were the buildings of the military staff, the regional and municipal governorate, and the state councilor's offices (Moushir Sarayi). Nothing seemed to have happened there. Only the government had changed.

But this deception did not last long. When the cart turned to the right, I saw the empty Yegeghyats Square in front of me, the large square that always used to be crowded. The orphaned St. Sarkis Church, the center of my Easter games, was still standing. Just opposite, in front of the square, was our house. Jumping out of the cart, I had a strong urge to run home, but a sharp, unpleasant feeling stopped me. The uncertainty was greater than anything I could feel. I headed to the left, to the Getronagan School [Central School], the Holy Trinity Church, and the Prelacy.

The Getronagan School had been turned into an orphanage-hospital. It was headed by Dr. Arshag Boghosian, a broad-shouldered, slightly hunch-backed, calm and intelligent looking, amiable man of about 40. My hope of finding relatives were dashed. I had no family member among the orphans. There was no one from Yerznga; everyone was from the surrounding areas. There were only two or three families left in the city from Yerznga, including our neighbors, the Tarigians. I left not knowing what I should do. An officer was standing in front of our house.

"What do you want?" he shouted.

"This is our house. I would like to see it ..."

"Is this your house?"

"Yes ..."

"Where are you coming from?"

"Erzeroum."

"Are you a volunteer?"

"No, an official of the Union of Cities."

"Were your relatives here?"

"Yes."

"And now?"

"I don't know ..."

The man was sympathetic. He hung his head, took out a cigarette, and said, "Please, come in ..."

Our house had become a dormitory, but there was no one inside. Part of the side building had been destroyed. On the lower floor were the cellar and storage rooms for grass-fodder, flour, fruit, and wood, as well as the stone oven and kitchen. They were filled with unfamiliar items. Above, the large common room, where we used to sit, dine, and have dinner in the summer, as well as four other rooms, were occupied by ordinary military beds. In my eyes, our house had become a historical monument. A soldier appeared from my small bedroom. I did not understand what he said. My throat was tight. I could barely hold back my tears. I descended the stairs and went outside. All the trees at the side of the house remained in line and seemed like old and faithful friends. I knew all the nests and understood the chirping of the birds. From my window, I would throw tiny bread balls at them. I knew which tree would give resin in the summer. In the winter, I freed their branches from the heavy snow, so that they could remain upright. The row of trees stretched to the front of our large garden. Most of the fruit trees had been cut down or uprooted. There were also bushes and wild plants everywhere. Inside the garden, a few trees hung low, looking at me with sadness. Under them were bushes and scattered wild plants. There was no life here any longer. All my childhood memories had disappeared like a dream. Only in the depths of the garden was there an untouched corner where, as a child, my older brother Avedis would throw our mother's black shawl over his shoulders like a priest's mantle and sing, "*Sourp Asdvatz*" [Holy Father] and various other psalms like a priest. But there was also a large bush here. How and why was it there since the trees remained in their places? I shivered and cold air hit me. I smelled warm blood and felt a dizziness. I backed away in terror, and collapsed ...

When I came to my senses, it was twilight. I left the garden, trembling. The noisy crows were perched on the trees on the square. My mind was in disarray, and I did not know where to go. I was shivering from time to time. I noticed someone in the yard of the Tarigians. What was this, a dream or reality? He looked very much like my elder brother, Misak. This was such a surprise that I hardly had the confidence to call him. It was him! My brother Misak! He had arrived from Serbia and joined the volunteers in the fall of 1915. After the Russian advance of 1916, he came to Yerznga, when it was under Russian control.[*] We, two brothers, had met up in Kanaker, after the retreat of 1915, in Antranig's army, when it was being reorganized [late 1915]. During the reconquest of Van and the advance on Bitlis and Moush, we were together in the army up to Arjesh. While in Arjesh, I contracted spotted typhus and was taken to the military hospital in Van. We thus lost touch with each other for a while. A few months after the occupation of Yerznga, we found each other again.

"Are you sick?"

---

[*] These two sentences regarding Misak's movements been changed according to Tehlirian's corrections which were not entered into the final Armenian edition of *Remembrances*. See *Vem Hamahaygagan Hantes*, pp. 345-46.

"No, but I got a little cold on the way last night."

"Let's go inside, I am at the Tarigians."

He was there with his wife and children. I remembered them. They thought that my brother had found me. Tarigian embraced me, his wife cried with joy ... tea, cheese, bread, boiled eggs, the cheerful gestures of old hosts, but all in a half-ruined and empty house.

They had escaped and miraculously survived. After a long march, they had fallen into the hands of a Kurd in Dersim, who had saved and looked after them on the condition that they converted to Islam. What they had gone through was still fresh, and Mr. Tarigian had a need for people to know the horrors they had experienced, as well as their ingenuity in surviving. My brother listened to him intensely, asking additional questions about the hellish role of the city's police chief, Memduh Bey, the massacres of Kemakh-Boghaz, and other such incidents.[*] I wanted to leave, just leave, but where could I go?

His wife, probably sensing my feelings, went upstairs and came down after a while. She told me that I could go upstairs to rest if I wanted. Upstairs, in the room given to my brother, the window looked over the garden of my uncle's house, which was associated with countless childhood memories. Clouds passed through the sky, occasionally obscuring the moon. I pulled the window shutters down and went to bed, but the old blanket had no warmth. My head was burning like a furnace, my body was trembling. I covered myself with my coat. It did not help; my body was shaking. I started thinking that I was useless, helpless. I felt disgust with myself. Unlike me, other people had a purpose, a will. For example, Hamo did his job well, he kept the Armenian public informed of ongoing events. What happened with the tombstone notes? Wasn't it strange to record the graves of dead people when there were no stones left in the country, and the bones of the unburied were scattered in the mountains and valleys ...? I could not understand how only a few families out of 20,000 Armenians remained in the city, including our friends, the Tarigians with

---

[*] The massacres of Kemakh-Boghaz would have included the Tehlirian's ancestral village of Vari Pakarij.

Fall, 1915, Yerevan-Kanaker. *(Left to right)* 1. Misak Tehlirian, Soghomon's brother, a volunteer from Serbia. 2. Sahag Tehlirian, Soghomon's cousin, volunteer from Selanik. 3. Soghomon Tehlirian, 1915, Kanaker, in 1st army.

their children. They were chosen by providence as witnesses to unprecedented massacres. "No, it couldn't be like this, unless a powerful hand continuously commanded the massacres with a clear conscience," as Hamo had once told me when we talked about the killings. Again, I saw Talaat's puffy, smug face in front of me, and he seemed to be raising his furry paw in the darkness ...

Ah, if only I could have cut off that hand and let the monster bleed, to make him feel and understand the terrible magnitude of his crime ... Could I believe that one day there would ever be a just judgment? A warm feeling uplifted my spirit, a feeling that I had felt in my little bedroom seven years earlier, on the other side of the wall, when every night I had muttered with my mother, "*Hayr mer, vor hergins es ...*" [Our Father who art in Heaven.]

I had come home from far away in dusty boots. Oh Lord, how far had I come! Through mountains and valleys, I finally reached Ghuybashi, and from there walked straight home. On the threshold of our house was a head under the poplar trees that jumped and rolled towards me. It was my mother, my mother's head, but I was surprised because it was not covered. It had a thorny headscarf around her neck, under the ears.

"Come here, so they don't see you, my child," she said, at my feet.

"Where, mother?"

"There, there, in the garden under the bushes, we're all lying there."

"And where is your body, mother?"

"It's there, there, my child, come quick!"

And I followed my mother's head, which disappeared into the bushes ... Indeed, everyone was there, silently stretched out under the bushes. There was my brother.

"Avedis, hello," I whispered ...

"Avedis" ... "Ssss" ... The poplars whistled under the gentle breeze. My brother looked at the sky with open eyes, and my mother's head was asleep near her body.

"You here, like this?" I muttered, astonished. "Hripsime, Markar, Baydzar, get up!"

Suddenly, my brother looked at me and said:

"Who are you and what do you want from us?"

"Don't you remember?" I said, trying to smile.

"No," said my brother gently and then shook his head.

Suddenly the moon came out of the clouds and looked down. I only now saw that my brother's head was chopped off.

"I am Soghomon, Avedis!" I said, terrified, and wanted to hug his head. But, suddenly, his face darkened, and a cold smile appeared on his lips.

"Oh, you ... yes, you look like him, but where were you when we ran away? Why aren't you lying with us, and why did you come to caress me like a thief at night? Go, go, I don't know you."

And, on my knees, under the bushes, I cried like a little boy ...

"Soghomon!" ...

I was suddenly woken up.

"Hey, boy, why are you roaring like a bull?" asked Misak.

The sun was rising ...

CHAPTER THREE

With Mourad

I introduced myself to Mourad in the morning. I had only seen him once before, seven years earlier. It was in Yerznga, on Yegeghyats Square, and later, at Trinity Church, where he had spoken before a large crowd about the Turkish Revolution and the "general Ottoman fatherland." At that time, he was a bronze-tanned man with deep, fiery, restless eyes, under thick, black eyebrows. His head rested on his masculine neck and his bush-like hair was combed backwards, reminding me of the lion's mane pictured in my childhood schoolbook. Now, there only remained the eyes and hair of the former Mourad. There were wrinkles on his face. He had lost his vitality and had become sorrowful. There was pain in his eyes, a very deep pain that could not be expressed in words. His proud, imperious face had become sad.

There was so much work to do, and so few people to do it, that Mourad immediately took me into his group, which was based at the Krisdiniants girls' school. First, Vahram Der Manouelian, who was called "Chemishgadzaktsi,"[*] caught my attention. He was the spirit of Mourad's special squads searching for Armenian orphans. He was a tall, handsome, and charming young man, barely 25 years old. His posture was strong and firm. His answers were short and sharp. He was respectful, always waiting for the other person to speak. During work, there was no trace of hesitation on his face. He listened attentively to the instructions given to him, his eyes fixed on Mourad's face. Without any unnecessary show of confidence, he would nod affirmatively. He had one foot in Dersim and one other in Yerznga. He had managed to establish contact with Kurds, amongst whom Mourad's "*meg hay, meg vosgi*" [one Armenian, one gold] policy had become very popular. Chemishgadzaktsi followed that order

---

[*] Vahram Der Manougian from Chemishgadzak (1889-1918).

strictly, paying one Ottoman gold coin for every Armenian handed over to us by the Kurds. New orphans were handed to us every day.

Another notable presence was Jebeji Sarkis,[*] who would embrace the liberated orphans and squeal like a bear, "Hey, who are your parents?" Joyful, cheerful, bold and brave, Jebeji was like a new bride in Mourad's presence. Mkhitar from Kemakh (from Avak Monastery), Kalousd from Pakarij, Mardiros from Govdoun, Haroutiun Chachanian, Avedis Moushmoulian and others, none lacking in courage and self-sacrifice. Apart from Hovnan, one of Mourad's comrades on the Sivas-Samsoun-Batumi escape route, Nshan, Armenag, and Vartan stood out. Vartan had the strength of a bull. He would suddenly pick up a friend, turn him up upside-down, and laugh, silently, as he shook him like the carcass of a sheep. In general, all of them were devoted, experienced, young people, ready to make any sacrifice.

Mourad's close associates were Dr. Arshag Boghosian and his old comrade in arms, Gaydzag-Arakel.[†] Dr. Boghosian was the representative of the Union of Cities in Yerznga. He cared for the orphans and the patients. Judging from the outside, there was hardly anything impressive about him. He would sit quietly during meetings, his mind seemingly wandering in distant places without paying attention, lost in his thoughts. But, he had a thoughtful, witty face, and spoke little, in short sentences, and he almost always made a practical suggestion. His comrades would listen to him intently. Gaydzag-Arakel was in his forties, a man made of nerves and bones, with sunburnt skin, whose battles against the Hamidian regime were known to all. Currently, he was dedicated to the cause of rescuing orphans. One of his most prominent features was his wolf-like, protruding jaw.

The tireless work of these dedicated people yielded great results in a month or two. The announcement of "one Armenian, one gold coin" policy had a big impact. Hundreds of youngsters from the surrounding Kurdish villages were released from captivity.

---

[*] Sarkis Jebejian (1879-1920).
[†] Dikran Abajian (1869-1917).

Fate also smiled on us, as one of my brother Misak's children, his 10-year-old daughter, Armenouhi, was found.

In a short time, the empty Armenian quarter of Yerznga began to come to life again. There was feverish reconstruction as the ruined houses were repaired. Smoke rose again from chimneys, and the fields were plowed. There were preparations for autumn sowing. The remnants of our people, who were back under their roofs, were showing unparalleled vitality.

All recaptured areas were in the same situation. In every region the villages were being reconstructed and the fields were turning green. There was intense building everywhere. The Armenian villager was rinsing his native land enthusiastically with his sweat, rebuilding what had been destroyed by the enemy and the war. There was a resettlement program, run by a special department. Large sums of money and loans were provided to help the refugees return to their homes. In addition to government institutions, charitable and cultural bodies worked in the recaptured territories: the Armenian Benevolent Society of the Caucasus, the Brotherhood Relief Committee, the Moscow Committee, the Union of Cities, the Central Refugee Committee, various patriotic unions, and others. Observing the peace and reconstruction in Yerznga, one might have concluded that the existential threat against the Armenian people had vanished.

But that threat was one aspect of many threats. After the retreat of June [*sic*, August, 1915] the previous year and the disbandment of the Armenian volunteer army, the Russian monarchy's attitude towards Armenians had changed. By the winter of 1916, there was no more talk of "Armenian autonomy." According to information received, it was now considered enough in Russia to grant Armenians "school and church autonomy" and even that was, "as far as the local conditions allowed." Nicolay Nicolayevich, the great prince and ruler of the Caucasus, oversaw the recaptured territories. General Peshkov, whom he had appointed as governor-general, filled the Armenian-populated areas with anti-Armenian officials.

General Kaletin, military commander of the Yerznga forces, and chief-of-staff Lastochkin, were such agents of the autocratic regime. The police chief of the city was a Georgian who was a

Gaydzag-Arakel.

Turkish citizen. Khayri Bey, a former Colonel in the Turkish Army, was appointed mayor by Kaletin. Turkish spies, who had remained in Yerznga as civil officials after the Turkish retreat, were all over the place. If needed, the Turks also sent more people from their army. Thus, for example, Commander Moustafa Vefa Bey, from the Kemakh front's 8th Battalion, was settled in Dersim after Khayri Bey's letter of invitation. He had supposedly "fled" the Turkish army, as an "enemy" of the Unionist government, but was engaged in intelligence gathering for his country. These were the conditions when we celebrated the New Year in Yerznga.

***

In early February [1917], after a short illness, Gaydzag-Arakel died in Yerznga. A distinguished revolutionary, the guiding spirit in numerous mortal clashes, he died in his bed, just like Giumoushkhanetsi Avo. He lay in a simple coffin, sunk into a pillow, his head leaning to the side with his broad, beeswax-yellow forehead, and his jaw protruding forwards. The expression on his face was more remarkable than when he was alive. He seemed to say that he had already done what he had to do and died because there was no more work.

For us, his death marked the beginning of significant events. The February Revolution broke out in Russia. The czar was overthrown on February 28th, and that movement with deep, social foundations would not be mollified with simple political changes. The revolution deepened and expanded, embracing soldiers, and destroying the army. In this process, "Order number one" of the Petrograd Labor Council's Executive Committee, on March 11th, was a major turning point. This order meant that elected bodies would accompany armies to control their military commands and eventually take over the general affairs of the armed forces. In a short time, discipline broke down, and the army began to disintegrate. March and April were marked by internal struggles among various political parties, currents, and internal governmental circles. Under these conditions, in June, the worker-soldier masses turned their backs on the Russian offensive on the European front, so that, after one or two initial successes, it gave way to the desertion of troops and created new and larger

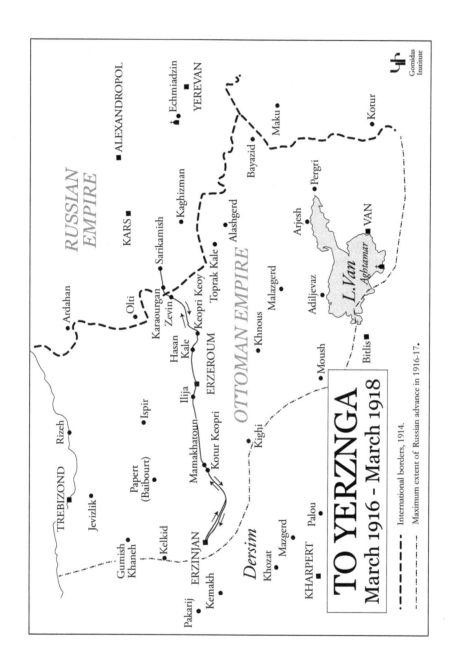

TO YERZNGA
March 1916 – March 1918

International borders, 1914.

Maximum extent of Russian advance in 1916-17.

movements in the rear. In August, after General Kornilov's speech, the Russian army was disbanded and was unable to continue the war.

These events in [European] Russia had consequences on the Asian fronts as well, and their influence was felt in Yerznga in the spring. Far from their homeland, tired of three years of fighting, angry soldiers began to leave the front and head for home. The movement was especially strong in the Yerznga region.

A very difficult situation was being created for us. To replenish the abandoned fronts, we needed forces that did not actually exist. As long as desertions of the Russian army were partial, the situation was under control. But when desertions began to spread to various parts of Russia and the Caucasus, and civil strife escalated, the situation worsened.

It was under these conditions that the October Revolution took place in 1917. The revolutionary right to expropriate landowners' lands and talk of "honorary reconciliation" triggered a mass exodus of soldiers from the front lines. For Russia, the war was over. The Soviet government offered an honorable democratic reconciliation without annexations or reparations. Yerznga was part of the Russian-occupied lands that were to be ceded to the Turks in the event of an agreement. Even for the remaining few Russian soldiers at the front, it was no longer necessary to stay and protect it. Soldiers hurried home to get their share of land and unite with their families.

Deprived of resources and real support, completely isolated and facing the Turkish armies, as well as the Kurds in the rear, we tried to hold the abandoned front with our small forces. We endeavored to take possession of the countless weapons left behind by the Russians and to replace the local authorities. However, the course of events had its own momentum. On November 17th, a ceasefire was established between Austria, Germany, and Russia. On the same day, the commander of the Turkish forces, Vehib Pasha, made a similar proposal to the commander-in-chief of the Russian Caucasus Army. In the middle of December, A[rshag] Jamalian[*] came to Yerznga with a

---

[*] Arshag Jamalian (1882-1940), ARF activist and politician.

Russian military commission to conclude the ceasefire. The bright-eyed Armenian revolutionary did not hide the dire situation. It was already abundantly clear that if the demoralization of the Russian army and the return of Russian soldiers to Russia continued at the same rate, we would be unable to defend the more than 500 kilometers of our front stretching from the Black Sea to Kelkid-Yerznga-Khnous-Van with our own forces. According to Jamalian, the Turks wanted the ceasefire to actively contribute to the disintegration of the Russian front, and then, by redistributing their forces, to launch an attack. There was no hope that the Council of Commissioners formed in the Transcaucasus would defend the front. The Georgians sought independence, and the Tartars sided with the Turks. The Tartar movements in the Caucasus were particularly worrying. The Caucasian Muslims were ready to embrace Turkish armies. The secretive pro-Turkish sentiments during the old regime had turned into public Turk-loving displays. Muslim movements had begun to expand all over the Empire, which was deepening the chaos in the Caucasus. These movements were led by Turkish agents. They provoked riots and carried out bandit-attacks on trains, food supply convoys, Russian soldiers returning home, and Armenians. These movements were especially prevalent in the provinces of Kars, Yerevan, Kantsag, and Erzeroum.

The ceasefire was signed on December 18th by Captain Omer Lutfi Bey and Colonel Vishinski. At the same time, General Lyakhov, the commander of the Russian forces in Yerznga, who had replaced General Kaletin after the February Revolution, was recalled. Lyakhov's departure resulted in the collapse of the Yerznga front. For the Russian soldier, it was pointless to stay any longer. Thousands of miles away from home, when his country was in turmoil, and it was obvious that these captured lands would be returned to the Turks.

After the departure of Lyakhov, there were barely 500-600 troops left at the Russian military base in Yerznga, and several Armenian and Russian officers who no longer had any influence on the remaining Russian soldiers. There was a brief interlude in the middle of January [1918], when Colonel Morel arrived from Tbilisi to take over command.

This course of events forced us to adopt a different policy, but we clung to our decision to defend our country to the last breath. A general conscription was immediately announced for the Armenians in Yerznga, up to the age of 70. The dedicated and brave Armenian population of the surrounding villages, who had barely survived and were reconstructing their houses, were gathering at the Prelacy Square, to take up arms again. On that day, 200 Russian-Armenian soldiers of the Trabizon front reached Yerznga. It was as if an entire army had arrived. The excitement was overwhelming. It was assumed that new, larger groups would arrive. The conscripts were taking part in the military exercises enthusiastically. The officers of the former Russian army in Yerznga, including the two young officers from Karabagh, Der Agopov and Der Petrosov, with whom I had traveled from Kars to Erzeroum a year earlier, were engaged in this work. There were others as well, like Lieutenant Tanielian, the military doctor Arslanian, Gafian and others. There were several Russian officers, among whom Mrouzov stood out for his zeal and self-sacrifice.

Something like an Armenian government was established in Yerznga, headed by Mourad. He had appointed Yousouf Effendi mayor, and had ordered mosques to open so that Turks could freely practice their religion. He had set a salary for hojas, muezzins, and ulemas. He spared no effort to win over the local Turks and to establish friendship with the Kurds of Dersim. However, these efforts could not yield results because there was no force to defend the front. By early 1918, very few groups remained of the 300 Russian battalions of Caucasian troops. On the contrary, the Turkish forces, with accompanying artillery and military equipment, had 142 battalions of infantry and 41 battalions of cavalry, about 150,000 fighters in all. Against this huge force, the Armenian forces numbered only six battalions. Of these, only 1,200 men were on the Yerznga front, 200 of whom were dedicated to the protection of communication lines. The Yerznga forces were completely isolated, separated from the Erzeroum fortress by 150 kilometers.

Everyone understood the difficulty of our situation, but we were all hopeful that reinforcements would soon arrive. Every day, Mourad called Colonel Torkom, who was in charge in Erzeroum. But his calls were in vain.

One day, Giurintsi Sahag ran over to us. He was looking for Mourad, who was at Dr. Boghosian's. We called Mourad and were excited. Colonel Torkom wanted to talk to him, and there was no doubt that reinforcements were coming. We gathered near the office door, impatient to know how strong the forces would be, where they were coming from, and when they would arrive in Yerznga. Mourad came with Dr. Boghosian. His long-darkened face shone so brightly that he did not even notice our greeting. Picking up the phone, he shouted:

"Yes, yes, it is me, Mourad. Hello, hello, colonel, are they on their way ... what ... I didn't understand ... what independence?"

We later learned that Colonel Torkom had announced that the following day, at 10 o'clock in the morning, he would declare Armenia's independence in Erzeroum and was asking Mourad to do the same in Yerznga ...

***

The Turks, fully aware of the situation, began to create pretexts to violate the ceasefire. In mid-January, they mobilized Kurdish collaborators, who began to attack us from the rear. However, they encountered strong counter-attacks and losses everywhere, and withdrew.

Mourad, who feared that, were the Kurdish movements to our rear to expand, we would be in a dire situation, spared no efforts to reach agreement with Kurdish tribal leaders. Amirkhanian and Chemishgadzaktsi were sent as envoys and one day, through their mediation, Suleyman and Hasan Aghas from Dersim, surrounded by about twenty armed Kurds, arrived in Yerznga in a cart sent by Mourad.

They were received like princes, as much as that was possible under the circumstances. After the reception, well meaning

64

negotiations took place. The next day, the Kurdish leaders received a horse and a watch each and left satisfied. Attempts were made to develop similar relationships with the people of Purukantsi Memish Agha, a Kurd from Terjan. Some measures were also adopted to avoid certain problems arising in the city, with round-the-clock guards in the Turkish districts and banning Turkish women and girls in the streets.

But these efforts and precautions were ineffective. Our forces did not exert the required influence on the Kurds, and their attacks did not stop. Willing to break the ceasefire, the Turkish command exploited the Armenian-Kurdish clashes that they had provoked, during which both we and the Kurds suffered casualties. Every day, General Otishilidze, the commander of the Russian forces in Erzeroum, would pass on to us the accusations he had received from the Turks. Supposedly, on January 12th, we had set fire to the Turkish village of Zeggiz, 18 kilometers southeast of Yerznga. They said we had raped the women and massacred the men of the village of Kesk, in the southeast of Ardas. Allegedly, after the Russian military unit had left Yerznga, killings had taken place in the region.

Then, these absurd accusations began to take on a more serious format. It was claimed that we had tied the hands of "many" Turks in Yerznga and driven them to military barracks and massacred them. Allegedly, on January 28th, "many Turks were burned alive in Yegeghyats Square." Allegedly, we had burned Turkish mosques everywhere near Yerznga. We had also supposedly massacred countless Turks on the southern route from Giumiushkhane.

Eventually, their imagination became so aggravated that they started characterizing their complaints as large-scale "Armenian atrocities," in which they described events remarkably similar to the Armenian massacres they had carried out. We had supposedly gathered 650 Turks in Yerznga and deported them in an unknown direction. We had supposedly packed 500 Turks into Vehib Bey's house and set it on fire on all sides. It was claimed we had similarly filled three large houses with Turkish women and children and burned them. We had set fire to more than a thousand houses in

General Torkom (left), Smyrna, 1922 standing alongside a British officer, overseeing a military exercise of the Armenian Legion.

the city alone, and so on. The truth was that the Turks had also suffered casualties during the Kurdish offensive and their losses had not exceeded 200.

On February 10th, the Russian-German talks in Brest were interrupted. We were looking forward to the outcome with fear and trepidation. Two days later, Vehib Pasha finally broke the truce and, on the pretext of punishing "the Armenian villains," started an offensive. In the evening, our patrols in Chardakhlou came under fire from Turkish reconnaissance units, and immediately there appeared 100 soldiers and 16 cavalrymen, who tried to slip past our rear guards in the north-east. Then, other forces appeared from different directions. An unequal battle began against superior enemy forces. From the first moment it was clear that our resistance was hopeless. It was only essential to gain time, to save the civilians and to secure our retreat. Everyone was fighting to the death, especially Mkhitar from Kemakh, Kalousd, Jebeji Sarkis, and Hovnan.

But what could be done with a thousand men against the regular Turkish army and the Kurdish hordes? Fortunately, Mourad, despite our hopeless situation, did not lose his cool, and became even more vigilant as the situation worsened. He endlessly redeployed our meagre forces, assisting those guarding the bridge and the roads to Vaghaver and Kemakh, where the situation was more severe. He succeeded in halting the enemy's advance and made them retreat and wait for sunrise.

In the morning, our post on the Kemakh road was attacked by 200 Turkish infantry and 25 cavalrymen. Stopping the Turkish advance, the guards retreated to the southwestern edge of Yerznga. At 7 am, a 700-strong Turkish military unit headed towards Yerznga via the Kemakh road. About 10-12 kilometers away from the city, the unit moved towards Khashkhash and Vasgerd villages, which were the same distance from the western edges of Yerznga. Then, the Turkish army's advance stopped due to heavy snow. In the afternoon, at 2 pm, four to five kilometers outside the city, we saw the Turkish forces attacking us at the western and southern edges of the city. At the same time, we learned that a 6,000-strong Turkish force was moving from Pulumer towards Mamakhatoun. The news spread at a lightning speed, creating an indescribable panic. The people were terrified. The possibility of retreat was diminishing. Mourad ordered Jebeji to move forward with 20 cavalrymen to check with the men guarding the roads. But, at the same time, news came in that Chardakhlou's 70 guards were under siege and were requesting help ...

There was no possibility of sending assistance. The situation was more than disheartening. The terrified people were running around in panic. In this chaos, Chardakhlou's guards, who had managed to escape from certain death, entered the city. They were immediately deployed to the cemetery, where a fierce battle was raging.

Suddenly, the ground shook. Our soldiers had blown up the bridge over the Euphrates to stop the Kurdish advance. The panic intensified. People were running to the barracks. Heavy flakes of snow were falling and it was very cold. The noise and bluster were deafening. The women, children, and elderly were screaming out loud, "God, God!" and running towards the barracks. Yet again, suddenly, it was as if the ground had been torn asunder, and the terrible shaking instantly silenced everything. Mourad led our fateful struggle with amazing skill. The main military arms depot in the city had exploded. The enemy was stunned for a moment, giving us time to gather our scattered forces. But they resumed their attack. Bullets were falling like hail. Men, wearing threadbare coats, blankets, and tablecloths were falling over themselves as they ran in panic. The women and children were following them with tears in their eyes.

In less than an hour, the convoy moved out. Six thousand people, including the soldiers. The Turks entered the city, where the seriously wounded and several old women had remained, preferring to die in their birthplace ...

***

Colonel Morel led the retreat while Mourad and his cavalry defended the rear. The cannons and machine guns were distributed among the front and the rearguards. At the front were the wheeled carts carrying provisions. The rest of the Armenian and Russian soldiers moved with the displaced civilians. The scene was dreadful. Women and children wrapped in rags, tearful and dismayed, were falling on the snow and getting up again. The little ones, like adults, understood everything. They made no demands and had no grievances. Shivering from the cold, they remained solemn and self-contained, as they walked or ran after their relatives like small calves. On account of the cold, some of them had their hands covered under their clothes, which were then tied over, around their chests and waists, making them look like moving toys. Any one of them could always be seen on Jebeji's horse. He would rub their nose, mouth, hands, and feet, encouraging them, and then put them down again.

We had barely been on the road for two hours when Kurds opened fire from the mountains around Ptarij village. However, faced with our swift and strong resistance, they dispersed. But, as we approached the village of Khan, heavy gunfire erupted from both sides and from behind. There was pandemonium with people falling down, running, and shouting. The battle lasted a long time, until it was dark. By that time, the snow had stopped, and it was a crystal-clear night. The cold could crack stone. The air melted like ice cream in our mouths and a frosty northern wind blew from the mountains. No matter how weary people were, they did not sit still for a second to avoid the inevitable danger of freezing to death.

After midnight, we fought the Kurds who were attacking us from the nearby heights of Norgakh and Iratoukh. The refugees' march gave us away, and the Kurds had already taken up strong positions against us. It was impossible to fight continuously in those conditions, and the people faced freezing to death. At the same time, it was dangerous to move forward, not knowing what awaited us ahead. We could only advance, send reconnaissance teams ahead, and fight. During that nightmare, Mourad shouted:

"Men, who among you wants to save the lives of these people?"

"I," said Chemishgadzaktsi, who was well acquainted with the area.

Sahag from Giurin and the brave commander Mrouzov, one of the few Russian soldiers who had irrevocably linked his fate to us, joined him. They snuck by the sides of the gorge and disappeared into the semi-darkness. The shooting was still going on, but we could not move. We tried to, but the Kurds intensified their gunfire. They obviously wanted to pin us down until sunrise. Mourad resorted to the machine guns, and under their constant fire, the people moved ahead. It was a fierce battle, but we managed to get through with only five killed and several wounded. We could still hear gunfire to our rear and ahead, but the danger had passed. The Euphrates, squeezed into gorges, had sunk under the ice. From time to time, the ice was powerless to hide the river, and we could hear the water. We could also sometimes hear screaming and shouting from the front, but this had now become common. Someone was frostbitten or dead. Suddenly, Sahag appeared in front of us. Chemishgadzaktsi and Mrouzov had been killed.

"Oh, damned news, how were they killed?" shouted Jebeji in a daze.

"How many ways can one be killed?"

"Alas, may your home be safe!"

Jebeji cried.

I accompanied Sahag to the rear, to Mourad, who listened to Sahag's brief account. His eyes were shut, as if he were asleep, only the light movements of his face made it clear that he was listening.

In the darkness, we saw Vahram's Arabian horse approaching us in a bewildered manner. The cold had intensified and the moon began to rise. The eastern sky was slowly brightening. The long clouds hanging from the far horizon were burning. It was light, and a corpse was lying on the road ahead. There was no sign of Mrouzov or his horse. Chemishgadzaktsi was stretched out on his back in the snow, one of his hands horizontal above his head. He seemed to be asleep. Was there anyone who did not love him?

We reached Chelig. The crying of the freezing children, even of the adults, caused a stir. Among them was the guardian of the children, Jebeji. Caressing one, pretending to be angry with another, he was trying to soften their grief.

"Hey, aren't you ashamed? Did your mother raise you feeding you cakes?"

"Hey, what's happening to you? Look at me ... yes, see? Tears are no good. There's a good child!"

"Hey, your voice, eh!" ...

He was talking to them, and the children would listen to him.

The only wish of the tired and broken people was a day's rest in Chelig, to take a breath. But, for their own salvation, time was now of the essence. We had to move quickly and pass through the gorges.

Two hours later, we left for Chors. Halfway there, gunfire erupted from the mountaintops of Terjan. The people panicked anew, and the shooting became more intense in the dangerous gorge of Sansar, when the Kurds opened fire on us from the heights of Dersim. Hiding behind the rocks, they fired relentlessly. They were better positioned than we were. Our main difficulty was looking after the civilian refugees. There were screams and cries for help everywhere. In the most intense moment of the battle, when we were climbing the snowy mountain to try to outmaneuver the Kurds, more than fifty Kurds took up positions on both sides of the Terjan mountains and began to fire. It was a moment of complete annihilation. We had to slide down the mountain slope. Now, despair overwhelmed everyone. Our cries and screams filled the gorge. However, Mourad found a way out of this situation by resorting to cannons, the only weapon that intimidated the Kurds. We quickly moved two of them to point to the Kurdish positions. Now, everyone's salvation depended on the efforts of two young Russian-Armenians, Der Agopov and Der Bedrosov. The first shots confused the Kurds, and then, their otherwise inaccessible positions were destroyed. Half an hour later, they fell silent.

We moved ahead, leaving behind 25 dead fighters and 38 dead or wounded horses in the gorge. We also had 60 wounded.

At night, we reached Chors, where one could find the wooden barracks built by the Russians. A hundred Armenian soldiers were guarding the barracks. The people charged into them. The screams doubled when they realized the extent of our casualties.

At least 50 soldiers and 200 refugees had frozen to death on the road that night.

At the end of the night, we moved to Vzhan. Due to the number of wounded, the frostbitten, and the loss of some horses, we were forced to leave three field and one mountain cannon, plus half of our supplies, which were all destroyed in Chors.

It was almost daylight. The sky was gray, the wind was blowing, and the snow was striking us hard like grains of rice. It was as if nature and human beings had conspired to destroy us. We were driving the tired civilians like the ruthless horsemen of Shah Abbas.* There was no other way to salvation, everyone was the master of their own destiny. Whoever wanted to be saved, had to keep walking ...

The sun had already come up when we discovered that the forty-meter-long bridge on the Chors-Vzhan road had been burned down. It was clear that the enemy pursuing us had decided to annihilate us there. Indeed, before reaching the depths of the gorge, they opened fire. The people were running and hiding in little crannies in the side of the gorge. Mourad was running left and right, giving instructions. The Kurds were firing from favorable positions on the opposite side. We were firing at them from the bottom of the gorge.

A fierce, fateful battle began. I was overwhelmed by shivers and had a high temperature. I was gnashing my teeth, but that had nothing to do with fear. When it became clear what we had to do, my trembling subsided, a strange calm came over me, and my consciousness began to function clearly and quickly.

On the foothills of the mountains, a group of Kurdish horsemen and cavalry were moving back and forth to take up favorable positions. Others, firing constantly, tried to approach a small, conical hill in front of us, overlooking the gorge.

"Take that hill at all costs," shouted Mourad to Jebeji.

We sometimes crawled, fell, ran, jumped, climbed, and slid back, but we moved forward, replying once to every ten shots they fired.

---

* This is a reference to Shah Abbas who relocated Armenians to Isfahan during the Ottoman-Safavid war at the beginning of the 17th century.

Bullets were flying over our heads. Others were following us to take the hill.

"Yes, men, yes, *ghourban!*" we could hear Mourad's heartfelt cries from below.

It was not possible to keep count of those falling from the bullets fired by the Kurds. It was here that people were subject to the whims of fate. At that moment, a person could either live or die, depending on what fortune decided.

"Hushh ..." someone whistled and fell on his face right next to me.

"Hey, hey, brothers ..." It was Vartan who, with a heavy machine gun on his back, was climbing up towards us on all fours. There was gunfire everywhere. Vartan lay down on his back, facing the bullets, and suddenly, a cannon roared from below.

"Hey, hey ..." Luck had saved Vartan. He came past us, rolling on the snow.

The cannons were firing relentlessly now. Jebeji, Hovnan, and Sahag threw themselves onto the path leading to the top of the hill and we followed them. A torrent of bullets landed there. There was no way we could move. All that was left was to take up position and fight, but we could not find a suitable position.

"To the left, to the left," came Mourad's shouts from below.

The storm was roaring, the cannons were thundering, and the surroundings were shaking from the sound of rifles and machine guns. Turkish-Kurdish bandits had taken up secure positions everywhere and were firing at us. Somebody lay low and slid past us. Jebeji and Hovnan were crawling and we followed them.

"To the left, to the top," Mourad kept shouting from below.

Suddenly, Jebeji stood up and jumped over the crest of the hill to our left. Then Hovnan and Sahag managed to climb up and reach the rocky peak of the hill. The Kurds kept the hill under heavy fire but were unable to dislodge our men. It was a great success. The progress of those of us below became easier. Suddenly, new forces appeared behind the hill. Regular volleys followed one another. The Kurds were firing constantly, moving from position to position, and opening up in the form of a large crescent. In the chaos, it was impossible to understand what was happening. But it was obvious that the Kurds, familiar with the surroundings, were tightening the ring, trying to get behind us. Suddenly, they spread out in a daring half-circular motion forwards while other forces appeared behind them. We did not know what was going on below us, in other positions, and we could no longer hear Mourad's voice. The commotion and noise had silenced everything. A state of despair ensued. "Fire at the opening end of the chain," shouted Jebeji.

With our first volleys, the Kurds stopped and collapsed. They seemed to have gone underground. We waited for a new attack at any moment when we suddenly heard, "Hey, hey!"

It was Vartan again, a little below. He had fallen on the snow like a buffalo and could not move. We went to him. He was breathless and exhausted. We helped him stand up and immediately set up the machine gun. Suddenly, the Kurds jumped out of their positions and charged at us, guns blazing.

"Drr, ada, da, da, da ..." thundered the machine gun, mowing down the first row of Kurds. The Kurds retreated in panic and hid below the cliffs. More than a dozen corpses and many wounded remained at the scene of the attack as they tried to crawl over the snow to hide. Very few of them succeeded. At the same time, an unbelievable scene appeared. More than a thousand Kurds were fleeing on horseback and on foot across the vast plain beyond. They had been hiding behind the crescent-shaped heights, hoping to exterminate and plunder the retreating civilians. One single machine gun had frightened them.

We were firing at the front of the mountain, as well as the center and the farthest points at the back. The panicked Kurds were sustaining losses while our good marksmen were picking off the rest. Horses and men, rolling and jumping, were running like possessed demons. We were the masters of the situation here, but a deadly battle was still raging on below. The cannons were fired more often and the gunfire was more ferocious.

It was only now that I realized the importance of the captured hill. We could only pass at the lower part of this hill where the water was shallow and frozen, thus bypassing the burnt bridge.

People had already started to move to the other side, but it was a difficult task to get them to the rear of the hill. The Kurds

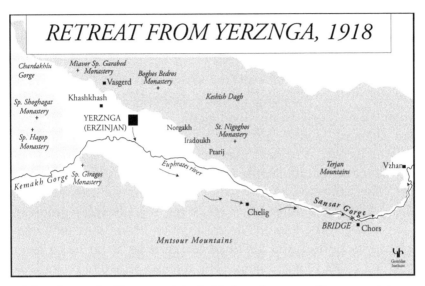

Map shows the Yerznga plain (white) and surrounding mountains (shaded), the movement of the retreating Armenian forces, including the vital crossing of the Euphrates near the village of Chors.

continued to fire endlessly at us from distant, invisible positions. The cannon and machine gun were powerless against them now, and it was inevitable that we would lose one in ten people. The people's passage was defended by good riflemen under the direct leadership of Mourad. Corpses were lying everywhere. The transportation of women and children, as well as the frozen and the wounded was very difficult. We took them over the shallow water on our shoulders, carrying them in our arms, or with the few surviving horses. The severely wounded were crawling on the snow, like mythical serpents. Dr. Boghosian, with the help of several people, was pulling and dragging them towards the passage, but how many could he help?

By 9 o'clock in the morning, the crossing was over, or more correctly, we were forced to stop it, because most of the volunteers defending the retreat had been killed. But, by that time, the wounded and frozen, except 30 refugees, had already been carried across the river. Other than the latter refugees, eight wounded volunteers also remained on the other side. The total number of our casualties, including fighters among the civilians, was around

500 people. Two hundred Russian soldiers had [also] frozen, as had 300 of the refugees.[*] All our food carts, cannons, and machine guns remained on the other side ...

We had passed through the gorge and the shooting had stopped. Those pursuing us were probably busy robbing the wounded and corpses, and dividing the abundant spoils. The wind had changed course and was now coming from behind us, pushing us over. The road was rocky and the snowstorm did not allow us to see ahead. People were falling, breaking their arms and legs. The condition of the wounded and frozen was perilous. Many, seeing that they were hindering the caravan's progress, were asking to be killed. The cavalrymen Morel sent to Vzhan reached us halfway and only had five carts for us. It was a great relief to be able to move faster. The convoy seemed to be static as it crept on silently. It was not clear who had been lost or frozen. Those who had miraculously escaped death showed great drive, a certain supreme effort that turned a person into a machine. But even if we had escaped persecution from the human-beasts, nature still wanted to have its way with us. We had hardly descended to the plains when the storm started to roar fiercely. It was the storm of Dersim haunting us. After a while, it began to rush down the rock face, lift up piles of snow, roll into snow-capped crevices, climb up hills and, changing course over our heads, blast snow at us. Suddenly, everything was in turmoil. It was as if a general earthquake was about to open up the earth and swallow us. Thick white clouds kept coming towards us. They cast such a shadow and cut out so much light that it felt like dusk. The snow was moving around us like strands of cloth. It whooshed and landed on our greying faces, or piled up elsewhere. It was colliding, coalescing, and tumbling around, then floating upwards and disappearing behind the clouds.

Anyhow, we arrived in Vzhan at 9 o'clock in the evening. The people entered the newly-built wooden dormitories. Whatever was available was broken up and burned in the tin stoves that remained in their places. We learned from the local guards that

---

[*] These figures suggest that the grand total of casualties, including those who died in battle as well as those who froze, was 1,000 people.

our patrols in Fam and Vartagchu had been ambushed by the Turks and killed. Some of us in that dormitory began cleaning our weapons while others rested. I could not sleep, although I felt broken, as if I had been crushed under a cart. Next to me, Jebeji was snoring. I was listening to the late-night commotion. The storm was still roaring, blowing with fixed intensity, scraping away at the walls outside, knocking on doors and windows. It was as if the roof was about to be torn off and the walls fall in. Suddenly, a window slammed down on the floor. Jebeji jumped up and looked around anxiously like an animal in danger.

"Hisous Krisdos!"

He crossed his face and turned onto his other side.

In the morning, we took the Baghche-Erzeroum route. There was no pursuit involved. It was a clear day and the sun was shining on snow-covered fields, smiling at yesterday's snowstorm and other developments. People were still mourning their losses. In the afternoon, we reached Karjil. According to the order received from Erzeroum, all guard units were to be concentrated in Mamakhatoun, which we reached on the evening of February 17th [1918]. There were food stalls, blankets, clothes' depots, and huge arsenals of limitless ammunition. The civilians could recover there.

Colonel Morel, with the help of Captain Gafian and other strong-willed Armenian officers, was working to form a small but reliable force to defend Mamakhatoun. But, under the circumstances, his efforts were doomed to failure. After the collapse of the Russian front, the Turks threw their best forces at us. According to information received, Vehib Pasha's two armies had been supplemented with other forces, and they were all moving in the direction of Yerznga-Erzeroum. At the same time, the Kurdish bands and irregular soldiers were mobilized on a grand scale, as they were interested in the easy-to-obtain loot that lay ahead – plentiful Russian goods, full warehouses, and numerous other riches scattered everywhere.

We left on the morning of February 19th [1918]. Mamakhatoun was burning. Mountains and valleys were thundering, as ammunition depots were being blown up ...

In Karabeyli, Sebouh joined us with his cavalrymen, volunteers, and some of the Armenian and Greek refugees who had migrated by the Papert-Aghsonk-Maden-Kopkhan-Prnagaban route. Most of the deportees from Papert had already moved in the direction of Ilija.

We arrived there in the evening, and the next day we were in Erzeroum ...

CHAPTER FOUR

"We Lost Our Fatherland"

Erzeroum had become an Arshagavan.[*] You could find people from everywhere: Trabizon, Van, Papert, Khnous, Constantinople, Alashgerd, Tbilisi, Moush, Tabriz, Karabagh, Yerevan, and other places. It seemed that surviving Armenians from all over the world had fled and taken refuge in Erzeroum. There were all kinds of Armenian and Russian "authorities," but the city was in a state of anarchy and chaos. It was unclear who were the leaders and who were the subordinates, what steps were being taken for the defense of the city, our political direction, or what we would do. There was only one heartwarming conviction in the general turmoil and disintegration: Erzeroum was a renowned fortress. Its fortifications and artillery were [supposedly] enough to withstand the most powerful armies ...

I was now staying with Sahag and Hovnan at the Sanasarian school, where displaced people had gathered.

Barely an hour or two had passed when Hamo Paraghamian visited us. He was just the same person, except that he had lost his energy. Obviously, we embraced upon seeing each other, but he was not one for emotional displays, so he immediately pulled out two long sheets of paper from his pocket to interview us for his next report. None of us was willing to talk. We were interested in the situation in Erzeroum and the defensive possibilities of the city. Hamo had to put his paper away to respond to our inquiries.

The fortifications of Erzeroum had a strong artillery defense with 400 fortress and field cannons. But most of them were unusable, having been abandoned and buried in the snow. Barely a dozen or two cannons were ready for action. The artillery force consisted of 40 officers and 400 soldiers whose morale was poor.

---

[*] A new capital built by King Arshag II in the 4th century and populated by fugitives of all descriptions.

The Russian officer corps had already moved from Erzeroum to Sarikamish and the defense of the fortress and the command of the "troops" had passed into the hands of Armenians. Antranig, who was still in Alexandropol, was appointed head of the fortified region of Erzeroum. After the retreat of our forces from Yerznga and Papert, including the forces in Erzeroum, we numbered 3,100 soldiers, 400 cavalrymen, and eight artillery units. Leaderless, abandoned and demoralized, our discipline was declining with each passing day. The refugees were gathering at the doors of various institutions and making demands. We lacked the necessary organization to overcome the difficulties caused by the retreat and displacement.

The next day, we went to the commissariat, hoping to see Mourad and understand what we had to do. There was no one there. A smartly dressed soldier was sitting alone in a room next to the hall. Upon seeing us, he quickly pushed back the sword resting on his thigh and asked in good Armenian.

"What do you want?"

He spoke at an astonishing speed.

"Who are you?" he asked more anxiously.

"We are Mourad's soldiers," said Hovnan.

He extended his hand.

"Colonel Torkom."

I recalled the telephone conversation with Mourad and Colonel Torkom's proposal to declare Armenia's independence. Now, the colonel was interested to know why the people of Yerznga had not been sent to Erzeroum earlier, before the fighting had started, as that would have facilitated the defense of Yerznga, and civilians would not have suffered as they had during the retreat. Sahag explained that many of Yerznga's defenders had relatives among the local population; had they been sent off earlier, the city's defenders would have left with them. This was particularly the case because people did not want to leave for Erzeroum without significant defensive forces to accompany them for fear of Kurdish attacks on their way.

Colonel Torkom hung his head, his coal-black shiny eyes looked around the table as if seeking something, and said, "Yes, it was necessary to look at matters from that perspective. Since day one, I was saying that we could not withstand Vehib Pasha's armies, we had to change our orientation, but no one was listening. Now they are blaming me. I heard that Sebouh's soldiers are insulting my dignity and threatening me. They are saying that I did not send them help, nor to you." He spoke in a sad voice, elongating the words "did not." As if our retreat had taken place for such reasons, he continued in the same sad voice. "What can 50-60 new soldiers do, when the enemy sends armies against us, not counting the Kurds. Isn't that reasoning irresponsible? What can a colonel do in such a crisis, even if he is appointed by a powerful authority like the National Council, when people do not want to submit to his authority, and someone else tries to undermine that authority?"

The colonel looked at us, emphasizing the words "someone else," but that did not interest us.

"He thinks himself superior to me, though I have been appointed by the National Council in Tbilisi. I gave him the rank of colonel only a couple of days ago and nobody knows who appointed him to be the head of the military. I formed a group of fifty people to come to your aid in Yerznga, but he opposed it, saying that they were needed here ..."

"Who?" asked Hovnan.

"Don't you know? Colonel Karakeshishian. I formed another group to go to Papert [Baiburt]. I ask you, how could I send auxiliary forces under such conditions?"

This conversation revealed more than Mourad could tell us.

"The past is over, Colonel. It is important to know what you have decided for the defense of this city and what we have to do."

"Everything has been 'decided,' but that means nothing, as we have no power."

"In that case, wouldn't it be wise to immediately move the civilians to Kars, so that they won't be harmed during our retreat?"

A bitter smile appeared on his pale face.

"You are right, but where will we take these unfortunate people from Kars?"

"So, you assume that the Turks will reach Kars?"

"What 'assume'? Don't you know that it was agreed at Brest to give Kars, Batumi, and Ardahan to the Turks?"

"When?" exclaimed Hovnan, probably thinking that the Turks were already there.

"Yesterday, my dear. We received a telegram about it yesterday."

"What are you saying, *hey vakh!*"

The news was a surprise to me and Sahag as well.

"What do you think about that?" Sahag asked.

Colonel Torkom's face suddenly radiated; his black eyes sparkled. His lips moved like the lid on a jar, as he opened his mouth in proportion to the words he was uttering, emphasizing them one by one.

"I do not consider you ordinary soldiers. I consider you compassionate, knowledgeable young Armenians, and I speak honestly. If I were sure that the situation would be saved by personal sacrifices, I would not hesitate to sacrifice myself for my people. Unfortunately, neither I, nor thousands like you, under the current circumstances, can do anything. The situation is more than complicated; they are fighting against us not only with weapons, but also with politics. Thus, if we cannot use weapons against weapons, at least we can pursue politics against politics. We must change our orientation. Let us forget the Russians and declare independence."

"Do you think the Turks will take our independence into account?" Sahag asked curiously.

Colonel Torkom replied emotionally.

"Oh, my dear, if we had taken that step two months ago, when our issue had not been discussed in Brest, our situation would have been very different now. I told them, I called the National Council, Mourad, Sebouh. They thought I was crazy. But it is not too late now. It is necessary to confront the enemy as soon as possible. Once we do that, the Turk will not dare set foot on the borders of the independent state of Armenia."

"Why?" asked Hovnan pensively.

"Because, in the near future, they will face our allies, Great Britain and France, who will definitely be victorious."

These last words made everything clear to me. I did not reply.

"Can't you talk to Mourad about that?" the Colonel asked Sahag.

"We are irrelevant people, Colonel. What can we do?"

"Do you think it is useless?"

Sahag's face took on an expression that could have meant either a "yes" or a "no," depending on what the colonel said.

"Pity," he sighed, extending his hand to us.

***

In those days of general collapse, there was extraordinary excitement when news came that General Antranig and his army had reached Hasan Kale from Alexandropol. When the news was confirmed, the enthusiasm of the people peaked. The people, having forgotten everything, were singing in the streets, *"Tsayn muh hntchets Erzeroumi hayots lerneren"* and *"Iprev ardziv savarnoum es ler ou jayr."**

The 20,000 Turks at Erzeroum, who had been joyful with the hope of imminent freedom, were suddenly demoralized and locked themselves in their homes. All their hopes had been dashed. Antranig was coming.

Antranig arrived. He was received with an extraordinary ceremony. The crowd had taken to the streets all the way to Kars Kapou. "Long live Antranig!" shouted the frenzied people.

"Long live!" echoed the streets ...

The following day, it was back to reality. The poor people had expected a miracle that did not happen. They were now drawing conclusions that were not very favorable to the leaders, even to Antranig.

"Why was he so late?"

"Where had he been up to now?"

"What can be done at the last moment?"

---

* These were two well-known patriotic songs of that era, "A Call Has Sounded from the Mountains of Erzeroum" and "You Hover Like an Eagle Over Mountains and Rocks."

Such questions led to various discussions and expectations.

We were not concerned by rumors. When Mourad called, all surviving comrades gathered around him again.

The Turks had already made Erzeroum the target of their military operations, and the Armenian vanguard, under pressure, was retreating step by step towards Ilija [just outside Erzeroum].

On March 11th [1918], the adversary, gathering its forces at Ilija, launched a powerful attack. We retreated, suffering heavy casualties. An extraordinary military consultation was convened by Antranig. The next morning, the evacuation and retreat from Erzeroum began, in the most difficult circumstances. By 9 o'clock, the Turks were already in the city. They captured an enormous amount of ammunition, food, clothing, and other military equipment. More than a hundred Armenians, who had remained in the city, were massacred. On the way, Armenian fighters from Khnous and its displaced population joined the thousands of refugees. Then, one could see even more masses of refugees over vast areas, a scene I was already familiar with from Yerznga.

We were now approaching the borders of Russian Armenia. The moon was rising in its majestic splendor, promising a fine day. It was very cold. The dome-like shining, snowy peak of Mount Masis [Ararat] was standing tall and looked majestic in the darkness. In the distance, in the early morning light, one could see the golden rocks of mountains. The horizon was burning. Shortly afterwards, the sun began to rise. The gold-colored peaks of the mountains shone through the haze.

I looked around with the sorrow at losing our homeland. I, one of the remnants of the last generation of my ancestors, knew very well that we had lost our homeland at that moment. And my responsibility to previous generations felt very heavy on my shoulders. It was bitter and unbearable. The feeling of revenge born of personal grief became a matter of conscience, a way of making up for our generation.

In mid-March, the pursuing enemy encountered us in the Kars-Ourgan region. After our strong counterattack, their harassment slowed down but did not stop. They pulled in the Kurds who were behind us. On March 13th, following overwhelming Turkish attacks, we retreated to Khan-Dere. On

April 2nd, a large force of Turks moved on to the Karakurt and Partos areas, and then attacked Khan Dere. After a series of bloody battles that lasted several days, on the night of April 6th, Sarikamish was evacuated, warehouses were blown up, and everything of military importance was destroyed. Our losses were significant, especially in the Karakurt gorge, where many volunteers fell. I was wounded in my upper right arm and was removed from the ranks of fighters.

***

Sarikamish was still standing when I was about to depart for Tbilisi with a group of other wounded men. The mindless commotion at the station was indescribable. Crowds had surrounded the train. People were running around in groups, with huge sacks on their shoulders that seemed to contain mutilated corpses. It was as if the carriages were under attack. Footwear, hats, bundles, blankets, and pieces of cloth were abandoned as people, with disheveled hair and torn collars, threw themselves furiously into the carriages. The animalistic drive for survival had overwhelmed human judgment. An armed group of Russian soldiers returning home threatened to smash everything if they were not given a place on the train. The Armenian stationmaster was running along the platform in panic and shouting at the doors of the carriages, begging for a few seats. Seeing that no one wanted to give in, he suddenly twisted his thick neck like a bull, near our carriage, and broke through the crowd with his fists. The commotion and unspeakable noise deafened everyone. Finally, the Russians settled down and the train moved off. The crowd was now criticizing the intolerable transportation system. There was no authority, no power, and especially no order. The harshest critics were the ones who had lost their belongings and were looking for their bags that had been thrown out of the windows. A tall, stocky Caucasian-Armenian with a puffy face, straightened his long, dense black hair, and cried out with emotion:

"Alas, poor Armenia, what have they done to you?"

In the neighboring compartment, a western Armenian, with a full baker's face and wide-open eyes, was describing various events in an exaggerated manner. Another man, with a thin neck, was nodding his head in agreement with whatever he was saying.

The effect of this panic was felt in Kars, too. However, there was still discipline at the station there, as the ancient fortress inspired faith. There was no reason to be too frightened. In the afternoon, we arrived in Alexandropol, where the snow had melted on the station platform, forming a muddy puddle. Three years earlier, we had been greeted by a theatrical mob here who were playing *davoul-zourna* music. They were the same people, flexible and agile, with cold red noses. Excited and disturbed by the news, it seemed that everyone was looking for someone. One person, with his clothes and hair disarrayed by the wind, grabbed another by the neck, turned him around, and shouted:

"You, son of a donkey, what were you doing? Let's go and register as volunteers."

Volunteer, evacuate the refugees, save the lives of those left behind. That was now the motto of the day.

Further north, in Karakilise [modern day Vanadzor] and Sanahin, people were calm, rational, and peaceful. The unfolding events were far away, and whatever was to happen would happen. Only elderly people were at the train stations. They walked along the platforms with their thumbs tucked in their belts, occasionally stopping and looking disinterestedly into the distance. Nothing could surprise them anymore.

The lush vegetation of Lori was still covered by snow. Naked tree trunks, with bare outstretched branches, were still awaiting their green shoots.

It was morning when we arrived in Navtlough, meaning Tbilisi. A succession of misty mountains remained in the background. We then came to Mount Mama-David, cut through the chain of mountains, and stopped in amazement, enchanted by the view of the city. Navtlough was on the outskirts of the city. It was spring here. Dark blue-greens were spread in the direction of Gochori. Lower down was Tbilisi, whose distant slopes were lost in orchards. Here was the Kur river, like a silver ribbon, dividing the city into two equal parts. The spring sun shone on the windows of houses that seemed to have been washed and cleaned. My God, how stable the city seemed, and how uncertain the destiny of its people.

When the train came to a halt, I remembered our departure three years earlier. The changes were immeasurable. The station was now filled with confused soldiers returning home. Yerevan Square was quiet. People were just talking.

Several people were standing in front of the city hall on Velyaminovskaya and Behrutian streets, and a crowd of exiles had gathered nearby. The fourth hospital we were sent to was in this area. Only five of us could be accommodated there, thanks to the efforts of Dr. G. Saghian. There was no more room, so the rest received tickets to be treated at the clinic next to the Aramian building and to remain there. The normally busy Yerevan Square was almost deserted. There were no longer bespectacled, long-haired intellectuals at the Sakayan café, who three years earlier had been arguing about political events and drawing conclusions, none of which had come to pass. Instead of militant volunteers, refugees from various parts of Western Armenia had gathered at "Anatolia" restaurant. There was a little more life on Golovinian Avenue. High-ranking Russian servicemen were grouped inside the iron gates of the Russian church near the palace. They were probably attending the funeral of a prominent person. A little further down, on the other side, before reaching the entrance to Alexander Park, rose the five-story house of the Aramiants family, which had been taken, against the will of its wealthy owner, by the Armenian National Council and its affiliated organizations. Everything was topsy-turvy with the past and present all mixed up in my head.

A few days later, a hand rested on my shoulder in the spacious restaurant on the first floor of the Aramiants house. It was Mr. Tatigian.

"You have returned and you don't remember us! What happened to your arm?"

"It's all right, sit down," I said, surprised.

"No, if you have nothing here, let us go home. It's lunch time."

Although three years had passed, the Tatigians' house and the first feelings and emotions that had awoken in me towards Anahid seemed like an old childhood memory. Now, the closer we got to the apartment, the more excited I became.

"Can they at least stop the advance of the Turks at Kars?" Tatigian asked when I clarified the hopeless state of the front in a few words.

"Maybe."

Only girls can blossom as Anahid had done. She had grown up. She was more beautiful than ever, and her attitude had become serious and meaningful. She quickly approached me in the corridor, but when she spoke, she found it difficult to connect her words. "I knew you had come, but I did not see you. Oh, no, I did see you once, in front of the Aramiants house. Mr. Yanikian said that it was you."

Her mother and elder sister appeared. Gradually, the warm atmosphere of that family invigorated me. The younger sister, Setig, who had been barely one and a half years old at the time, now spoke freely, pronouncing "g" as "d." Anahid had maintained the habit of listening with her head tilted when her father spoke. And Mr. Tatigian kept asking me about sad things.

"So, no one from Mardiros' large family survived."

"Nobody."

"Why do you think our Shahen is alive?"

"There are still Armenian officers serving in the Turkish army."

I knew that his favorite nephew, Shahen, was amongst the 2,000 or so Armenian soldiers and officers around the Kharpert region, where they were working on road construction as "ameles,"[*] but my information was so unpleasant that I was forced to remain silent.

"How hard I tried to bring him here. I wrote to him so many times."

"And what happened to the Momjians?" asked Mrs. Zvart.

"They were taken away and killed, ma'am."

"What about our neighbors, the Tanielians?"

"Enough," said Mr. Nshan.

---

[*] Amele: conscripted laborer in the Ottoman army.

***

I was already aware of the situation. There were shelters for the refugees on the outskirts of the city, in Havlapar, behind Sheytan Bazar, Saltatski Bazar, Khojavank Cemetery, and other places. A large group had gathered in the Bakouriani area, very far from the city.

Although the so-called "Armenian evildoers'" – the pretext the Turks had used to violate the ceasefire since Yerznga – had already taken refuge in the Caucasus, the Turks had annihilated the Western Armenians and were seeking the end of Caucasian Armenians as well. For the Georgians, the Turkish threat was not an existential threat, but a political one. The Tatars [modern day Azeris] had openly sided with the enemy and were no longer trying to hide their allegiance; they were leading the Turks to Transcaucasia without hesitation. They organized riots and other movements everywhere. They were spying on a massive scale and destroying the rear by all means.

The movement of Kurds and Tatars, which had begun in mid-March [1918] in the Kars region, took the form of organized military operations. Armed Muslim groups surrounded Merdinek and Ardahan, where fierce fighting was taking place. Thousands of bandits were exterminating Armenians in the border areas.

In Transcaucasia, disagreements between the three nations, especially Armenians and Tatars, were growing and deepening in both the Seim[*] and the Transcaucasian Commissariat.[†]

Under these circumstances, the peace talks that began in Trabizon became a plaything in the hands of the Turks. Vehib Pasha continued to advance in the direction of Batumi and Ardahan, conquering new areas day by day. Rauf Bey spoke of the "preconditions" for reconciliation, the only purpose of which was to undermine the already weak Armenian-Georgian partnership. Astonishing telegrams were being sent to Tbilisi signed by Kars regional commissar Tsamoian, Ardahan regional commissar Shagalov, executive chairman of the city and regional committee

---

[*] Seim: short-lived Transcaucasian Parliament (1918).
[†] Transcaucasian Commissariat: the government of Transcaucasia [South Caucasus] (1917-18).

Saralidze, and treasurer Ivanov regarding attacks, massacres, pillage, and mass exodus. At a time when touching speeches were heard from the podium of the Seim directed at the "internal enemy," there were rumors of secret Turkish-Georgian negotiations, according to which, Chkhenkeli was working in Trabizon to keep Batumi within Transcaucasia in return for handing Kars and Ardahan to the Turks.

On April 13th [1918], the Turks entered Batumi. Shortly afterwards, the delegation from Trabizon arrived in Tbilisi, and the rumors of a Georgian-Turkish secret agreement were verified. Chkhenkeli had handed Batumi to the Turks on the condition that it would be returned to Georgia after signing the Brest-Litovsk treaty. The Armenians were in shock. On April 22nd, Georgian and Tatar politicians declared Transcaucasia an "independent state," which was the first of the "preconditions" for reconciliation demanded by the Turks. On the same day, Gegechkori's government resigned and a new one was formed in which Chkhenkeli was everything: the foreign minister, prime minister, and head of the delegation for "peace negotiations." Compared to the former government's wavering pro-Russian orientation, this government's pro-Turkish orientation was quite firm.

On April 24th, Akaki Chkhenkeli ordered General Nazarbekian, the commander of the Armenian armed forces, to hand Kars over to the Turks. The Tatars were overjoyed because the surrender of Kars meant the unimpeded advance of the Turks into southern Transcaucasia. Georgian politicians were now negotiating with the Turks to retake Batumi and form an independent Georgia. The Armenians of Tbilisi were living days of unprecedented tragedy.

Mourad and Sebouh appeared in Tbilisi during those days. My wound was healing and I took the opportunity to meet them in order to determine what to do. But I wish I had not seen those two old fighters of the Armenian liberation struggle in that condition. They were unrecognizable, bitter, desperate, and demoralized. Mourad, however, told me that he intended to form a group of cavalrymen to travel across mountain roads to Alexandropol as soon as the National Council approved the move. He promised to include me in that group. A few days later, I learned that he had left for Russia via the North Caucasus in order to offer his forces to Lenin ...

In mid-May [1918], the Turks captured Alexandropol [Gyumri]. Then, the fighting moved to Karakilise [Vanadzor], where, after several clashes, the Armenians were forced to retreat and take up new positions in Bozikiugh and Nikitina, blocking the road to Yerevan.

After capturing Karakilise, a Turkish force moved to the north, in the direction of Tbilisi. At the same time, the Muslims of Sadakhlu and Sandar region cut off the railway connection to southern Transcaucasia. In those days, convoys of refugees from the occupied regions began reaching Tbilisi. Thousands of helpless and hungry people appeared every day in the city and there was no end to it.

One day, in the midst of such a crowd, I suddenly noticed Hovnan. He was walking like a seriously ill person and was crouching forward.

"Hovnan!"

He stopped and stared hesitantly at the sidewalk, as if he did not know what to do. I approached and pulled him out of the crowd.

"So, it's you. How are you?" he asked happily, taking off his *papakh* and wiping the sweat from his forehead with it. He had a soldier's kitbag in one hand and a pillow and blanket under his other arm. As if he was trying to remember something, blinking his small, deep-set eyes, he continued:

"This time we barely escaped death, brother. We barely came out of the flames. But I would still stay, if it were not for this lack of leadership. Everything has gone poorly since Mourad left. I now want to see him, to understand what our end will be. I want to take orders from Mourad, become a member of the Bolsheviks, and fight against the Tsarist Russians. They destroyed us," said Hovnan, wetting his dry lips with the tip of his tongue.

"Mourad is not here."

"What?" he cried in despair.

"Yes, he has left for the North Caucasus."

"Ohhh ..."

It was as if the ground had collapsed under his feet, leaving him in such a desperate state.

"Can't you ask the National Council for a way for me to go?"

"Where?"

"After him, what do I know?"

***

The Armenians of Transcaucasia were living through fateful days. They were fighting fierce battles against Turkish military forces in the Ararat Valley, around Sardarabad, in the spirit of the Vartanants War.[*] The situation was chaotic in Tbilisi. Thousands of displaced people were scattered everywhere. The Seim and the Transcaucasian government were on the brink of collapse. The Georgians were seeking to overcome future difficulties by declaring Georgia separate and independent. Day by day, the Armenian-Tatar conflict was deepening, and the latter were leading the Turks to Baku. The Armenians had been left between blood and fire. In those conditions, there was no point in wasting time in Tbilisi, and the next day Hovnan and I went to Batumi. Due to the ongoing civil war, it was not easy to cross to Russia quickly at that time, and we hoped to join Mourad in the north Caucasus. The train was full of displaced people, most of whom were Armenians from Tbilisi. The number of refugees in Poti was greater. All the hotels, inns, canteens, and restaurants were full to the brim. It was raining heavily, forming deep puddles on the rough sidewalks. We went straight to the harbor, where a boat was leaving for Tuapse. However, all tickets had been sold and it was impossible to travel. We returned to the city, when, suddenly, Hovnan shouted:

"Hey, look!"

In a corner of the waiting room, Colonel Torkom was talking to a beautiful, young woman. There were travel bags stacked on top of each other. There was also an old woman standing next to the girl, probably her mother.

"Let's approach him and see what he is doing here."

---

[*] Battle of Vartanants was the epic battle at Avarayr between Christian Armenia against Sassanid Persia in 451.

Soghomon Tehlirian, 1915.

It did not seem to be a good time, so we approached to greet them briefly. Seeing us, Torkom interrupted his chat and greeted us with a slight movement of his hand.

"What are you doing here?"

We told him that we wanted to go to Tuapse, but because we could not find tickets, we had had to return to the city.

"Tickets are no problem. Wait here for a while, I will arrange it."

We stepped back, surprised by Torkom's confident attitude. Perhaps he had some official contacts or acquaintances there.

Colonel Torkom was talking about an interesting story or war. The young lady was listening intently. From time to time, the mother would look at the colonel and cover her mouth when yawning. It seemed the story was over. The colonel moved lightly towards us, striking the ground with the heels of his shiny, long shoes.

"Hello, guys," he said cheerfully, as if he had just seen us. "Where do you want to go?" He turned to me, closed his mouth, and straightened his jaw forward.

"Tuapse, then Armavir."

"Well, wait here, we will go together."

Less than a quarter of an hour later, he brought us two tickets and asked for help carrying his luggage.

It was noon when the ship set off. The rain had stopped much earlier, the sea was beautiful, and the sun's rays shone through the cracks of the clouds over the water, projecting the pattern of a huge golden feather. Behind the disappearing horizons, like a mirror over the blue sea, one could see the foggy outlines of the Pontic Mountains. Beyond them lay my homeland. Everything seemed like a nightmare ...

Colonel Torkom was talking to the woman. Her mother was sleeping in the sun. Towards evening, when the lady and mother went below deck, the colonel approached and took me by the arm to the other side of the deck.

"I would like to talk to you about an important issue, but first I will explain the current situation. The war is coming to an end," he said, inspired like a prophet and closing his mouth tightly with the last word. Then, he continued:

"The German attack in the direction of Flanders, Ypres, and La Bassée was not successful. They barely broke through 20 kilometers and stopped, while their goal was to strike a crushing blow on the British forces. Their last attack on Paris was unsuccessful. The United States has been an active force since April 5th, and it is now the driving force to end the war. The British army, thanks to the work done in the previous three months, is now of great value. Under these circumstances, it is obvious that developments on the Russian front are not enough to save the day for the Axis powers. Austria-Hungary and Bulgaria are already begging for peace. The situation of the Turks is worse. They are being crushed on the Mesopotamian front. The British have occupied Baghdad since March 26th. In Syria, the Turks are retreating on the Jaffa-Jerusalem line ..."

I listened to the colonel's comforting information with great interest, which was new to me.

"Let's see what happens now," he added. "The course of the Tatars is clear. They want the Turks to dominate Transcaucasia by dividing the region between themselves and the Georgians as semi-independent states. The course of the Georgians is more complicated and instructive in many ways. Three days ago, in Tbilisi, I learned from a reliable source that they had had a secret meeting to declare Georgia's independence. They want their independence and territorial integrity to be guaranteed by Germany. The latter will be represented by Count Schulenburg to the Georgian government. A number of secret agreements have already been signed with the Germans to exploit the country's communications and resources. Chkhenkeli, Nikoladze, Jordania, Surguladze, generals Kvinitadze, Otishilidze, and other Georgian statesmen are holding such secret talks day and night. Khan Khoyski, Khas Mamedov, Mafikiurtski, Usubekov, Jafarov, and other Tatar statesmen are aware of their activities. The Georgians agree that Eastern Transcaucasia should have freedom of action and control its fortunes with the help of the Turks. Thus, with such lowest level of betrayal, we Armenians are once again abandoned between blood and fire. The German delegation headed by Von Losov left for Poti yesterday. The Turks do whatever they want and nobody cares, while we have no allies against them. Now, I ask you, what shall we do under these circumstances?"

His black eyes, filled with vengeance, were focused on me, his face frozen. The conspiracies around us were not news, but it was the first time he had given me a full account.

"Well, it's hard, isn't it, to find an answer?" he said in a rather overwhelmed tone. "But I have an answer to it, and it is not only now that I say it; it is necessary to stop the traitors and immediately declare the independence of Armenia," emphasizing his words one by one.

"Three days ago, I made a last attempt in Tbilisi. Again, they thought I was crazy. Neither the members of the National Council, nor our politicians could understand the necessity of declaring independence as soon as possible. Now, I am going to Moscow, and from there I will cross to Arkhangelsk and take a boat to London to take action in favor of Armenian independence. I have done all the initial work and I have no doubt of success. I know for a fact that the British agree with that. Now, I ask you to join me in this work. I will take care of your travel expenses, even after getting there, it is easy. What do you say?"

I wasn't expecting the last part and looked at him in amazement.

"Give up your 'volunteer' plans; not one, not even ten Mourads can save our situation. It is not us who will decide the fate of the war. Enough is enough, let's save a little of our blood and look into politics. You can be useful to me in this regard, working with Armenian communities. This offer is good for our nation and promises a great future for you personally."

"Colonel, I'm sorry, but I do not have any calling for a diplomatic mission. That's not my job," I said ...

"It's a pity," he responded, and left with the measured footsteps of a soldier.

Once again, the sun shone behind the clouds with its fiery eyes and disappeared. Below, Russian anti-Soviet travelers lined up on the open deck of the ship, singing and drinking. I often heard them toasting the name of Kaletin, a well-known figure who had committed suicide a little while ago, thus ending his adventurous life. Once more, like a nightmare, Yerznga came to my mind again ...

***

We arrived in Tuapse late in the morning. We said goodbye to the colonel, thanked him for his support in Poti, and got off the boat. Tuapse was beautiful from a distance, with amphitheater-like buildings stacked on top of each other. However, it was not particularly attractive when one was closer. Armenian refugees crowded the areas along the coast. They were either intending to go or actually on their way to the north. The Georgians were in a festive mood in the city. Georgia had been declared an independent state [on May 26th, 1918]. Unlike the mood of the Georgians, in this Babylon of peoples, the Russians also had their own concerns. Civil wars were raging throughout the country. The Don Cossacks, led by Ataman Krasnov, started a movement in the south of Russia and were roaming the country since April. They ruled over most of the coast and the Don area, and were now moving west and north, as well as threatening to occupy the North Caucasus ...

Armavir was also crowded with Armenian refugees. A week earlier, a large group had arrived from Tbilisi. Those reaching Armavir were branching out in two directions, some to the north-west, towards Rostov, and some to the south-east, towards Vladikavkaz. The Armenians of Tbilisi and the Caucasus in general went in this latter direction. I heard that the Tatigians had left in a group to Essentuki. Most of the refugees were Western Armenians who had been moving from place to place for the third year in a row. They said that refugees from Tbilisi, along with thousands of carts, carriages, and vehicles loaded with household items were moving to Vladikavkaz. One person's place on a coach was worth up to 10,000 roubles. The Armenian world was uprooted and on the move. Perhaps that is how our people had migrated to Poland, the Balkans, and elsewhere centuries earlier ...

Mourad was not there. He had left with Sebouh for Tsaritsin with the intention of going to Moscow or Baku. Hovnan insisted

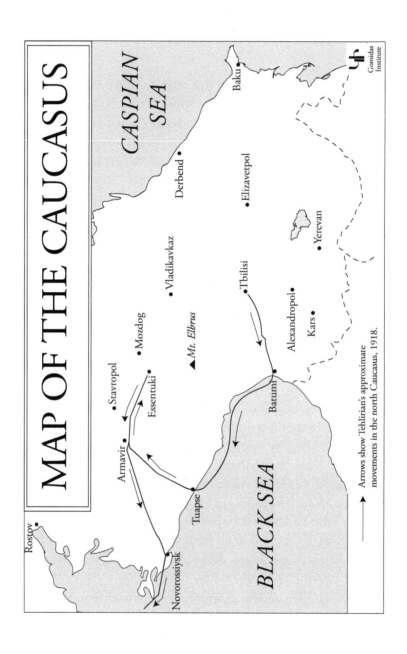

MAP OF THE CAUCASUS

CASPIAN SEA

BLACK SEA

Baku

Derbend

Elizavetpol

Yerevan

Vladikavkaz

Tbilisi

Alexandropol

Kars

Mozdog

▲ Mt. Elbrus

Stavropol

Essentuki

Armavir

Batumi

Tuapse

Novorossiysk

Rostov

Gomidas Institute

Arrows show Tehlirian's approximate movements in the north Caucasus, 1918.

on going to Tsaritsin. Without Mourad, his life was worthless. I no longer thought of wandering around, especially since we didn't know whether we would find Mourad in Tsaritsin, nor what we would do when we found him. We had to take other steps to deal with the widespread misery. Colonel Torkom was right in saying that scattered individuals could no longer do tangible work. I shared the money I had received from my brother in Yerznga with Hovnan, and he left for Tsaritsin on the same day, promising to keep in touch.

I spent most of the day with refugees at the station. Newcomers were piling on top of the earlier ones, and there seemed to be no end in sight. The migration was disorganized. The newcomers were left on their own. The number of sick people was increasing every day. The attitude of the local Russian residents was becoming more and more unfriendly. Forced to save their own lives, the Western Armenian refugees appeared in the market with all kinds of trades and goods to sell, threatening the livelihoods of the Russian shopkeepers. The Armenian peasants became "Jews" in their eyes ...

I supported the work of a local Armenian refugee committee and spared no effort in helping alleviate the misery in any way I could. Every mother and child reminded me of my relatives, whom I still imagined alive in the deserts of Arabia, of course, in more difficult conditions. But this did not last long. I had headaches, exhaustion, fever, and sometimes dizziness, as I had once had in Yerevan. It turned out that I had typhus. In those days, my only relatives were the Tatigians. Although it was very unpleasant, I had to go immediately to Essentuki while I could still move.

A group of Caucasian-Armenian refugees were arguing on the train over the Treaty of Batumi, according to which Armenia was declared an independent state. I understood nothing. I vaguely remember Poti, the ship, Colonel Torkom. I felt as if I were in a furnace ... the train's vibrations made my head throb. Sometimes, I managed to strain myself and understand something of the conversation.

"It's a trap, brother, not independence," someone shouted. "Twelve thousand square kilometers and a million Armenians surrounded by Turks on all sides ... How can such a state survive?"

"Do you understand what is happening? What could they do? How else could one breathe a little in this ongoing nightmare?" screamed someone else.

"So, if we count our victims at a minimum of 1,200,000 people, we will come to the conclusion that we have sacrificed one person for every square meter of land in the newly created Armenia," said a third person bitterly ...

Everyone was very kind. Although I told them I had typhus, they were not afraid to take care of me in every possible way. I do not know how I got to the Tatigians in this very difficult situation with the help of a fellow traveler. The Tatigians lived in a two-story building with a garden.

"Don't worry, it's nothing, it will pass," said Mr. Nshan, helping me to remove my clothes.

I then became aware of Mrs. Zvart, Anahid, Zepiur, and a Russian man who was a doctor. My head was very heavy, my bones felt as if they were broken.

After three weeks, I owed my life and existence to the Tatigians and especially Anahid, who spent long, sleepless nights taking care of me. She listened to the doctor's instructions carefully and carried them out strictly. During my illness, she ruled over me, and that often annoyed me. But something made me obey her like a child. It was Anahid who ran around to find milk and yogurt, which were not easy to find in those days. Day by day, I was convinced that this girl was different from all the women I had ever met. Sometimes, I felt that my life was very precious to her. She expressed very warm concern toward me. But looking closely, I always came to the conclusion that she was more interested in the fight against my illness than in me. Sometimes, she had an argument with her father about me. According to Mr. Nshan, eating should not have been forbidden when a patient had an appetite, and he was right, because I had never felt so hungry in my life as in those difficult days. But it was in vain. Anahid did not deviate even slightly from the doctor's orders, even if I died of starvation. The following week, when the doctor announced that

Mt. Arakadz (background) with ruins of Ani (foreground).

the "crisis" was over and the "recovery period" was about to begin, mother and daughter now seemed to have decided to stuff me with a special diet. While Mrs. Zvart only scolded me for "failure" with her maternal generosity and affection, Anahid instructed me to stick to the doctor's orders and eat only what was allowed.

Since the retreat from Yerznga, the strong love I had built in my heart for her three years earlier had been tainted. Yet again, her care and unconditional caring filled my idle soul with incredible joy, and I was filled, day by day, with an overwhelming sense of mental rapture. I waited impatiently whenever she was out of the house.

As soon as I recovered, Anahid toned down her behavior, cooled off in a way, and seemed sad that she had nothing left to do any longer. Now, her attitude was the same as in Tbilisi. Polite, friendly, and only sometimes, intimate. Most of the time she spent reading in the spacious garden, under the lush, dense trees.

By the end of July, I was well enough to consider returning to Armavir. But what would I do? I was imagining myself on projects that did not actually exist, such as working with the refugees' commission, which had probably already dissolved. I just realized how unprepared I was for life. I had left my homeland to study with rosy prospects, but I had got involved in bloodshed and destruction. I had become a semi-accomplished guerrilla fighter.

Was this to be the course of my life? Wasn't a major change needed? Sometimes, it seemed that the real meaning of life was in finding personal peace. A modest job, family, children, as most people lived their lives. But every time I remembered my past life, the unburied graves of my relatives and friends, I felt that I could not be happy with such a [settled] existence. What did Anahid think? Were all the books she read really useful, or did she want to be busy with something else? At home, at lunch, and dinner, she expressed a scattered state of mind and was often reprimanded by her mother or father. Sometimes, she was overwhelmed with unbridled cheerfulness, which was expressed with laughter. In any case, our relationship had become so complicated that she avoided being alone with me.

Full of uncertainties, I spent most of the summer days in the south of the residence, where the sun-drenched Caucasus mountain range with its snow-capped Mount Elbrus looked magnificent in the background.

One day, it was dusk. When I went home, I took a different path that extended along the wooded area of the summer house. Countless birds flocked to the dense deciduous trees, screeching in the air with their loud, incomprehensible language. Despite that commotion, trees and hills slept in their eternal peace. Coming down from the hills, I saw Anahid walking with a book under her arm. Suddenly, like a child caught red-handed, she cried out, "Aah, I didn't know that you were here ..."

"No, of course. I just thought of coming this way for once," I said, barely controlling my anxiety.

She immediately composed herself and began talking cheerfully about the day's events, the neighbors who had broken up during my illness, and how they were now trying to get back together. Unaware of the widespread disasters, she remained untroubled by the world around her. Then, suddenly, she was sort of delighted that the neighbors had been morally compromised. She was smiling, looking at me from time to time with half-open eyes. All her words were mostly simple utterings, but she radiated a deep, inner joy. Yes, she was happy. Her sixteen years had left her with nothing but innocent contentment. "Now or never" I kept thinking. But how? I could hardly hear what she was saying, but I felt I had no right to disturb her carefree cheerfulness. When we got home, I was angry that I had missed the best opportunity to speak up.

The next day, I was sitting in the garden with little Setik, who had gathered a bunch of twigs and asked me to cut them down to size with a knife, when Anahid appeared with a letter in her hand. It was addressed to Armavir, care of the refugee commission's chairman, Seferian, and meant for me. It was from Hovnan. He wrote that he had reached Tsaritsin and joined Mourad, that the local commander of Soviet forces, Petrov, had welcomed Mourad and Sebouh with great pomp and given them all the opportunity to travel to Baku to fight against the Turks. "Leaving immediately, here on the Volga River, we will be in Baku in three days," Hovnan said. But the letter had been written about a month and a half earlier and there was no postage stamp on it.

"Who brought it?"

"An Armenian man."

"Didn't you ask who he was?"

"An Armenian merchant from Mozdog, I forgot his name. Is it important?" Anahid asked thoughtfully.

"Never mind, perhaps he is still there. I will find him."

"I can help you, I remember his face. Round like the moon, with very red cheeks, and a big belly," she said, drawing a semicircle in the air and laughing out loud ...

We easily found him at the neighboring "Astoria" hotel. He was sitting at one of the tables in the shade under the trees in the yard. We sat down.

"It is peaceful in Armavir," he said, answering my questions, "but there is commotion in Mozdog."

"Who rules there?"

"It is very difficult to say. The other morning we hung a white flag from the store. But when we learned that the Bolsheviks had won out, of course, we immediately took it down, but by the time the red flag reached the store from home, the whites had won again. Naturally, we hung the white one up again. The next morning, I sent the young shop worker out to find out who held power. It was the reds. I took down the white one, hung up the red, and came here. Now, who can say which side is in control?"

"Excuse me, but how did my letter get into your hands?"

"Yes! I was going to say that I was in Baku, and I came to Armavir from there."

"Were you in Baku?"

"Yes!"

"When?"

"A little while ago."

"How are they?"

"Who?"

"The city, the Armenians ..."

"The city is not well. There is fighting. Armenians are not harmed. They are fighting like lions," he said, putting his fists on the table.

"So, is the fight still continuing?"

"Of course."

"When did you leave Baku?"

"About four or five days ago," he said, waving his fingers. "I took the opportunity and went to Derbent with Bicherakhov's military unit, and from there to Armavir ..."

"Did you say Bicherakhov?"

"Yes, he is a very brave general, but on the night of July 25th, he had to retreat."

"Today is August 8th, so you left Baku two weeks ago."

"Well, you are right. We went here and there, and lost count of the days."

"Is the Derbent-Balajari road still free?"

"Of course. Balajari is in the hands of the Armenian commander, Hamazasb."

"Is Mourad there?"

"Mourad?"

He pulled a large colored handkerchief from his pocket and wiped the sweat off his forehead. Unfortunately, he did not know anything about Mourad, but he had heard of him as the "Armenian commander." Then, turning to Anahid, he asked about life where we were living, letting me understand that the conversation between us was over. Judging from the prices in restaurants [he added], life looked quite expensive.

But Anahid, carried away by her thoughts, did not understand the question and smiled innocently. We did not get much information from that tormented Armenian. But what he had said was enough to make me nervous ...

I had never experienced such mental anguish as I did that night. Hovnan did not leave my sight with his slender, tall stature, and his colorless, bony face. His small, suspicious eyes seemed to stare at me from the surrounding darkness with bitterness. Yes, for better or worse, he continued on his path. And weren't they all like that? Mourad himself, who had had the courage to allow his beloved wife to commit suicide, who had watched with a telescope from the top of a mountain how his relatives were being led to their deaths, who had gnawed at the barrel of his gun in pain, unable to fire on the executioners so that the deportees would not be harmed.

There was no doubt that I had to go to Baku, but I felt really constrained. I could not reconcile my personal and objective judgments ... There was only one way out. I had to cut and throw away the knot that held me back. I could already see Baku with its balmy air, dust everywhere, tired trees in its park, passers-by running around like crazy, little fast carts, and huge buildings sitting there, just as I had seen them three years earlier on my way from Rostov to Tbilisi. It seemed to me that, at every step, I bumped into one of my comrades: Jebeji, Hovnan, Sahag, Vartan, Nshan. I felt that the only meaning in life was meeting a comrade somewhere. Then, I remembered our hellish journey: Vzhan, Chors, Chilig. I remembered Chemishgadzaktsi, his corpse lying in the snow under the bright moonlight, his cold eyes wide open, and his perplexed horse running towards us ...

I woke at dawn from a deep dream. It was as if I had died and was in a grave, where my relatives were. The grave was large, made of stone, and damp. Only a lamp illuminated the impenetrable darkness. My people were very happy that I was finally dead, especially my sisters-in-law and the children. The latter jumped on my shoulders, overwhelmed with joy. But my mother was distraught. She cried and accused me of dying too soon, coming to the grave without taking their revenge ...

It was raining outside. The wind rustled the leaves of the trees. It was dawn. One of the upright branches of a poplar tree scraped against the edge of my window.

In the morning I looked outside. The sun was shining above the trees. The ground was undoubtedly damp. But, as usual, the tea table was set there. Anahid was standing next to it, filling the teapot. I went down, determined to talk to her. "Yes or no," I would demand to know. But when I approached her, I lost my nerve.

"Good morning."

"Good morning."

"I wanted to talk to you about something because I'm leaving tomorrow," I said at last.

She shrieked, "Where to?"

"Baku."

"But why?"

"You heard that man yesterday, you know, the letter ..."

"But you are not fully recovered," she exclaimed, and then, suddenly regretting what she had said, smiled.

I felt that she was really concerned. My heart was trembling and I could not find a word to say.

"Of course, it's your choice, but I do not think your decision will be pleasing to dad," she said, recovering her composure.

"Mr. Nshan will understand me, but the issue is ..." and I stopped.

"What issue?"

"I think it's obvious to you."

She was staring at me with her bright eyes, as if she was holding her breath. "If she denies me, it means everything is off. I will not say another word," I thought. Suddenly, she blushed profusely, lowered her eyes, and made a vague expression with her face. I found the courage to go on.

"To be honest, I do not understand myself. At first, I thought I had overcome the feelings I had for you, but with time, they actually deepened. Sometimes, I felt I could hope for reciprocity. But, but, of course, you did not give me any grounds ..."

I lost the thread of my thoughts.

"Anyhow, it is still early, but can I hope that in three or four years?"

"Daddy is coming," she said, looking confused.

"My daughter, isn't it damp? Wouldn't it be better to drink the tea inside?" Mr. Nshan said, as he approached us.

"No, dad, the sunshine has already reached us," and she continued with an air of indifference:

"Do you know what, father? Soghomon is leaving."

"Where to?"

"Baku."

"Baku?"

It seemed to me that Anahid did not take me seriously and I felt very bad.

"Yes, I will leave tomorrow evening," I told her father, who was looking at me, surprised.

He read the letter I had received and I told him what the man from Mozdog had said.

"What can I say? Since fate brought you to our door during these difficult days, it is natural that I consider myself responsible for you before your father. At least that's how I feel about it. If, God forbid, something happened to you! But I think your father could not say anything either in this case. We grew old prematurely, we became useless. Now, if we hold you back, how could we live with our conscience? Go, but be careful."

Anahid, who was arranging the teacups, threw all the spoons she had in her palm into a cup, and sat down.

"Fill them, my daughter," said Mr. Nshan, and then spoke about Mourad, whom he admired.

The next morning, Essentuki was in commotion. A large group of refugees had arrived from Baku. Active, well fed, and their stomachs protruding, they were better clothed, with beautiful, shiny travel bags, unlike our usual refugees. Oil producers, managers, merchants, women and girls dressed in jewelery. Then came rows of men, who honked like geese. They stopped near the

"Astoria" hotel. At night, a group of these young men came out and kissed the women, whose searching eyes looked far and wide under their summer hats. Someone very thin was complaining about the difficult conditions of Essentuki. And, suddenly, among the crowd, I saw Bolsetsi Levon, my comrade-in-arms in Araul. I approached him, but my joy did not last long. I was informed that Mourad had been killed, and the days of Baku were numbered, as the Turks had reached the suburbs.

CHAPTER FIVE

In Constantinople [Bolis]

I was trapped in Essentuki and could not see a way out. Anahid, after avoiding me for a few days, resumed her friendly manner. Nothing had changed in her attitude, except that she was now addressing me with the informal "you." I, in my turn, did not raise the issue close to my heart. I was spending most of the day at the neighboring "Astoria" hotel. In the evenings, when I returned home, Anahid would ask me questions about matters that were actually obscure to her, but she slowly turned the conversation to the people from Baku – who was married to whom, what were the girls' names, what was the level of their education, didn't I think the girl with the blond hair was quite beautiful, perhaps her nose was a little long, and other questions that made no sense to me.

In the second half of September [1918], the Turks entered Baku. The great stream of refugees that followed also came our way. Some of them fled to Persia, some to Petrovsk, and some to Krasnovotsk. The number of people massacred in the city was around 20-30,000.

In those days, the situation in all of Russia was still complicated. Anti-Soviet armed movements were growing day by day. Organizations opposed to the Soviets were emerging everywhere. Local clashes were turning into large-scale civil conflicts. The Czechoslovaks occupied Kazan, Sembersk, Ufa and the Middle Volga region, declaring the area "Country of Constitutional Assembly." Fierce battles were taking place in the south-eastern parts of European Russia, in the Don, Kuban, and Orenburg regions. Anti-Soviet forces were organizing conspiracies, intimidation, and uprisings in the center. Then, Denikin's army was conquering the entire North Caucasus, from the shores of the Black Sea to the Astrakhan deserts. General Dudov's forces were roaming the Orenburg region. In Siberia, cut off from the center by the Ural-Volga front, the "autonomous" Omsk and Vladivostok "governments" were formed.

In addition to internal class divisions, the ethnic forces of the different peoples of Russia also played a critical role in developments. Apart from every nation, every region also declared "independence." Newly formed states were emerging in the Far East, the Transcaspian region, the Urals, Arkhangelsk, Finland, the entire Baltic region, Ukraine, the Don region, Kuban, Dagestan, and the Transcaucasus. Even in Kharbin, people wanted to have their own "provisional government."

These internal counter-movements were greatly stimulated by external enemy forces, as well as former allies. The Germans controlled the whole western part of Russia, Ukraine, and Finland through various local agents or "authorities." The Far East was ruled by the Japanese, backed by British, French, American, and Italian troops based in Vladivostok. In Siberia, former allies were supporting Admiral Kolchak with weapons, money, and supplies. The British and Americans had landed on the shores of Arkhangelsk. In the south, the French supported the famous adventurer [Symon] Petliura. The Basmachis invaded the Transcaspian region at the instigation of the British. In fact, the Germans and the Turks ruled in Transcaucasia.

In those days of general collapse, news broke that the Mudros Armistice had been signed on October 30th [1918] and that the Turks had laid down their arms. They were obliged to immediately vacate the lands they occupied in Transcaucasia. The allies were to control Constantinople and the Straits. According to another condition of the armistice, surviving Armenians were to be gathered in Constantinople, and the organizers of the mass murders were to be brought to justice.

The days of reckoning were near. The idea of going to Bolis and killing Talaat came to my mind again, and I felt it dictated to me by the ghost of my mother. At the same time, I hoped that one or more of my relatives might be in Constantinople, or that it would be easy to find out about them in that city.

Now, everyone was in a hurry to return home. On the very first day, a large number of Baku Armenians left. Levon was with them and apparently had a hard time separating from such a sweetheart, just as I had found it hard to leave Anahid. He preferred a long winding road from Baku to Batumi and then Constantinople, as if it were difficult to find a suitable boat to Constantinople from other Black Sea ports. The next day we left for Novorossiysk.

"Forget that accursed country; we barely broke free of it," Mr. Nshan tried to convince me.

Mrs. Zvart urged me to go to Tbilisi and stay with them until the war was over and I could return to my father in Serbia. Only Anahid remained silent and seemingly indifferent.

It was night. Deportees were filling the train at every station on the way. They were going to Kherson, Odessa, and the Romanian border. Distances meant nothing to them. A Russian villager joined us at a station and settled in our carriage. He wanted to ask me something, but the train started moving at that moment. He took off his hat, crossed his face, and began to whisper a prayer. At the end of the prayer, he crossed himself three times, covered his head with his hat, and adjusted himself on the seat. He then asked me, "What time is it?" It was three o'clock in the morning. He put his head on his knees and began to snore immediately. The Tatigians were also asleep, except for Anahid, who remained seated like a statue. I believe she understood everything I felt and thought about her. That night, more than ever, I thought of Anahid in the highest terms. I had found the solution to my predicament. I would first avenge the death of my mother and relatives, and then remain inseparable from her until death, if fortune smiled on me. I wanted to calmly tell her all these things, but alas, that opportunity was not given to me.

The conductor came in and saw that the wick of the oil lamp in our carriage was about to burn out. He did not replace it. I could no longer see Anahid well in the semi-darkness. The peasant kept snoring and making strange noises from his nose. The windows of the train were vibrating in unison. There was commotion in our carriage all day long, as people came and left, each passenger traveling in a different direction.

We reached Novorossiysk in the evening. A ship was leaving for Poti and Mr. Nshan took the opportunity to board it. The closer the departure time, the more I felt the need to talk to

Anahid. But even now, Mr. Nshan would not leave me alone. He kept trying to persuade me to go with them. I was disappointed with myself and thought it would be better to express what I had to say to her in a letter.

They were about to leave when Anahid approached me and said with a sad smile:

"So, this is it ..."

"Yes, but I did not get a response from you ..."

"What response?"

"The answer to my question two months ago in the garden."

"What good is it now?"

"It matters a lot to me."

"Come with us to Tbilisi, that's my response."

"I give you my word of honor that I will come; just promise me that you will wait for me."

"Oh, my God, what can I say?"

"That you will wait for me," I insisted.

"Well, let's see which one of us will keep the promise."

Their ship departed and gradually disappeared, becoming smaller and smaller on the horizon. From afar, far away, I could still see a hand, a white handkerchief.

***

It was dusk and raining lightly. I was walking towards the station, encountering a small number of passers-by. I do not know what I was thinking. I felt as if I were on a path from which there was no turning back without success. There was unusual commotion at the station. Everyone was buying a newspaper to read with their own eyes. The war was over! Germany had accepted the terms of an armistice [November 11th, 1918]. I left for Odessa two hours later.

Immediately after the Mudros Armistice [October 30th, 1918], the allied powers became the masters of the Black Sea. Anglo-French warships appeared on the Russian shores. British troops were in Ukraine, the Don region, Finland, Estonia, and Latvia. The French were landing in Crimea.

Odessa was under Graeco-French rule. It took me about a month to sort out my papers and secure a place on the "Euphrates," which was to sail for Constantinople. All travelers were in the same position with new difficulties arising every day. Everyone was eager to reach Constantinople, hoping to get some news of surviving relatives.

We finally left in mid-December. The next morning, the ship stopped in Constanza. Due to quarantine regulations, we were not allowed to disembark and spent a boring day and night on board. On the morning of December 18th, we approached the Bosporus. The air was crisp with white clouds in the sky. The sun's warm rays sometimes broke through and fanned out like a golden umbrella, creating a pink haze on the horizon. The rays would break through the jet-black waters below. The colors of the sky and sea changed constantly, as if they were two eastern queens, competing with each other with their colorful costumes. The steamer, with its sharp bow, cut through the waters and approached the Bosporus strait, sending the parting waters left and right. Standing at one end of the deck, I watched the valleys and hills appearing in front of me, my mind wandering into the depths of that blood-stained country: Van, Khnous, Erzeroum, Yerznga, Chelig, Chors, Vzhan. The sun now brought with it cotton-white clouds gliding across the sky. It was a solemn procession of scattered clouds, which, like many dead souls, accompanied us steadily in the direction of the meandering strait. The number of travelers increased on the deck, and they pointed in different directions, enjoying the sight of familiar places again, so many years later. The waters of the Black Sea were now behind us and we were well into the narrow passage of the Bosporus.

Among the travelers on the deck were many Armenian and Greek deportees, as well as others. As the ship got closer to Constantinople, joyful cries were heard from them. Hagop, a fellow traveler from Yenikeoy, who knew the area like the back of his hand, was now silent and emotional. Here was he, in his birthplace, Yenikeoy, with its 10,000 or so Greek and Armenian inhabitants. The town was below some hills on the right shore of the Bosporus. He was probably wondering about his mother, sister, brothers ... Which one of them was still alive and what had they lived through? I understood his feelings.

We passed other settlements but everyone focused on Bebek near the shore, where the temple of Artemis had once stood. We passed Kourou Cheshme, Ortakeoy, Beshiktash, and Chraghan Palace on the European side. We practically touched the famous Dolma Baghche, behind which, on a hill, was Yildiz Keoshk. There were so many painful associations with those snow-white palaces.

Uskudar [Skiudar] began to appear on the Asiatic side. There were people from Uskudar on the ship. According to them, "uskudar" meant place of resistance in Persian. Xenophon rested there prior to crossing to the European side. There was nowhere in that country that was not soaked in old or recent blood. Its old name was Prizibolis, named after Agamemnon's child. The Byzantines built three memorials there for the Athenian help against Philip the Macedonian. Now there were many sharp minarets reflecting in the sun.

We then passed Karakash on the European shore, where the silver waters of the Marmara opened up in front of us, flowing past Saray Bournoun.

Across, on the water, was the lonely Kiz Koulesi. The tower was built in the days of Manouel Komneni, to control the Bosphorous, while, according to Turkish tradition, it was built by Sultan Mehmed when a gypsy foretold that his daughter would die of a snakebite. The tower was thus built to protect his beloved daughter. Many years passed and the world heard of the beauty of Mehar Shehid. Then, the Persian Shah's son came to marry her. And here also came fate, when a venomous snake among the flowers he had brought bit Mehar Shehid. However, as one may have expected, the prince sucked out the poison, saved her life, and married her ...

We were now in the Golden Horn. Constantinople was really a dreamlike place. According to Byzantine tradition, Apollo himself pointed out the location where the city was later built. The Asian part dazzled the onlooker with the countless minarets, and the European part with magnificent palace-like buildings that seemed to float on water.

The steamer slowly approached the quay of Galatia and stopped. The dock was filled with a colorful crowd waiting for the ship. Porters passed the luggage from hand to hand, as if the belongings did not have owners. I was surrounded by deafening shouts, curses in many languages, and red fezzes. Everything was the same, as if nothing had changed. The police checked and collected passports. However, I was very disappointed when we came out of the quay. As charming as the city was from afar, it became more unattractive from closer up, with its narrow and murky streets, dirt everywhere, and the labyrinth of miserable wooden buildings bearing traces of fires ... Seen from the sea, no city was so enchanting, yet so disappointing close up, as Constantinople. I bought the *Jagadamard*[*] newspaper from the first newspaper seller I encountered. The last two pages were filled with notices placed by people looking for their deported relatives. From Galata Saray to Taksim, a throng of people rushed in different directions. Armenians, Greeks, Turks, Europeans of all nationalities and religions, all mingled as if Constantinople was the cradle of humanity. At every step I noticed British and French soldiers, the only indication of foreign rulers.

I finally reached the editorial office of *Jagadamard* through the incomparably cleaner and more attractive Pera Street. It was a great consolation to see this building in such a wonderful state, despite the disasters *Jagadamard* had been through. There were young people, fiery faces, and women and girls huddled in the dimly lit front of the editorial office. Next, in a quieter, brighter room, sat a man with the appearance of a wrestler, probably a young writer or a poet. I approached him.

"Excuse me. I would like to place a notice that I am looking for my relatives, but I do not know where I should go."

"Here. Who are you looking for?"

I understood from his tone that such work had become routine for him.

---

[*] *Jagadamard* newspaper was a well-known Armenian newspaper published in Constantinople. It was also the organ and center of the ARF (Tashnagtsoutiun) in Constantinople.

"My mother, my brother, the wives and children of my two older brothers."

"It is not possible to include all of them at once. If you find one, that would be a big deal."

"Write: my mother, my brother ..."

"Your address?"

"I do not have an address, I've just arrived."

"Where from?"

"From Russia."

He put his pen down and looked at me.

"How did you get here?"

"By boat, from Odessa."

He stood up.

"Did other deportees come as well?"

"Of course."

"Come here."

There was a large group in the adjacent hall.

"Mr. Krikor," he called out. "This gentleman has just arrived from Russia."

"When? How?" responded Mr. Krikor.

And then, he and others began a detailed inquiry about the number of deportees from the North Caucasus, their disposition, developments in the Caucasus and Russia, the people who had arrived on the "Euphrates" steamer, and so on.

Then, a pale girl, who was listening attentively, asked directly:

"Sir, might you have heard of Levon Madatian?"

"Bolsetsi Levon?"

"Yes. He is from Bolis [Constantinople]!"

"Of course!"

"Is he alive?"

"Yes, miss. He is my close friend."

"What do you say!"

"Believe me, we were together in Essenduki, but he left earlier than I did. He should have been here by now." Apparently, Levon was very close to the girl, and she lost herself completely.

Miss Yeranouhi Tanielian.

"Sir, if only you knew the despair of his parents. They cry day and night. Where do you live? Could I have your address, sir?"

"I have no place yet, miss."

"Maybe you'd like to go to Levon's parents with me."

"Happily, but first I would like to put a notice in the newspaper and rent a room."

She seemed to be afraid of losing me in the crowd.

"Sir, I know of a room. There is no need for a notice."

"No, another kind of notice! I am looking for my relatives."

"Oh, sorry, let us get acquainted. I am Yeranouhi Tanielian. Would you like me to help you? Here, please ..."

We left after returning to the earlier room and placing the notice with the young man.

***

Miss Yeranouhi was like a nun. She did not fit my ill-informed ideas about the Armenian women of Constantinople. There was nothing naïve about her. She was a teacher and quite aware of political developments. She was involved in Armenian affairs. She was a close relative of Levon and lived in Pangalti with her mother. The first thing I found out from her concerned the escape of those responsible for the Armenian massacres.

"Yes. Talaat, Enver, Jemal, Halim Pasha, Bedri, and practically all of the 'famous' killers fled on the eve of the armistice."

Although it was hard to imagine that these criminals would be living in the open, such news still caused me deep disappointment.

"Didn't you know?"

"No!"

"Talaat Pasha was the first to escape."

"Why couldn't we get that monster before the armistice?"

"Oh sir, if only you knew how hard our comrade Mourad tried, but he was himself killed by the monster."

"Mourad, you say?"

"Yes, Hampartsoum Boyajian, one of the pillars of our party, who was known by his pseudonym 'Mourad.' Haven't you heard of Hunchag Mourad?"

"Are you a Hunchagian?"*

"Yes, you probably thought I was a Tashnagtsagan. Admit that I disappointed you, sir!"

"What are you saying, miss! What's the difference?"

"Yes, there is no difference for me. I have many friends among them."

The room that she had in mind in an old Greek woman's home next door was fortunately still available. Afterwards, she took me to her mother, who was overwhelmed with my news about Levon. While she [Yeranouhi] set glasses, plates, and spoons on the table in the next room, her mother asked me many questions. They immediately set the table with many things I had not seen for a long time: milk, butter, coffee, cheese, and so on. It was noon when the young lady led me like a detainee onto a trolleybus to Levon's parents in Beshiktash. I had to be careful that Levon's sick father would not suddenly die of joy! There was no one else in the

---

* Hunchag or Hunchagian: A member of the Social Democratic Hunchagian Party, one of the main Armenian political parties of the 19th century.

***

In those days, nobody in Constantinople bothered with the traitor Haroutiun, Talaat, or other fugitive criminals. The mood was different. The focus was on Armenians and Armenia. Religious and earthly divisions were put aside. There was an attempt to gather all the remnants of Armenians under a single national umbrella. Above restless political circles, "Araradian Armenia"* was now the subject of loving affection among the masses. The light of dawn illuminating those lands could now revive the dark horizons of Armenia and the nation.

This excitement intensified in January 1919, when a delegation from Armenia arrived in Constantinople, led by Avedis Aharonian. The delegation stayed at the Tokatlian Hotel in Pera, which our compatriots visited day and night, excited by the news from Armenia. I had the opportunity to listen to Avedis Aharonian, when he spoke at the Armenian Club in Pera and explained in his eloquent and fluent language, to the applause of the large crowd, what great efforts the Armenian soldier had made to push the enemy out of the country, and how hard the birth of "Infant Armenia" had been. It really was a miracle in those times. The powerful speech of the talented speaker both moved and excited those present. Later, as he was leaving for Paris, a large crowd gathered at the port of Galatia to bid him farewell. Before the eyes of the bewildered Turks, the crowd chanted, "Hurrah! Hurrah!"

There was even more excitement in late February when the British warship HMS *Caesar* arrived at Galata and Patriarch Zaven returned from exile. We were just beginning on our path to statehood and spiritual authority was still everything. The patriarch had returned safe and sound, and this meant that the nation was still standing and would survive. From the shore below the Ottoman Bank, thousands of Armenians were on the streets of

---

* The reference is to the new republic of Armenia, which was expected to be awarded new territories around Mt. Ararat at the Paris Peace Conference in 1919.

Patriarch Zaven Der Yeghiayan.

Constantinople. The return of the old patriarch symbolized the return of all the refugees ...

Armenian-Turkish relations were not bad at that time. Armenians did not have much reason to be dissatisfied with Turks. The political conditions forced the latter to compromise. After the death of Sultan Reshad, Prince Vahideddin was enthroned under the name of Mohammed VI. He was considered an admirer of British politics and a pro-Armenian. Respectable Armenians were testifying that the enlightened and artistic heir to the throne, Abdul Mejid, had said to an influential Armenian, that "our current sultan is extremely kind and would extract vengeance on behalf of Armenians." But from whom and how, he had not said. *Ikdam*, a Turkish newspaper, had written that all deported Armenians would return. The same respectable Armenians had appealed to the pro-Armenian heir to the throne, and he had replied, "Yes, by all means, all exiled Armenians, wherever they are, will return."

And what if they didn't return? The Armenian people were like infants, like "Infant Armenia," at that time.

By now, relations between the two unfortunate peoples during the massacres, Armenians and Greeks, had become more fraternal. The administration of the Greek Patriarchate held a magnificent liturgy and requiem service at the Aya Triada Church in Taksim, in memory of the Armenian martyrs. Many moving sermons were delivered.

For their part, the Armenians held an even more magnificent liturgy and mass in the Church of the Holy Trinity, in memory of the Greek martyrs, with the participation of metropolitans and the Greek Patriarch of Fanari. The service included the Armenian hymns and prayers, "*I Verin Yerousaghem*," "*Kanzi Zkez Orhnemk*," "*Hokvotsn Hankoutselots*," and other hymns and prayers.

Naturally, they were undertaking projects for the benefit of the Armenian nation, and the Armenian Patriarchate succeeded in forming a pan-national committee with the participation of Catholic and Protestant religious leaders. This committee was to take care of orphans and the needs of the returning deportees, as well as assist the Armenian Red Cross. Civil society was also in motion. The Armenian Red Cross, which had hospitals in Shishli, Pangalti and Beshiktash, worked particularly hard. The committee had feeding stations in various districts as well as orphanages that were in a better state than those in the Caucasus. The Armenian Medical Association had opened an accelerated training course for nurses and attracted hundreds of people. Former literary clubs were being re-formed day by day, and new associations and unions came into being, such as the Relief Society for Armenia, the Relief Commission, the Labor House, the Women's Union, and so on. Theatrical performances were presented once more and various events and parties were also organized for the benefit of Armenia. Numerous tea parties and dinners were organized in honor of the generals of the allied states or the correspondents of foreign countries who were already sympathetic to Armenians or were in the process of being won over during such lavish events.

The political situation was considered favorable to Armenians in Constantinople. On March 20th, at the suggestion of [US President] Woodrow Wilson, the Versailles Conference decided to send a commission to the Middle East, consisting of representatives of the United States, France, Great Britain, and Italy to assess the needs of the peoples and new countries to be formed by the dissolution of the Ottoman Empire. Armenian political circles tried to move the interest of the United States of America in favor of the Armenian Question. The American representatives at the Conference, and especially President Wilson himself, considered the Armenians very close to his heart and showed a willingness to take care of Armenia.

With hopes and expectations, having passed through blood and fire, the remnants of the Armenian people everywhere showed the strongest desire and extraordinary stubbornness to survive and live as a nation. Previously, they had only seen good in the motives of powerful nations so that, by the time they realized their mistake, it was already too late. Now, the remnants of that people were holding onto anything that could be useful for their survival. The only thing that was really noticeable was the silencing of revolutionary sentiments. The counter-revolutionary and inhuman blow [dealt by the Genocide] and the atrocious murder of revolutionaries left such sentiments [within Armenian communities] to the side.

I already had friends and comrades who unanimously testified to the sad role played by the traitor Haroutiun Mugrdichian. It was he who had informed Talaat of developments at the patriarchate, just before the deportations. It was he and Hamazasp, the well-known monk, expelled from Armash Monastery, who kept watch on the members of the committee working on Armenia* a year earlier, during Talaat's government. Mugrdichian was the one who had compiled the list of Armenian revolutionaries and intellectuals who were exiled and massacred. He was the one who had zealously persecuted Armenian community activists in Constantinople. It had already been verified that the blacklist compiled by the traitor and handed over to Talaat through Chief of Police, Bedri, consisted of 250 intellectuals, of whom barely ten had survived. Those ten survivors had been on the blacklist by mistake. For example, instead of Minas Cheraz, Mugrdichian had included his intended victim's brother on the list, Kasbar Cheraz, who was a lawyer. The latter managed to correct the mistake and was saved from death. Not knowing who exactly the Tashnag party member Mgrditch Hovhannisian was, he had listed two people of the same name, one of whom survived. In addition to the famous revolutionary Hayg Tiryakian, he had also listed another Hayg, who only managed to survive because of the real Tiryakian's intervention to correct the mistake. Levon Shamdanjian was confused with Mikayel Shamdanjian, who managed to return from exile, and so on.

I had been seriously pursuing that monster for two weeks. I was in Beshiktash for several hours every day at different times. But the traitor had realized that times had changed and did not go out

---

* This is a reference to a series of reforms that were championed by foreign powers between 1912 and 1914 for the better administration of the Armenian provinces of the Ottoman Empire. This reform process was due to be implemented under the supervision of two European inspectors. It was scuttled by the Young Turks with the outbreak of World War One.

much. One could only get to him inside his apartment, but his front door was always locked.

In this once-famous district were the remains of Chraghan Palace, which had been burnt down. The traitor resided in that part of the district. Opposite the house was a taverna, which belonged to an Armenian. There were also some grocery stores around it. There was no point in looking for an apartment there, a necessary vantage point to monitor the traitor closely. Around this district were patisseries, oriental shoe sellers, and sleepy rug-dealers, who slowly played with their rosaries and waited for customers. On the upper floors, here and there, were some apartments belonging to Armenians. Levon's parents lived there. Below them was a row of coffee-houses, where old men with green and white hats, snow-white beards, and proud faces, sat against walls or around doorways, lazily sucking on hookahs, and sometimes, slowly, lifting tiny coffee-cups to their lips.

At the end of March [1919], I made an attempt to befriend the owner of the café, but knowing that I was a refugee, he cold-shouldered me. It was on that day that a young boy appeared at the entrance of the traitor's house, hurried straight to the taverna, bought a bottle of "Martel," and returned home. In the evening, I informed Miss Yeranouhi about it, who was my only supporter in this matter. She had managed, through acquaintances, to contact some relatives of the traitor and obtain his picture. The boy I had seen was his only child.

The next day was Sunday. A mourning ceremony was to be held at the Holy Trinity Church in Pera on the occasion of the martyrdom of Armenian intellectuals. There was a large, mixed crowd. The Gomidas Choir performed the polyphonic liturgy. The whole atmosphere was extremely moving and heart breaking. Most of the attendees had lost family members. After the liturgy, Patriarch Zaven spoke, "If a grain of wheat falls onto the ground and dies, it dies alone: but after it dies, it brings forth much fruit," and with this analogy, he stated that all the martyrs would sprout like grains of wheat and give life.

In the evening, the Pangalti Youth Union had organized a mass mourning ceremony in the spacious hall of the Red Cross. When I got there, all seats had been taken, and I remained standing. The mourning ceremony was opened by the editor of Gavrosh Y[ervant] Tolayan, who was a survivor himself. In a few words, he highlighted the meaning and significance of the martyred intelligentsia, drawing the youth's attention to the importance of literary, social, and revolutionary activities, and urging them to fill the voids created by the martyred intellectuals.

One of the surviving intellectuals, Dr. Melkon Giulisdanian, recalled his own arrest, as well as those of his friends, on that Saturday night, when all prominent Armenian public figures in Constantinople – clergymen, civic activists, revolutionaries, editors, teachers, doctors, clerks, pharmacists, merchants, etc. – were taken to prison one after another late at night.

"The newcomers came with happy and contemptuous smiles," he said, "but upon seeing hundreds of well-known old and new prominent figures around them, all of them gloomy and lost in their thoughts, they too became worried."

"Gradually came daylight," he continued. "Everyone was mentally prepared with the hope of receiving help from outside. There were expectations that the "misunderstanding" would soon be resolved. The muezzin's *"Allah ou Akbar"* could be heard from a nearby minaret. But in the central prison of "Mehderhane," the darkness of night would gradually return. Only the roar of British warships could be heard from outside.

"Then came the third act of the tragedy. The checking of names on the blacklist, searches, separation into groups of twenty people or less, and the exodus. Police Chief Bedri was there in his special car. The groups of prisoners marched along Hagia Sophia boulevard to the seashore, toward Sirkeji. There were cries and sobbing ... And then Saray-Bournou, Giulhane Garden. A turbulent sea with huge waves ... The separate groups arrived and enjoyed the divine grace of seeing each other again. And the "Shirket No. 67" steamer. Two hundred and twenty people, the cream of the Armenian nation, accompanied by as many policemen and soldiers. We were then on the Marmara, our troubled souls reminiscing ... The fear of death. Haydar Pasha. A train with its lights out. Then Sinjan Keoy station. Darkness. The head of the Central Prison reading the list of the first group of martyrs. Murmurs. Those whose names were read out embracing others and leaving. Seventy five people to Ayash, Agouni, Khajag, Zartarian, Jangiulian, Shahrigian, Siamanto, Pashaian, Parseghian, Daghavarian, Varoujan, Achukbashian, Zakarian, Levon Larents, Chavoushian, Tomajanian ..."

And the speaker monotonously read out the names of 75 people. A woman in the crowd was sobbing loudly. Whispers were heard in the hall, "Who is she? ..." "His sister ..." "Whose? ..."

The speaker continued calmly.

"Dawn. From Kalayjik to Chankiri ... a large barracks, its windows covered with boards." A new list of 56 people. Names unknown to me. But where were the large empty barracks, their windows shuttered with wooden panels? I was no longer able to follow the speaker ... *"Bila tereddüt ve merhamet, bir aylıktan doksan ya?ına kadar itlafı"* read Talaat's order in Turkish.

I understood, "To destroy mercilessly and without pity, from one month to ninety years old ..."

There was a large crowd. The air was heavy. My head was spinning, and I was suffocating. I could hardly understand the speaker. His words were bouncing in my head. "Jelal-Aleppo," "Cherkez Mehmed," "Vartkes, Zohrab." I strained my full attention.

"Vartkes, I will not let you go to Bulgaria. I know you want to save yourself. Whatever happens to us, you will share the same fate."

"Who said that?" I asked the person standing next to me.

"Talaat to Vartkes."

"Zohrab, feeling that they were being led to their deaths, asked his landlord Mahmoud Nedim to intervene," the speaker continued in a monotonous voice ...

And again, a commotion disrupted the grave silence in the hall.

"Finally, under the supervision of the mounted gendarmes, Zohrab and Vartkes were taken away in a coach," continued the speaker ...

Again, I understood nothing ... again the same person, "Cherkez Mehmed" ... some Khalil ... Dikranagerd ... Karakeopriu ...

I felt I had a helmet on my head, which was gradually squeezing my brain. It was a nightmare, not a remembrance commemoration ... Suddenly, I felt dizzy, I could smell cold blood, I was overwhelmed by horror, and I was about to pass out. Putting all my strength in my legs, I only just reached the door and left the room, shaking ...

It was cool outside and the sky was clear. I was thinking of going to Beshiktash, to Levon's parents, and asking for permission to live there, so that I could be close to the traitor's house. Otherwise, nothing would have been possible covering that vast space. Perhaps Levon had already returned. If so, it would be easier, as I could tell him my intentions.

Passing the military school, I entered Nshantash Avenue, whose lights were shining on the waters of the Bosporus. Before reaching Okhlamour Keoshk, I could see the white marbled Hamidiye Mosque in the distance. Its pointed minaret played under the glimmer of the stars. Talaat's spiritual father, [Sultan Abdul] Hamid, was supposed to die there 14 years earlier, but the bomb missed "the great assassin" and his carriage blew up in front of him. Who could have imagined that this land would give birth to much greater killers than him?[*]

Upon reaching the building of the traitor, I just froze. The light was on. The curtains in the windows overlooking the street were open. A woman was working around a wide table covered with a snow-white tablecloth in the hall. She was setting the table with spoons, knives, forks. She suddenly looked outside, and I immediately left, crossed the sidewalk and turned to enter the taverna. The owner, who was sitting at a round table with two people, looked at me.

"A bottle of beer."

---

[*] The reference is to the attempted assassination of Sultan Abdul Hamid II, in a bomb plot called the "Yildiz bomb," organized by the Armenian Revolutionary Federation in 1905.

"If it weren't for Boghos Nubar Pasha, who knows what it would be like," said one of the two elderly Armenians sitting under the wall, folding the notebook in front of him. Then, he moved his glasses from the tip of his nose to his forehead and looked at me.

"*Mashallah* [Praised be the Lord], seven provinces, the land is as big as the world," said the other, filling the glasses with raki.

"Is Cilicia also included?" asked the owner of the taverna.

"Hey brother, what kind of a person are you? We are talking about the seven vilayets, [plus] Marash, Kozan, Jebel Bereket, Adana Sanjaks, as well as the port of Alexandretta, all given to us, and you say, 'Cilicia'! Where else are those areas?" the spectacled man exploded in anger as if severely offended.

"*Ishde!* I say the same thing, Hamedos Agha," said the owner without hesitation and coughed as if clearing his throat.

"Good. A country without people is the same as a garden without water. Who will go and live there?" said the other person, smoking.

"Brother! Let's get the land first, then it's easy. Should a person think of the house first or the tenant?"

At the sign of the owner, they were silent. A young boy, whom I had seen before, came to them.

"Five bottles of 'Martel.'"

He then paid, took the bottles, and left.

"Who was that?" asked the bespectacled man.

"The son of the dog."

I suddenly remembered that the boy was the son of the traitor.

"What is this? Five bottles of 'Martel!'" whispered the other.

"He has guests."

I was so confused. I could have pushed myself into the house with the boy and had missed the opportunity.

"Eh, no one has been found to shoot the dog and wipe the dirt from the forehead of our nation," sighed the spectacled man.

"It is not the right time, Hamedos Agha, let the [Armenian] nation find its feet first," said the second man.

"It's not the time! And what if he escapes like the traitor from Armash?"[*]

"Wherever he goes, Judas' end is obvious."

Suddenly, their words set me off like a sprung coil. By the time I had paid and left, it was already too late. The front door was closed. Desperate, I ran to the window and saw more than ten men and women gathered around a table. The traitor was sitting at the head of the table, right in front of the window, toasting with a glass in his hand. I was overwhelmed with pent up fury. I wanted to pull out my gun and shoot him through the window ... His arrogance, self-satisfaction, slightly curved posture, sparkling little eyes, and thin-lipped, wide mouth. They all made me tremble.

"Shall I pull it?"

"Pull it!"

"Through the window?"

"Straightaway, straightaway!"

My entire being was in turmoil.

"To the head?"

"To the heart!"

Suddenly, the windows shattered. The traitor fell back and slumped on his seat.

Early the [following] morning, I read in the newspapers that the traitor had only been wounded. Everything shattered in my mind. I should have nailed the bullet in his head. My sense of failure was as heavy as death itself.

A little while later, Miss Yeranouhi appeared. Paler than usual, somewhat confused but smiling, she shook my hand:

"I congratulate you, my brother. What a development, how wonderful," and sat down, stunned.

"Are you ill?"

"Are you mocking me?"

"Why would I do that?"

"Don't you know that the traitor survived?"

---

* Mampre Vartabed Sislian (Hidayet). A notorious Armenian collaborator who worked with the Young Turks in the persecution of Armenians during World War One.

"Oh, don't worry. I have already visited the hospital where he is lying in bed. A Greek doctor, a friend, told me that his hours are numbered."

The traitor died the next day.

CHAPTER SIX

To America

The death of the traitor brought much joy to Armenians in Constantinople. Within the party [ARF Tashnagtsoutiun], the question arose of pursuing the mass murderers, and the need of cooperation between party branches and comrades in Russia, Transcaucasia, Berlin, and Geneva in this regard. But the enthusiasm only lasted a brief moment as more important political issues became of greater concern.

Babajanian, a member of the Armenian delegation [at the Paris peace conference], had just arrived from Yerevan on his way to Paris. In Yerevan, Western Armenia was already considered part of Eastern Armenia. The Armenian authorities were preparing to celebrate the first anniversary of "United, Independent Armenia" with great pomp and ceremony. The comrades in Constantinople were also preparing for the same celebrations. On May 28th [1919], Mr. Babajanian gave a rousing speech in the great hall of the Greek Sillogos [Philological Society] in front of a large crowd, creating great excitement among those present.

These developments seemed like the culmination of recent diplomatic successes. The Peace Conference had decided in January to liberate Armenia and appoint a trustee in accordance with Article 22, which referred to international mandates. Since February, the delegation of the Republic of Armenia had been in Paris and was working in coordination with the Armenian National Delegation. Now, in Constantinople, the urgent issue of the day was the "Memorandum" presented to the Assembly by the two Armenian delegations [i.e., the All-Armenian delegation].*

---

* The delegation of the Republic of Armenia was headed by Avedis Aharonian and represented the Armenian state, while the Armenian National Delegation was formed outside Armenia and headed by Boghos Nubar Pasha.

In addition to the demands for the seven vilayets plus Cilicia, Armenians were seeking reparations from Turkey for the deportations, massacres, confiscations, and all kinds of deprivations suffered by the Armenian nation. The abandoned Armenian communal and private properties in Turkey were to be handed over to the Armenian spiritual authorities of Constantinople and used to meet public needs. The custodial state was obliged to force the Turks, Tatars [i.e., "Caucasian Tatars" or modern-day Azerbaijanis], and others occupying Armenian lands to clear those territories, disarm the inhabitants, and deport and punish all those who had taken part in the massacres, violence, and looting. They also had to remove all elements causing public unrest, including all *"muhajirs"* [settlers] who had been settled in Armenia during the rule of Abdul Hamid and the Ittihadists.[*] Additionally, there had to be measures, both inside and outside Armenia, to return forcibly Islamized women, girls, and children to the care of the Armenian Church, and to release Armenian women from harems. Turkey was also required to pay Armenians compensation for properties seized during the war and other Armenian properties in Turkish lands. Finally, they had to return churches, schools, and monasteries with all their holdings and lands seized from Armenians.

This memorandum was a test of the political maturity of Armenians. In this respect, the Turks were moderate and practical. It was also no longer a secret in Constantinople that the Anatolian national movement was directed against the victorious allied states, as well as Greeks and Armenians. Everyone knew that Mustafa Kemal [Ataturk], the hero of the Dardanelles, who had been sent by the Constantinople government to suppress the Anatolian movement, had actually become the rebels' leader. The Turks sought to capture the western part of the Asia Minor peninsula from the Greeks, along with Smyrna, Bursa, and Constantinople; as well as Constantinople and the Straits from Allied forces, and a narrow strip in European Turkey to secure Constantinople. Then, once and for all, they wanted to gain full independence, ignore the interests and demands of national

---

[*] A member of the Committee of Union and Progress (political party).

minorities, and create a new Turkey for the Turks. Mesopotamia, Syria, Palestine, as well as parts of European Turkey were considered lost, at least temporarily.

At the same time, Turkish statesmen everywhere were channeling the responsibility for the deportations, massacres, and destruction onto the shoulders of three or four Ittihad leaders, thus deflecting punishment on the country. At the end of May, it was announced in the press that Grand Vizier Talaat, who was a fugitive, Minister of War Enver, Minister of Education Dr. Nazim, and Maritime Minister Jemal Pasha had been given ten days to appear before the Constantinople War Tribunal. Otherwise, they would be deprived of all civil rights and have their properties confiscated.

During those same days, the Turkish press in Constantinople re-evaluated the causes of the recent catastrophe in the country. New revelations were made public every day. The Ottoman entry into the war had been decided by the governing body of the Ittihad without the approval of Parliament. One of the party leaders, Riza Bey, confirmed in his interrogation that long before the declaration of war, armed groups had been sent to the Caucasus to provoke unrest. Minister of Foreign Affairs, Javid Bey, Minister of Public Works, Mahmoud Pasha, Minister of Post and Telegrams, Vosgan Bey Mardigian, and Minister of Commerce, Souleiman Bey had resigned from their posts for the same reasons. The looting of the state coffers was described in gloomy terms. At the time of their escape, it was alleged that Talaat alone had tens of thousands of Ottoman gold coins. The main enabler of fraud and deception was the inspectorate under Ismail Hakki Pasha, who was in charge of wartime requisitions and supplies. The abuse of the so-called "wagons trade" amounted to millions.

On June 10th, the Turkish military tribunal in Constantinople sentenced the main culprits for the massacres, Talaat, Enver, and Jemal Pashas, to death in absentia. While they were sentenced for the systematic annihilation of an entire nation over the course of several years, these three nominal death sentences came to erase the country's historical stain from the face of the earth.

***

One of my friends in Constantinople took me to see Patriarch Zaven, who had asked to see me. The Patriarch had suffered significantly from Haroutiun Mugrdichian's betrayal. A large part of the Armenian National Assembly[*] had been ousted and murdered because of him.

The Patriarch was the most miserable man in the world, the most unfortunate pastor in our history, a clergyman who had been left without a flock. Since the end of 1913, Archbishop Zaven Yeghiayan had been writing and complaining about massacres, land grabs, and looting in the Erzeroum, Van, and Bitlis regions.

At the end of 1914, when events escalated and turned into large-scale massacres at Boghaz-Kesen, Pelou, Bashkale, Harazan, Satmanis, Apsham, Hasan-Tamran, Tash-Oghlou, Kara-Tsorig, and in other Armenian villages, the newly elected patriarch had spared no effort to prevent the approaching disaster through lawful means.

He was then deprived of all his influence on the government. After the start of the war in Turkey, until March-April 1915, the role of interceding with the authorities on behalf of Armenians was played by three members of the Ottoman Parliament, Vartkes [Hovhannes Serengulian] and [Krikor] Zohrab in Constantinople, and [Arshag] Vramian in the provinces. However, their interventions ended with their own deaths, and the Patriarch was exiled and barely escaped the same fate in Mosul. Now, with his sad, dejected eyes fixed on me through his glasses, he blessed me and said, "Yes, my son, traitor Haroutiun Mugrdichian was three times worse than Vasag."[†]

My only purpose for that visit was to request the Patriarch's support in pursuing Talaat. I had exhausted all means at my disposal and he was my last hope. However, at that moment, some

---

[*] The *Azkayin Zhoghov* (National Assembly) was the officially recognized body leading the Ottoman Armenian community.

[†] Vasag Suni is considered the archetype betrayer in Armenian history, as he sided with the Persian enemy against Armenians at the Battle of Avarayr, in 451 AD.

members of the National Assembly appeared, and we were forced to part.

Wherever Talaat was, it was clear that his tracks could be traced in Constantinople with the help of his political opponents, and for that purpose, we needed money, which was not readily available. All the efforts of Miss Yeranouhi to find financial resources within her own [Hunchakian] party were unsuccessful. Now, in a difficult situation, she was about to leave for America, where she had been invited as a teacher. I did not know what to do.[*]

By the end of the summer [1919], the influence of the Anatolian national movement was considerable on the Turks of Constantinople. Day by day, they became haughty and arrogant. The previously balanced and respectful relations between Armenians and Turks was weakening.

The Turkish intelligentsia was divided into two parts, or rather, two political currents: "Westerners" and "Easterners." The former believed that the salvation of Turkey was only possible by agreement with the Western states; otherwise, it would be impossible not only to rebuild the divided country, but also to hope for a settlement of the difficult economic situation. Only by agreement could Constantinople and the Straits be saved.

The Easterners, to the contrary, believed that the West had always been an evil for Turks and there was no reason to expect salvation from it. It was necessary to rely on the Muslims of Persia, Afghanistan, the Arab lands, India, and especially Russia to fight against the Western powers to protect national interests.

The ranks of the latter current were growing rapidly. Young Turks, ex-servicemen, and Ittihadist figures fled Constantinople and joined the Kemalist movement, which already had a clear plan of action. The Westerners, in fact, now constituted the few supporters of the "sold out" government of Favzi Pasha and the "captive" Sultan.

At the same time, the mood of Armenians in Constantinople was noticeably regressing and disappointment was setting in

---

[*] She was a member of the Hunchakian or Social Democrat Hunchakian Party, one of three "classical" Armenian political parties. Founded in 1887 in Geneva, Switzerland, it is still active today.

regarding the "Great Allies." A number of "pro-Armenian" generals in Constantinople, having little or no contact with Turks, became "pro-Turkish" and strained relations between Armenians and Europeans. There were also former "pro-Armenians" who now did not hesitate to say that Armenians were not that good either. The average citizen was deeply affected by such unpleasant developments. The paramount consideration for informed people was, of course, the broader political situation, which did not seem favorable.

First of all, General Harbord's mission as caretaker of Armenia came to an unfavorable conclusion. There were no Armenians in Armenia ...[*]

"Our allies should have taken into consideration our graves," said people with tearful eyes. Yes, it was not possible to form a state with graves!

The news coming from Yerevan was also not comforting: famine and disease were still raging. Great Britain no longer wanted to rely on Armenian forces in the Caucasus. It turned out that Armenians were more Russian than the Russians themselves, and the British could not rely on Armenians since they, the British, were now fighting against Russia. Armenians were indignant at the British approach to the Zankezour-Karabagh issue. The British wanted to annex those lands to Azerbaijan, despite strong protests from the local population. Kars and Sharour-Nakhichevan temporarily became British provinces, under whose control Turkish rule was effectively established.

Empowered by British policies, the Turks were trying to destroy the newly-created Armenia from within. Kars, Sourmalou, Sharour-Nakhichevan, and other areas formed local "independent republics" with their own governments, "shouras," and fought against the authority of Armenia. On the territory of Armenia were the "Republic of the Western Caucasus" with the

---

[*] The General Harbord Mission was sent to Asia Minor and Armenia by President Woodrow Wilson to report on social, economic and political conditions in those regions in 1919. This was part of President Wilson's interest in the United States assuming a mandate over a future Armenian state in the region.

"shura" [council] of Kars, and the Eastern Caucasus or the "Republic of Araks," which included the basins of Sourmalou, Zanki and Vedi Bazar, Milli, Sharour and Nakhichevan, with Nakhichevan as the center. Each of these "republics," in turn, was divided into smaller, provincial unions with their own local "shouras." These republics kept their own armies, armed with Turkish artillery, machine guns, and rifles under the command of Turkish officers and cavalry. Bloody battles took place in Karabagh, Zankezour, Beuyiuk-Vedi, Tavalou, Koghb, Sharour, Sourmalou, Kars and Sarikamish regions.

There were divisions and disagreements within Armenian circles, the effects of which was also felt in Constantinople. Some groups did not want to accept the idea of a newly-created Armenia under those conditions. Some were even annoyed that Caucasian Armenians had appropriated the name "Armenia" to their country. The "Ararat Republic" was a separate Russian issue, while the longstanding Armenian Question concerned Turkish Armenia. At best, the Armenian Republic was the country of one segment of Armenians, but not Armenia.

At the end of August, Miss Yeranouhi left for Paris to go to America. She had high hopes to continue her pursuit of Talaat. She gave me hope and insisted that I persevere.

A month passed, and I received no news from her. I spent those days waiting, looking at the historical and artistic monuments of the city. I can never forget the dreamy impression I got from watching Constantinople from the Galata Tower one September evening. The city spread out like an amphitheater with its towers, the large and small domes of mosques, and elegant minarets. To the north were beautiful mansions and palaces among the trees on both sides of the Bosporus. To the east, on the Asian shore, lay Uskudar [Skiudar], among cypress trees, with its rosy buildings and spacious cemeteries. From afar I could see Kadikoy, the ancient Chalcedon. Each area had its own waters with sailboats, rowing-boats, and steamships of all sizes moving in all directions. The sky seemed to be burning with the light of sunset. The districts of Kazim Pasha, Dershane, and Galatia seemed to be floating in the fire. Pera, up to Shishli, was shrouded in bright copper rays. On the other hand, the tops of the minarets and mosques on the Asiatic parts of the city, and the glass windows of countless buildings, created an illusion of flashing flames, as if Constantinople was basking among them in the evening.

I also visited the world-famous Hagia Sophia and was astonished by it. It was not surprising that Justinian the Great, stepping into the newly-built temple for the first time, shouted, "O Solomon, I have vanquished you." The huge building was divided into innumerable, multicolored and arched sections, in the center of which a fantastic dome seemed to hang from the sky by gold chains. I did not know by what laws of nature that huge mass could remain there at a height of about 60 meters. I think that question had only been solved by the ingenious Armenian architect Drtad, who rebuilt that building of the world-famous architects Anthemios Tralatsi and Isidore Melidatsi, after it had collapsed. If it is true that Byzantine art is a unique blend of Christianity, Hellenism, and the East, then one of the supreme embodiments of these elements is Hagia Sophia. The kind and humble Christ stood strong, victorious, and worldly. Although the exquisite sculptures and decorations on the walls of the building were carefully plastered with the outward signs of his religion and the faces of the apostles were covered with gold stars, the radiance of the majestic old world had remained forever. The finest stones of all the ancient shrines, all the finest specimens of the world's marbles, were here. It seemed that they radiated light. The floor, made of multicolored marble beads, looked like a beautiful rug under my feet and stretched like a petrified flower garden. Apparently, there was no need for major changes to turn this magnificent temple of the world into a mosque. The traces of Christianity were covered with plaster, the cross on the dome was replaced by a crescent, and four minarets were added to the building, the first of which was built by the victorious Mohammed, the second by Sultan Bayazid, and the last two by Sultan Selim.

The large number of Turkish monuments in Constantinople were similar and bore the general features of Hagia Sophia in their structures. This was the case, for example, with the famous Kahriye mosque and the ancient temple of Archangel Michael at Edirne Kapou; similarly, the Hoja Moustafa Pasha mosque in the

Aksaray district, the Mehmed Pasha mosque in Atmeydan, the Giul mosque in Ounkapu, the Kilise mosque in Vefa Meydan, and the Fetiye mosque in Fener.

At the end of October [1919], I received a postcard from Miss Yeranouhi. "Always sing," it said. "The days will pass, a new spring will come again, full of roses. Forget your old sorrow, you will sing the love of a rose again." She signed, "Assurances of sincere sisterly love, Y. T." She was still in Paris, but there was no address. What did this quatrain of Ashough Jivani mean? I did not understand ...

Circumstances forced me to be realistic and take into account my everyday needs. I still had three gold coins left from the money my brother had given me in Yerznga. I did not receive the expected financial support from Serbia. The war had devastated my family's business and they were almost in misery. Now, sick of focusing on thinking about finding Talaat, I was being dragged into a meaningless existence. I had closed all options in life because of the solemn oath I had taken – as long as that monster was still alive. The nights were filled with nightmares, with my mother appearing as the main culprit. I almost always saw her in my dreams, in different places, and in different situations. Everything she said always revolved around the same issue: the death of Talaat. One stormy night, she knocked on my window. I looked and she showed me her blood-stained neck. I woke up in horror, got up, and approached the window. It was raining outside. No reasoning could free me from my obsessions.

While in Constantinople, I had thought that Patriarch Zaven, who was now in Paris, might be able to help me. The clergyman, having been through hell, could understand the pain consuming my soul. I could express all my feelings to him, like a confession, without hesitation. I left [for Paris] in November.

It was dusk. The ant-sized muezzins appeared on the pointed minarets to glorify Allah above the passing crowds. The sun was disappearing behind the immense sea, and, from its hiding place, changing the appearance of the sky with a magic brush, with new colors and shades scattered in the clouds. From afar you could see five or six allied warships anchored on the shores of the Marmara, sitting on the waters with their wings folded like mythical swans.

Their steel bows and silver masts shone in the rays of the setting sun. Cruising around the cape of Saraybournou, the steamer headed to the open waters of the Marmara. To the right was Makrikeoy, San Stefano, where diplomacy had issued its first verdict concerning our life and death.[*] Crossing from the left, we passed the Princes' Islands, the Dardanelles, and the historic Hellespont.

On the European shore, we passed the ancient Galibolis, now called Gelibolou [Gallipoli], on the peninsula. It was the first city to fall to the Turks in 1357, about a hundred years before the fall of Constantinople. Every event of the past, every place, seemed to be relentlessly confirming the path of historical destiny that was written for us in this country. Couldn't history have taken a different course, and in that case, what might have been our fate?

On the Asian shores were Chardak and Lampsace, the latter of which Xerxes had ceded to Themistocles on condition that he met his annual wine needs. Had anything changed over the centuries regarding the whims of rulers leading to blood and death?

Kala Ovasou, the ancient Aegospotami, appeared on the European coast, where the Peloponnesian War ended in the fourth century BC. Should the great powers of the time have shed blood for ten years for supremacy, when only their names would remain in history?

Further down, the straits narrowed, from left to right, between Cape Nazara and the port of Ak-Pasha, which formed the ancient Abitos and Sestos, the width of which was merely 800 or 900 feet. It was here that every night Leander crossed the waters of Hellespont from Abitos to Sestos, at the edge of which awaited the beautiful Hero, holding a torch in her hand, which guided his course. The only thing that is eternal ...

The strait reopened and widened. In the distance, sometimes face to face, Chanak Kale, Kilid El-Bahr, Set El-Bahr, and Koum

---

[*] This is a reference to the aborted treaty of San Stefano, following the Russo-Turkish war of 1877-78. The treaty included an article calling for reforms to ameliorate the condition of Armenians in the eastern provinces of the Ottoman Empire. This treaty was superseded by the Treaty of Berlin (1878).

Kale appeared one after the other; places where recently shed blood had only just dried. It was getting dark as we approached the open sea but we still remained in the shadows far below Yeni Keoy, where the memories of the Drovata war remained dormant.

***

I was stunned by what I saw in Paris: magnificent buildings, public squares, wide and endless avenues, people wandering about, bustling life everywhere, countless cars that gathered like flocks of crows and suddenly scattered. I, who already considered myself a "worldly person," felt that Paris was much bigger than I could have ever imagined. The speed of life was especially annoying. I wondered where people were going in such a hurry. It was as if there were fires that needed to be put out everywhere. I was on my way from Paris Gare de l'Est, and my journey had no end. I got a headache from everything around me. Perhaps it was also because I had deprived myself of food that day due to financial worries.

It was already dark when, after some searching, I finally found the Armenian church and bishopric. My visit was untimely. I explained that I had come especially from Constantinople to see the patriarch for a special reason. Archmandrite (vartabed) Kibarian gave in to my assertion. The patriarch remembered me but his inquisitive look confused me so much that my heartfelt speech, prepared in advance, fell apart. I could hardly answer the question about the purpose of my visit to Paris, to ask for his help in tracking down Talaat. For a moment, he looked at me sympathetically through his glasses, as people look at the mentally ill. He then hung his head and said softly, "I cannot take part in such endeavors, my son."

I stood up from my seat.

"No, sit down. You know what? I understand, I feel your inner turmoil, but neither my office, nor my position allow me to get involved in such a matter, but I can personally help you until you find a job."

I felt myself turn red.

"I do not need personal support, *Srpazan* [Your Grace]," I replied and left.

I stood on the street for a moment. What would I do and where would I go? I had been so convinced of success that I suddenly felt empty. It was raining lightly. In that foggy atmosphere, the streetlamps appeared like fading stars. I found myself in Etoile Square. Boissy [d'Anglas] Street had to be somewhere nearby, where the Armenian delegation [at the Paris Peace Conference] was staying at that time. Back in January, when Mr. Avedis Aharonian [the chairman of the Armenian delegation] had been in Constantinople, I had made several unsuccessful attempts to see him in person and ask for his support concerning the matter that was on my mind. I was now passing Etoile Square with the same intention when, suddenly, I saw many cars heading towards me. The square was very big and there was no way to run back or forth. I was like a standing corpse with flies crawling around me. Cars were passing close to me. With the slightest movement, I could have been under their wheels. A police officer pulled me out of that situation and showed me the way to Boissy Street. Here was Hotel Vouillemont, where the delegation was staying. However, this Armenian political center was silent and dumb, not the expected great hub of activity, where our national future was being charted. Aharonian was not there but a man in his fifties came over and looked at me.

"Why do you want to see Mr. Aharonian?"

"I want to discuss an issue with him ..."

He probably did not hear or understand me.

"He is very busy. He can hardly be useful to you. It is also difficult to find a job. It is better to apply to the Red Cross or the immigration commission."

I thought it useless to prolong the conversation and I turned to leave.

"Wait. Where are you from?"

"Yerznga."

There was discomfort on his triangular-shaped face.

"I thought you were from Adabazar or one of those places."

"No, I am from Yerznga, from the village of Pakarij."

"Do you have any skills?"

"No."

"Do you want to learn shoe making? I have a relative from Adabazar. We could possibly find you a job with him. Do you have any money?"

"Yes."

"Tell me the truth, I can help you."

"No, thank you."

I took his business card, which had two lines and an address on it. I then found a two-star hotel on one of the secondary streets. It was a room on the fourth floor for 12 francs a day. It was not expensive and I still had money to live for a day or two. I was very tired. I undressed and went to bed. Although I had been separated from my relatives for ages, I had only just realized what alienation meant. Evaluating the state I was in, I came to the conclusion that there was nothing left to do but shoemaking. Everything was so gloomy that this job seemed to be my only salvation. Who was that man and what happened to the business card? I was anxious. I looked in my pockets and found it. "Hagop Kocharian" was the name on the business card.

The Adabazartsi's workshop was located in the Belleville area. When I went to visit him in the morning, he was angry and rebuking the workers.

"If it weren't for me, all three of you would die of starvation!" he shouted. His mustache like a squirrel's thick tail, his wide mouth, and his hoarse voice did not bode well. When he looked at me, I saw that his eyes were kind, round and primitive, as beautiful as a sheep's eyes.

"Where are you from?" he said while looking at the business card.

"From Constantinople."

"Before that?"

"From Russia."

"And before that?"

"From the Caucasus."

"Oh, for God's sake, where are you from?!"

"Yerznga."

"Yes, now I understand. Sit there and watch what they do. If it weren't for me, all four of you would die of starvation."

***

Seeing the plight of the deportees in Paris, I came to the conclusion that my situation could have been worse. I survived, and I could earn a living by my own work. Although the Adabazartsi did not miss the opportunity to remind us that we all owed our existence to him, he was a kind person. The anger he often expressed at work lasted barely a minute, sometimes a little longer, when the issue was about his dignity. In general, he liked showing more power than he had. It did not bother me like the others. I was a shoemaker and that's how I treated my master. I was at work from 7:00 am to 6:00 pm, with an hour's break in the afternoon. At first, it was quite difficult, the work unfamiliar, but I got used to it little by little. The situation gradually became tolerable. I was now trying my best to forget the mission that stirred inside me. It was clear that finding Talaat was not easy. We needed organization, resources, and comrades. It was not something to be done by clergymen and community leaders. My work was also busy and I made real progress. I was already working with fabric and sewing shoes. In the mornings, I woke up motivated, eager to get to work, but after an hour or two, I felt I could happily give it up. I thought about finishing work early so that I could have free time to think about everything in detail. I had a miserable past and it was enough to make me feel worthless. Sometimes, I could not even think for days. It was enough to be in the cafeteria, where the deportees gathered after work and related stories, one after another, about recent events. I would again imagine Talaat's smug and puffy face, which seemed to mock me. I then began to imagine the various forms of murder: stabbed people, beaten, drained of their blood, torn apart, severed limbs, burnt... Those thoughts made me feel disgusted with myself. I thought that there was only one way to get rid of those nightmarish thoughts: work well, earn a lot of money, return to the Caucasus, and live a happy private life. However, I was obviously deceiving myself. The money I earned was barely enough for my needs, although I knew full well that I would not be able to return anywhere without money. I tried to go to the cafeteria as little as I could so that I would not hear anything about the massacres. I would avoid meetings. But being alone by myself only reminded me of everything and nothing changed.

The Paris committee of the Armenian Revolutionary Federation was busy with political projects and public events. The news coming from Yerevan at the end of the year created as much enthusiasm there as it had in the summer months in Constantinople. The insurrections that took place in heavily Turkish-populated areas of Armenia were suppressed and Armenian rule was established everywhere. In January, 1920, the Allies' Supreme Council recognized the de facto Armenian state. Recognition, although it did not predetermine the borders of that state, was a matter of days away. We soon learned that Metropolitan Chrysanthus, the agent of Venizelos and the head of the Pontian delegation, had signed a treaty with the Armenian government in Yerevan, whereby the entire region between the Pontic Mountains and the Black Sea, from Rize to Sinop, with about 1.22 million inhabitants, was annexed to Armenia as a federation. This diplomatic victory opened a bright prospect for us. Starting from nothing, we had suddenly become a ruling nation in Asia Minor.

In April, the Allies completed their negotiations in San Remo. It was already known that Turkey should give up the provinces of Erzeroum, Van, Bitlis, and Trabizon to Armenia, with the exception of some districts. Most of the western shores of the Aegean, with the city of Smyrna, as well as Thrace with its center, Adrianople, were to be ceded to Greece. On the European continent, Turkey was left with only Constantinople, nominally, with insignificant tracts of land on the outskirts of the Bosporus and Marmara, but here, too, there were restrictions. Elsewhere, Greater Arabia was broken up into Arab states so that Syria, Mesopotamia, and Palestine were torn away from Turkey. Finally, Kurdistan was also detached, to come under the care of a soon to be nominated state. In these historic days of the division of territories, only the Assyrian delegation, led by Agha Petros, were unsuccessful; they had nothing ...

In fact, they were tearing Turkey apart, and its domestic, economic spheres were falling under the supervision of international commissions. The Straits, customs, and all revenues and privileges were to be run by European commissions. The Greeks had already conquered Smyrna and were emerging with great vigor to take possession of their new lands.

What about us? It was amazing. It was said that Boghos Nubar Pasha was furiously protesting against the possibility of the Yerevan government occupying Erzeroum. He considered the move a "confiscation." He did not recognize the rights of that government as the "original" government of Armenia. The endless talks between the two Armenian delegations and the compassionate pleas of Armenians were in vain. The Pasha was stubborn.

Despite all this, the enthusiasm of the Armenians of Paris reached its peak in August [1920]. The Armenian diplomatic mission was crowned with success. The Armenian delegation signed the Treaty of Sèvres. Our country was free, the territory defined, the future was bright.

***

It was September. The horizons of Armenia were darkening again. The Karabagh-Zankezour issue was aggravated. The simmering Kars region was troubled. The Kemalist Turks had become stronger. Clashes were expected with them. I was about to return to the Caucasus when, one evening, the cafeteria owner, Tovmas Agha, said, "A beautiful girl, Miss Tanielian, was looking for you this morning."

I was surprised because I did not know any women in Paris. Suddenly, I remembered Yeranouhi, but she should have been in America a long time earlier ...

The next evening, as soon as I had finished my work, I ran to the cafeteria. Sitting at the corner table was a young woman who looked like Yeranouhi. Yes, it was her sister.

"You're finally here," she said, smiling like an old friend. "My sister told me about you. She wrote to you in Constantinople, but my mother told her that you had gone to Paris, and now I am meeting you here," she said, pulling a letter out of her handbag.

Miss Yeranouhi was asking me to go to America immediately for a task I knew about. I could not believe it! I could hardly contain myself. But why America? Was the monster there? The letter did not say anything else.

"What's that task, if it's not a secret?" asked the girl, narrowing her beautiful eyelids.

"To be honest, I don't understand either. I talked a lot with Miss Yeranouhi in Bolis about my desire to study. Now, perhaps, I have succeeded in doing so through my friends."

She didn't accept what I had said and made a mischievous movement of her finger.

"Whatever. Anyway, when are you leaving?"

"I can hardly leave, ma'am, because I need a lot of money."

"Oh, I'm sorry. I forgot to say that you have a letter at the Delegation with Mr. Hanumian. He is also looking for you. He wanted to give it to me but took it back in the end. He asked me to tell you about it. The letter was from Boston, maybe there ..."

The girl was going to continue talking for a long time, but I apologized and hurried to the Delegation before it was too late.

Hamo Paraghamian had written the letter! I was overjoyed. He had written that I should leave immediately for Boston. I had to get the cost of the trip from Hanumian, to whom Garegin Pasdermadjian [Armen Garo] had written at the same time.

Hanumian, who was prematurely bald, had an effeminate face, a pleasant smile, and did not ask me any questions. He just wanted to know when I could leave.

"Tomorrow."

He sorted out my visa issues within three days and I left at the beginning of October. Now everything was clear to me. The task was being handled by them in America. Paraghamian had learned about me from Miss Yeranouhi. There was no doubt about it. I was full of gratitude to that young woman of conviction. I remembered the quatrain she had written, which had disappointed me so much. "Days will pass, a new spring of roses will come again." She was confident in the success of the mission.

It was winter, but I was in the mood for a "rosy spring." I saw the ocean for the first time. Before that, my sea voyages had always had a shadow on the horizon, beyond which the land began. Now, that land was completely invisible, my high spirits began to drop, and I was overwhelmed with inexplicable sadness. It was as if I had been completely separated from the world and had fallen into obscurity. The ocean was calm, but after two days, it was suddenly covered with mist, thin at first, then gradually getting thicker. The steamer began to shake. The waves began to batter the ship on both sides, first as if playing with us, and then with more and more force. The steamer roared and roared. The waves were leaping up and down. With their heads held high, they spread their tongues far above the deck. The huge ship bobbled like a toy in the water. It was rising on the waves, as hollows and depressions opened in front of it. It seemed that the ship would be wrecked and crushed in those dark abysses, but each time it managed to pull its bow out and broke through the raging waters. The ship and the ocean symbolized struggle and victory.

In the afternoon, the storm subsided. The waves were now rising over the side of the ship, flowing over the deck, and sweeping over that part of the ship. Then, little by little, the fog began to disperse and gradually vanished. The rays of the sun shone on the endless expanse of water. Travelers hiding in halls and cabins reappeared on the decks. The women were laughing and giggling nervously.

It was a dream come true for me, on the seventh day, when I saw the shores of America on the horizon. I was so overwhelmed with joy, as if I myself was discovering the New World. Here it was, finally, as the exhausted steamer approached the port. The famous skyscrapers of New York had been visible for some time. The great hall of the ship was filled with many officials who began to examine our papers. I watched the thoughtful faces of the restless and somber Americans, their confident manners and movements, as I waited for my turn. My little French helped me through the questioning.

Even though it was not yet dark outside, electric lights were shining on the buildings, and the city seemed to be made of gold. This huge city of seven million people amazed me with its countless lights and electric advertisements. Finding the first cab driver that I could, I gave him the address of the ARF *agoump* [club-center]. My mind was blank. I was overwhelmed with a sense of gratitude to those people who got me there. I was trying to identify the sections of the skyscrapers, which probably consisted of 25-50 floors. A year earlier, I had been surprised by the commotion in Paris, but that was nothing compared to New York. Surprisingly, the driver of the cab did not lose his head in the commotion. We passed a bright circle of luxury shops and buildings. A large crowd was gathered in front of a movie theater. Life was boiling everywhere like a furnace. A little further down, in the center of a wide avenue where many cars had stopped, our car also slowed down and stopped. I noticed that directions were indicated by light signals emitted from a tower-like structure. Americans were walking on sidewalks with strong, firm, upright backs, their heads held high, looking into the distance. The lights changed on the tower, and our car was once again crawling in the herd of cars moving in a row. Next, we reached modestly built areas and stopped.

I was at the *agoump*. What a pleasant surprise it was to hear my sweet, native language on the other side of the world. There were three rooms, bright and clean, full of books, newspapers, and bright faces. What patriotic sentiments and feelings were immediately expressed by the numerous young people around me! At first, I tried to satisfy everyone's interest but, little by little, I started to get fed up. There was no end to the questions. People seemed to have a claim on me and I had to pay what was due to everyone immediately. Finally, I announced my departure and prepared to leave.

"Brother, you have not said anything about pressing issues. Where are you going?"

"I came here for help to get to Boston, not to give you a lecture," I said, barely controlling my anger.

"Well, brother, Boston is not going anywhere!"

"By the order of the Central Committee of the ARF, I must get there as soon as possible."

These words had an immediate impact. Suddenly, my stature rose, and they became obliging. We left, though they continued to ask me many questions on the way, taking advantage of every minute they had with me. I needed many days to talk to all those troubled souls about all our problems. Time was powerless to allow them to forget everything that had already happened.

I was fascinated by the fabulous city at night. My eyes were getting used to watching it. The high-rise buildings were no longer as imposing as before. They now seemed so light, as if made of paper. Countless streams of light poured down from countless windows and filled the abyss with light and darkness. The lamps on the domes of the sky-scrapers seemed to be waxing like the moon. To think that the poor people of our Pakarij were not allowed to live their lives even in their underground huts! With great difficulty, I was able to gather my thoughts and answer all their questions. They were interested in information I could relate, even though it was dated and imperfect. Apparently, it was different for them to hear my living words than read about the same issues in print. We finally arrived at the station, where I soon parted from those warm and patriotic young people.

CHAPTER SEVEN

On the Trail of the Prey

My experience in New York was also repeated at the editorial offices of *Hairenik* daily in Boston. The interview there was initiated by Hamo [Paraghamian], who began with his recollections of Erzeroum, where I had last seen him five years earlier. A friend from Divrig, with short, slender legs and rounded shoulders like a darkened moon, Hamo resembled a civilized Kurd. Nothing had changed in his inclinations and character. Nothing could distract him, even slightly, from his favorite job. Even during our informal visit, he had a pile of papers in his hand that could have been any kind of "regular correspondence." However, Hamo was not merely a correspondent there, but also a member of the editorial board of *Hairenik* and the secretary of the Central Committee of the ARF. What prompted me to go to Boston was Miss Yeranouhi, who was in California. Hamo found out about me from her. I also met the comrades of the editorial office – Setrag Baghdigian, the executive director of the Central Committee, our dreamy "Seto," Khosrov Yesayan, the executive director of *Hairenik* daily, and others. I became close with these latter two from day one and we became roommates.

Here in America our people also followed the events in Armenia with great interest. The impunity of the Turkish murderers was especially disturbing. At the beginning of the war, the Allies had made a solemn statement that members of the Turkish government would be held personally responsible for the Armenian massacres.[*] But the war ended with the victory of the Allies and the perpetrators of the Armenian Genocide remained unpunished and even came under their protection.

---

[*] This is a reference to the Allied declaration of 24 May 1915 stating that they (Great Britain, France, and Russia) would hold Turkish officials to account for the reported massacre of Armenians.

Autographed copy of Armen Garo's photograph for Soghomon Tehlirian dated Washington, October 5th, 1922.

The idea that Armenians should punish the Turkish murderers through their own means had matured among the Armenians of America. The spirit behind this sentiment was Armen Garo, under whose initiative a special fund had been created and work begun.

It must be said that this mood was not limited to America. Armenians everywhere were outraged by the Allies' attitude. An entire nation had been annihilated by barbaric means, and the victorious Allies, contrary to solemn promises, did not lift a finger to bring the perpetrators to justice. Everywhere people demanded appropriate action and everyone's eyes were on the ARF.

Naturally the ARF could not remain indifferent and considered an appropriate response. The 9th World Congress of the party that took place in Yerevan, Armenia, in the fall of 1919, dealt with this issue. Meanwhile, it turned out that what I had been dreaming about day and night was turning into reality in America. A lot of preliminary work had already been done under the leadership of Armen Garo.

While in America, I learned that the Ittihadists who had fled Constantinople were actively working in Europe. They had established contacts within European political circles and were trying to use them to oppose the Allies, negate the Armenian Question, and ensure a more advantageous position for Turkey on other issues. To this end, they had met with representatives of the Allies and held talks.

While Enver was in Russia, he had founded the Union for the Liberation of Islam, which had branches in Berlin and Anatolia. A conference had been convened in Berlin two months earlier to put pressure on Great Britain. The main focus of activities was Russia, especially the Transcaucasus, with the purpose of maintaining close cooperation with the Kemalist movement. According to the latest information, Enver, Ibrahim Talin, Kiuchiuk Talaat, Behaeddin Shakir, Moustafa Soubhi, Nouri, and Khalil Pashas had been in Baku, where they participated in the "Assembly of Eastern Peoples." The Armenian-Turkish war that had started in Armenia [September, 1920] was considered a consequence of decisions made at that conference. Talaat was thought to be in either Geneva or Berlin.

One day, I met Armen Garo, a tall, well built, impressive and friendly man. Although I had only seen him once before, I had heard a lot about him. He was a straightforward, honest, kind, and devoted leader. He knew that I was the one who had come from Paris and shook my hand in an intimate, open, sincere manner, with fatherly affection and brotherly warmth. My initial impressions of him were not misplaced. He had been born virtuous and pure, but the previous five years had taken their toll and created an unbearable anxiety in his calm soul. Under his round and slightly swollen eyelids, his beautiful eyes had lost their former radiance. There were now wrinkles on his face.

However, as in my first meeting, I was rather confused, because Armen Garo imagined me to be a perfect human being.

A group of us went to a nearby café run by an elderly friend. When he saw Armen Garo, he jumped up from his seat and exclaimed happily.

"Wow, Mr. Garo ..."

"Koko, tell us, how are you?" said Garo, turning to him like an old friend.

"How? May God help us. The condition of our people is dire ..."

Koko gave us a special, private room, and provided his services.

I learned from Armen Garo that, eight days earlier, they had sent a telegram to Hanumian in Paris to tell me to wait for someone from America, but I had already left.[*] Now, that person had to prepare for his trip to Switzerland. Armen Garo thought that person could do the preliminary reconnaissance work alone and, if necessary, draw on the help of local resources. He said I should leave when Talaat's location in Geneva or Berlin was discovered. That was also my wish. Taking caution into account, that is how we proceeded.

---

[*] The reference is to Shahan Natali (Hagop Der Hagopian, 1884-1983), one of the main organizers of Operation Nemesis, who was responsible for logistics. He was later expelled from the ARF and all references to him by name in *Remembrances* were masked by Simon Vratsian during the final editorial process of the book. He was referred to as "the representative," "our representative," and "my comrade."

It was apparent that Constantinople and Berlin had been instructed to look for Talaat's tracks.[*] The information gathered was to be centralized with the head of the intelligence unit. Photos of all the principal mass murderers were reprinted in three copies and ready. Financial means were also secured.

Although the problem still needed a lot of planning, I was overwhelmed with an inner joy that the work was in the hands of competent people and on the right track. All questions were clarified without argument or disagreements, as if we were members of the same family in which the word of the eldest held the most weight.

Garo was now sharing his impressions of Talaat and we all listened to him intently. For me, every story he related describing that scheming murderer was invaluable.

"When was the last time you met him?" I asked.

"The last time was on June 4th, 1914, when Vramian and I had a heated conversation with that monster at Khalil Bey's house about the planned Armenian Reforms," said Garo, as if speaking to himself, still buried in fresh memories.

"Talaat began the conversation with a long preface, trying to convince us that, despite their wish, they had not been able to meet our just demands ... that is, the land question, the schools issue, an increase in the number of Armenian officials, and so on. And then, addressing the reforms issue, Talaat accused us of resorting to outside interference instead of coming to an understanding with them.

"Vramian often interrupted him and pointed out the unsubstantiated nature of his claims with facts while Khalil Bey tried to persuade Vramian about the impossibility of dividing the number of officials on an equal basis. Talaat alluded to his negotiations with Hoff[†] and said that he rejected my candidacy [as

---

[*] The reference is to the ARF's intelligence network with its center in Watertown, Boston.

[†] Major Nicolai Hoff was a Norwegian military officer who was one of two Inspector-Generals who were appointed by the Great Powers and the Ottoman government to oversee the long overdue Armenian Reforms in the eastern provinces of the Ottoman Empire in 1914. This reforms project came to an abrupt end with the outbreak of World War One.

an aide] for the simple reason that, if I went with Hoff as one of his assistants, I would be the general investigator and not Hoff. Vramian said it was unnecessary to talk about my candidacy, as I had already asked Hoff to remove my name from the list. But, by rejecting the principle of equal representation, they were demonstrating that they were once again on the old path of obfuscation and trying to abort the reforms agreement they had signed in the first place. The three of them were arguing from 8:00 to 11:00 pm. I did not say a word. I watched Talaat's face intently, which seemed particularly intolerable to me that night. Every time Vramian got heated and said disagreeable things to him, a satanic smile appeared on Talaat's face, one of a smug man who was laughing at the other person. Eventually, both noticed that I was not saying anything, and Talaat turned to me and said:

"Garo, why didn't you speak at all this evening?"

"What shall I say, when I see that you have become so arrogant following your recent successes and want to toy with us," I replied.

"I do not accept your statement and ask you to prove what you have said," he responded.

"If Vramian could not convince you, I will not be able to do that at all. Let me just say that you are on the wrong path. This process that you have begun will lead the Ottoman Empire to an abyss. You are intoxicated by the latest successes; you are arrogant, imagining that you are a Napoleon or Bismarck."

"Am I Bismarck?" Talaat interrupted, smiling.

"Yes, but you are very wrong to think so. Unfortunately, you are all ignorant and unable to understand where you are going to lead this country. Do you want proof? Didn't you say to Vramian a while ago that you would turn the Kurds into Turks? How? By your cultural heritage? If you knew about history, you would not have said such nonsense. You forget that it was five or six hundred years ago that you, the Turks, came to our country. Many other nations, such as Persians, Romans, Arabs, and Byzantines came before you and left. We and the Kurds are still here. If none of them could assimilate the Kurds, how are you going to assimilate them? Last summer, I traveled to our three provinces and saw only three bridges in that vast area. Two of them were ancient Armenian structures, and the third was ordered by Tamerlane. I didn't see even a trace of your civilization. You should not take serious state affairs lightly.

"Coming back to our topic," I told him, "you are not being honest. You think you can put us to sleep here and create such economic and political conditions that Armenia is emptied of Armenians and you are permanently free of the Armenian Question. This is the second example of your ignorance. You are mistaken in your calculations. We will not give you enough time to implement your plans. Our national consciousness is so developed that we would prefer to demolish this great building, which is called the Ottoman Empire, than allow you to see Armenia without Armenians ..."

Armen Garo, carried away by memories of the past, stopped suddenly. His face expressed unbearable sadness.

"Alas, we miscalculated," he said.

"How did it end?" asked Hamo.

"When I finished, Talaat shouted. 'What are you talking about, Garo!? You seem completely changed.'"

"If there is a change in our midst, it is you! You are the ones who think you are great," I replied. "We are the leading Armenian revolutionaries and we will repeat what we have always said." Talaat went red in the face and began to look at his wristwatch. Then, suddenly, he rose and said that he had an appointment at 11 o'clock and was sorry that our conversation would remain incomplete. He left, asking that we meet again another day to convince each other. A little later, the war started, and I never saw Talaat again."

It seemed as if Armen Garo was making a confession, as if he was judging himself. He was so depressed. I wondered whether he really had had to talk like a revolutionary, with such simplicity and sincerity, with the executioner?

"Anyway," he said, emerging from his thoughts, "let's leave the past and look to the future. I need to leave now. Safe travels and good luck to you. I would very much like not to die looking back. In these difficult days, the death of that monster will be the greatest consolation for Armenians."

Just then, someone asked from the dining room, "What news from the homeland, Mr. Garo?"

"There is no new news, Koko. Everything is as you know."

***

Our representative left for New York in order to sail to Europe.

That night we sat with Seto and Khosrov, examining the photos of the criminals: Talaat, Enver, Jemal, Said Halim Pasha, Jemal Azmi, Behaeddin Shakir, Istanbul Police Chief Bedri, Dr. Nazim, and others. There were also pictures of Talaat and Enver's wives, which were apparently taken from group photos. Both were beautiful, angelic women. One was amazed at how they could live with these monsters.

Talaat was the most remarkable in his physical features: his strong arms, a square back, and the rock-like protrusions showed his strength and vigor. Anyone looking at his picture would have been amazed at how this seemingly inspired man managed to withstand the cries of an entire nation begging for mercy in order to carry out his extermination plan without changing course. In another picture, one could hardly see any white hairs on his scalp. A jet black, thick mustache extended to the left and right of his oriental lips. His neck protruded from a tight collar. A white jacket covered the arch of his belly and his face beamed sincerity.

And here was Enver. The idol of Turkish women at that time, a man who never proved worthy of a manly deed in his life. He gained fame during the recapture of Adrianople [Edirne] in 1913, when the work was already over. His baby-face and gentle expressions conveyed a desire to dance. It was said in Constantinople that on the wall of his reception room, on either side of his own portrait, were the portraits of Napoleon I and Frederick the Great, two ambitious geniuses who only resembled him in their short stature. Some said that Enver wore high-heeled shoes to look taller than he was. The decorated top of the Persian hat, which he wore and never lowered, served the same purpose. And indeed, in the picture, in his gold-threaded military uniform, he had quite a haughty expression. But two sets of medals spoiled this image, giving him a dandy, frivolous, child-like look. Again, he had the perplexed, fearful, wide eyes of a girl. In another

160

picture, his canine smile, barely noticeable under the small mustache, expressed a "dignified superiority." If only his dignity had not been severely wounded at Kardos [sic], where he might have earned the crown of "Turkish Napoleon," and perhaps the fate of our people might have been different.

The third mass-murderer, Minister of the Navy, Jemal Pasha, expressed a mixture of cruelty and arrogance. His staring large, sharp, and penetrating eyes showed cunning, ruthlessness, and selfishness. It was he who, as commander of the Fourth Army, starved and persecuted the remnants of our people in the desert.

As for Bedri Bey, looking at his picture, I was left confused as to how that nothingness of a person managed to exterminate approximately 500 brilliant intellectuals. The only claim of this unknown man with effeminate shoulders and sleepy, debauched eyes, was that he was close to Talaat. But that hollow man was again something compared to the scarecrow Said Halim Pasha, whose castrated, diseased appearance was an abomination. He was a man who had become Prime Minister with the power of money, hoping to be the ruler of Egypt after the war. This vain, inglorious Egyptian prince, deprived of real power, had enough courage to reject all appeals to end the massacres ...

With his knowledgeable and practical expressions, giving the impression of an insurance salesman, Behaeddin Shakir began the prelude to the great massacres in the summer of 1914 with the partial deportation and massacre of Armenians in the Erzeroum region. Then, together with the infamous Ittihad ideologue, Naji Bey, he spared no effort to raise ignorant Turkish mobs against unarmed Armenians from Erzeroum to Mosul.

Among the well-known, terrifying governors who were mass-murderers, was Jemal Azmi, with his almost square face and bloody jaw. He was a perfect monster who had the characteristics of centuries-old Asiatic barbarism. It was he who destroyed the 14,000 Armenians of Trabizon within two days. He first massacred the young Armenian conscripts in the army, and then arrested the 600 well-known men in the city, loaded them onto ships, and drowned them at sea. He then drove the women and children out of the city and destroyed them all near the village of Jevizlik with unimaginable cruelty.

It was past midnight when Khosrov shouted at us from his bed, in his sleepy voice, to go to sleep.

We went to bed, but I could not close my eyes. I could not fall asleep. I tried to picture Anahid before my eyes, to think of her, but the effect of the executioners' pictures was more powerful. Their monstrous faces remained at the forefront of my mind for a long time in the dark.

***

Established in a remote community but closely connected to the homeland, *Hairenik* newspaper and publishing house played an important role [in Armenian national life]. It is an indisputable fact that if Armenians had managed to maintain their identity in the diaspora, it was largely due to the organized work carried out by Armenian civil and political organizations, their newspapers, and publications. *Hairenik* had a major place in that family of publications. Founded in New York, it had just celebrated its 20th anniversary in Boston. Some comrades, Dr. Tashjian, Prof. Chakmakjian, M[anoug] Hampartsoumian, N[shan] Desdegiul, spent 10-15 years working at it, mostly under difficult, unbearable conditions. The *Hairenik* editorial office was a sort of "National Bureau," and nothing was done without it. All national [*azkayin*] donations were managed through *Hairenik*. It was an office and information source for immigrants. It received letters on behalf of displaced people. Although five years had passed, there was still a special section of announcements in the newspaper, where survivors of the Genocide posted advertisements and looked for their lost, exiled relatives. The doors of the editorial office were open during the day, and everyone had access to it. People were received warmly, listened to attentively, sympathized with, and helped spiritually, always displaying the belief in a better future.

As in Yerevan, Hamo was popular among people in Boston. I sat and watched the visitors for days, and always, with deep sadness, I had a feeling that this was a corner where Armenians could come to soothe their sorrows. They shared their pain together. They spoke of the loss of their children, with involuntary, trembling lips, as if they had fever. But there were also those who it seemed were born for an eternal struggle, and upon hearing of the Armenian-Turkish war, they came prepared to sign up as "soldiers of the nation," enrolling as volunteers for Armenia.

However, day by day, the Armenian horizon was darkening again. In the first days of November [1920] we received news of the fall of Kars; the Turks were moving towards Alexandropol. The same thing had happened two or three years earlier.

A few days later, upon receiving a telegram from Europe, I left for Geneva. I found the *Droshak* editorial office quite easily, where I hoped to see our representative who had not given his address. Geneva, especially the *Droshak* editorial office at the time, was seen as a place of pilgrimage for the Armenian revolutionary movement. It was not without concern that I approached the modest two-story building with a garden surrounded by iron-railings. The garden seemed to be neglected and had no signs of life. In the depths of the garden, amongst the trees and half-broken branches, were the remains of a pavilion. The fallen branches and bushes left the impression of a deserted block. The door to the main building was open and one could see pictures of martyred revolutionaries on the walls inside. Books were stacked on glass shelves in the central part of the two rooms. The clean, modestly furnished but cold rooms made it look like a memorial rather than an apartment. No one seemed to be there. The building was as silent as a grave. I came out, bewildered, when I heard a woman's voice from the basement.

"Who is it?"

"Excuse me, ma'am, where is the owner of the house, or anyone?"

"What owner of the house?"

And suddenly in front of me I saw a yellow face, like parchment. It belonged to a slender man who, with his hand placed on his side, rose with his dignity wounded.

"There are no women in this building, sir! You have come to the wrong address."

My involuntary rejoicing seemed to anger him.

"Who are you and what do you want?"

"Excuse me. Are you Mr. Anton?"

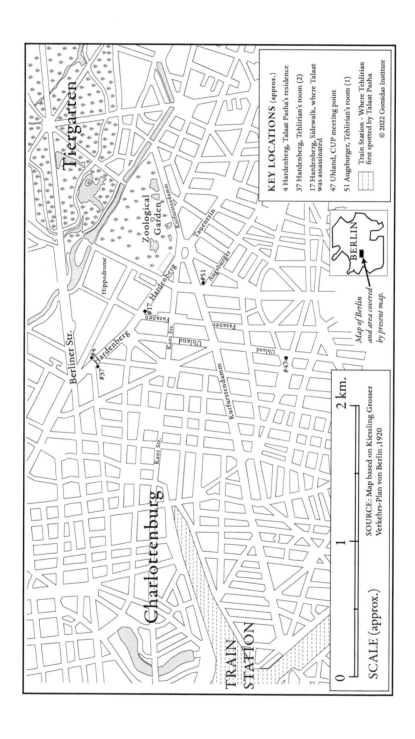

TRAIN STATION

Charlottenburg

Berliner Str.

Tiergarten

Hippodrome

Zoological Garden

Hardenberg

#4

#37 Hardenberg

17 Hardenberg

#51 Augsburger

Kurfürstendamm

Kant Str.

Fasanen

Uhland

Tauentzin

Kurfürstendamm

Fasanen

Uhland

#47

SCALE (approx.)

0   1   2 km.

SOURCE: Map based on Kiessling Grosser Verkehrs-Plan von Berlin, 1920

Map of Berlin and area covered by present map.

BERLIN

KEY LOCATIONS (approx.)

4 Hardenberg, Talaat Pasha's residence

37 Hardenberg, Tehlirian's room (2)

17 Hardenberg, Sidewalk, where Talaat was assassinated

47 Uhland, CUP meeting point

51 Augsburger, Tehlirian's room (1)

Train Station - Where Tehlirian first spotted by Talaat Pasha

© 2022 Gomidas Institute

"Yes!"

"The comrades told me about you."

"What comrades?" he said curiously.

"From America."

"Unger Tehlirian?"

"Yes!"

"Well, wouldn't you know it, you blessed man! Come in ..."

It turned out that our representative had left five days earlier, without revealing his destination, but leaving a letter for me with Mr. Anton. The representative stated that thanks to a letter he had received from Constantinople, he had learned of the whereabouts of a relative in Berlin and was heading there. I also had to hurry if I wanted to go to "university."

Mr. Anton had some revolutionary experience in the Balkans. Almost from the moment *Droshak* had been established in Geneva, he had become the meticulous manager of the building and its property. He realized that I had come for an important task, but he showed no interest. While he treated me to tea, I learned from the conversation that the editorial board of *Droshak* wanted to move to Paris and intended to sell the Geneva building to buy a new one in Paris. He spoke about it with bitterness. In his opinion, *Droshak* would lose its strength as soon as it was transplanted from Geneva. It was an irresponsible act, even a crime against the glorious past of the building. He could not understand how the "Echmiadzin of the Armenian Revolution" could be sold. Mr. Anton had no intention of leaving the building. Like a cat, he was more connected to the nooks and crannies of the building than the owner. He was almost certain that he would die in that building before it was sold; he had already aged and was ill. If it was sold, he would ask the new owner of the building to allow him to live there as a janitor.

I was listening, but my mind was elsewhere. I was moved and perplexed by the words, "his trace has been found." I had to be alone to consider the weight of that news. Mr. Anton helped me find a place to stay at a nearby hotel. Despite the urgency, it took me five or six days to get a visa to go to Berlin, where I was supposed to be studying mechanical engineering. I left on December 3rd [1920].

***

Germany was still in a difficult situation because of the war. In economic terms, the peace treaty had created a semi-colonial state in the country. Heavy war reparations had devastated the economy. Successive governments had been unable to find a way out since the end of hostilities. The country was in turmoil; industrial strikes would continually start and stop everywhere.

I arrived in Berlin in the evening. It was barely 10 o'clock but life in that city of four million people was already dead. It was snowing. The car stopped in front of the "Tiergarten"[*] hotel where the representative lived. I was looking forward to being briefed about the mission. "It's very good," was the reply. Talaat was in Berlin. Pointing to a German newspaper with some parts underlined, he said:

"This article was written by Mehmed Zeki and directed against Ittihad, especially against Ismail Hakki."

"Who are they?"

"The first of the Ittihad youth to be sent to Berlin by the party three years ago to study was Mehmed Zeki, a well-known charlatan and crook, a former Ittihadist freeloader. He is a shadowy person who used to publish a weekly newspaper in Istanbul called the 'National Defense.' Now, apparently, things are not going well with his former bosses and he has started exposing things. In this article, Mehmed Zeki writes about an article written by Ismail Hakki on the Armenian issue and says:

"'It is surprising that their leader is a guest of the German Republic ... and Ismail Hakki does not write anything about the committee of criminals residing in Berlin.' He then continues, 'We know that Ismail Hakki Bey is not only closely associated with Talaat Pasha, but also with Dr. Nazim and the former governor of Aleppo, Bedri. It is known that these three are the organizers and perpetrators of the Armenian tragedy, as well as

---

[*] The actual name of the hotel is not given, just its location in the "Tiergarten" district of Berlin.

those who eliminated the Turks who were considered unwanted by them. The government of Istanbul will not delay in administering the punishment they deserve. The Ittihadists in Berlin have recently begun to declare themselves socialists. You should not believe them. The head of the socialists is Prince Sabaheddin, who barely escaped the persecution of the Ittihadists. I will give a lecture in the coming days, examine all these issues impartially, and expose the activities of Ittihad ve Terakki.'"[*]

The important thing for us was that there was no doubt that the murderers were there in Berlin. They included Talaat, the former police chief of Constantinople, Bedri, Ismail Hakki, and the governor of Trabizon, Jemal Azmi Bey, who had started a tobacco business with a shop in his own name, where he also traded in carpets.

This latest news simply stunned me. To massacre fourteen thousand people, to create a business using their wealth, and to live peacefully in the capital of a civilized country ... I was eager to shoot that thug, but such action could have alerted the rest to escape, including the more important ones, especially Talaat, whose monstrous ghost was following me day and night. We had to move carefully and not allow our prey to escape, although it was unimaginable for me to think that the governor of Trabizon could be discovered yet remain alive ...

It turned out that several of these men were being followed and we were making progress. So I, too, had to get to work, first of all by undertaking surveillance work.

The next morning, before I left the hotel, Hagop Zorian, a dark-skinned 27-28 year-old student at the University of Berlin, showed up.[†] A wide smile appeared on his pleasant face when he met me. He said he had come to share some interesting information he had learned from Hrach Papazian.[‡] It was said that Enver was due from Moscow in those days to revive Ittihad,

---

[*] Ittihad ve Terakki Jemiyeti or Committee of Union and Progress.
[†] Hagop Zorian's name was obscured as Hazor in the original Armenian publication of *Remembrances*.
[‡] Hrach Papazian's name was obscured as Hrap in the original Armenian publication of *Remembrances*.

but there was rivalry between him and Talaat over this issue. Supporters of the latter wanted Berlin to be the center of the reorganized party and its activities, while Enver insisted that the center of the party should be in Moscow. Hrach himself thought that the reason for this disagreement was that Enver was very often in Moscow and Transcaucasia and wanted to keep the party under his influence. He wanted to be as close as possible to Anatolia and play a role in developments there. Meanwhile, Talaat's supporters thought that their intervention in Anatolia could cause a stir in Europe and harm the development of the nationalist movement that had begun there.* Supposedly, a few days earlier, there had been a meeting between Talaat's supporters, the Egyptian Sheikh Abdul Aziz, the Syrian Shekir Aslan, and several Indian Muslims. Talaat had not been present at that meeting.

Hrach received this information from some Turkish students he knew well. He himself, as they said, was no different from a real Turk in appearance, name, and knowledge of Turkish, but he was pure Armenian. He had close friendships with Turkish students and Turks and provided significant services to our diplomatic representative with important information.

Hagop left after conveying this information. We also left a little later. It was snowing and large flakes soared like butterflies in every direction and descended firmly to the ground. It was a warm, quiet, and pleasant winter day. We went for a walk, each in his own thoughts. Shortly afterwards, we entered a wide avenue that stretched straight from the Imperial Palace to Brandenburg Tor, the largest street in Berlin. I needed to get acquainted with the layout of the city, the main districts and streets. I needed to learn at least a few German words.

We turned left, passed a few secondary streets, and reached an irregular square. On the corner to the right, where the street entered the square, was Azmi's tobacco shop. We passed in front of the shop. I could hardly stop myself from entering the shop to

---

* The reference here is to the "milli" movement, which mobilized Muslims under the Turkish nationalist banner, led by Mustafa Kemal [Ataturk].

see that monster. We walked around the square, along a parallel street, and turned to the left side of the square. There was a canteen-café on that street. It was still early for dinner. We sat by the window overlooking Jemal Azmi's shop across the square and ordered some coffee. It was the third day that surveillance had been assigned here, but so far in vain. There was no trade, the store door did not open for hours. Paying thousands for rent and keeping the store closed meant the store had been set up for a specific purpose. There was no doubt that it was a front, but where were the accursed masters?

My mind was still on what Hagop had said. If Enver's point of view had won out, Talaat might also have gone to Russia or Transcaucasia. On the other hand, Talaat's presence in Europe was more important for Turkish national interests. It was known that he was conducting rigorous diplomatic work in Europe, no doubt with Kemal's knowledge and wishes. Although statements had been made by Mustafa Kemal that the nationalist movement under his leadership had nothing to do with Talaat's Ittihad group, there was no question that the Ittihad movement was rooted in Anatolia. The army and the "Grand National Assembly" were mostly composed of Ittihadists. What was the point of adding Talaat to that group? Both the negotiations in Russia and the weapons and ammunition received through Italy were the work of the Ittihadists in Europe. In fact, it was the Ittihadists, working with other nationalists, who controlled the fate of Turkey.

I was busy with these thoughts when I suddenly noticed a woman entering Jemal Azmi's shop. I left immediately and my comrade appeared on the sidewalk a few seconds later.[*] But the woman's visit seemed to have happened in an instant. I was forced, with some displeasure, to follow the woman across the square. A little further on, my comrade came, insisting that he had heard the conversation with Azmi.

---

[*] This reference, "my comrade," is to Shahan Natali, whose identity was obscured by Vratsian, the main editor of *Remembrances*.

The monster had said, "I hope you will inform me" and the woman had replied, "Definitely, if he allows it." Apparently, Hrach's information was correct.

In my opinion, it was the most dishonorable thing to follow a woman, but what could I do? The snow had stopped. The slender woman, who was in a black fur coat and round fur hat, walked slowly, as if she was very pleased to be walking freely. From time to time, she lowered her head to examine her own steps, and suddenly, bored with the task, she raised her head and increased her pace. Only a carefree person full of dreams could walk like that.

The woman continued down the avenue. Admiring herself, she walked for about an hour, sometimes looking at her feet, sometimes looking forward, and then turning to the right, she entered the neighborhood of villas. Here, she stopped in front of a magnificent house bearing the number 165. She gently pushed open the gate to the snow-covered garden, quickly ascended the wide but short stone steps, and went inside ...

The next morning, I watched that building. It was noon when I suddenly saw a young man in the yard who rang the bell and entered as soon as the door opened. It happened so fast that I did not realize when or where he had come from. Judging by his height, he looked like Enver from the back. I cursed my lack of attention. A little further down, I noticed someone else in the corner also watching the house. Was he spying on me? As soon as I stuck my head round the corner, I was surprised to see that it was Hagop.

"What are you doing here?"

"Let's go. He may come out and see me."

"Who?"

"Ismail Hakki."

"Was he the one who came in a while ago?"

"Of course."

"Hey, I thought it was Enver."

"Let's go so he doesn't suddenly notice us."

"You go. He does not know me."

I waited for almost an hour until Hakki came out and hurried down the steps. I was very excited. It seemed to me that he was going to lead me to Enver. I felt sorry that the gun was not on me. He reached the outskirts of the main avenue, went on to Uhland Street, and entered residence No. 47. I waited there for more than half an hour, but in vain. It was cold, snowing, and I was hungry. I headed to the cafeteria, but I was confused about my direction and found the "Tiergarten" hotel with some difficulty. It was dusk when my comrade returned.

"Where have you been, boy?"

I told him and he rolled his eyes.

"Uhland, you say?"

"Yes."

"Number 47?"

"Yes!"

He clasped his hands, sat down, and clenched his jaw. He then stated with a beaming face, "Don't call me a man if Talaat does not live at Uhland 47 residence."

"What?"

"At around 10 o'clock, the tall man I saw three days ago entered Azmi's shop. As soon as he came out, I recognized him. Do you know who he was? Behaeddin Shakir."

The success of the day made us feel so elated that we expected to get the two main murderers at the same time: Enver in the neighborhood of villas and Talaat in Uhland, possibly the two together when they met up, which seemed quite certain. How else could one explain the connection between these developments? Hagop came in with two new friends. One of them was Vahan Zakarian, a slightly taller than average, slim young man, with black-and-white hair that was carefully combed back.[*] He spoke firmly, with a restrained, calm voice, and without exaggeration. His face was thoughtful, especially his eyes. The other, Hayg Der Ohanian, was a student.[†] His oval, sympathetic face shone with a beautiful smile, a bright, clean, and surprisingly friendly soul

---

[*] Vahan Zakarian's name was obscured as Vaza in the original Armenian publication of *Remembrances*. He was an employee of the Persian Embassy in Berlin.

[†] Hayg Der Ohanian's name was obscured as Haygo in the original Armenian publication of *Remembrances*.

concealed under a restrained appearance. Both were aware of the issue at hand.

Hagop reported the information he had heard from Hrach, who was careful not to meet with anyone else. There was extraordinary commotion in the Turkish club. Kemal's success in Armenia had inspired everyone. It was not impossible for them to reach Baku again. Enver had not come, but he could have arrived at any time. After we considered the information and intelligence of the day, the meeting decided to keep a close watch on Uhland and Enver's wife's residence.

It was night and I was still struggling to learn some German words and expressions with the help of my incomplete French and a travel dictionary. At dawn, it seemed to me that I had already mastered enough, but when I went to bed, I had barely four or five words left in my head ...

***

We kept Enver's wife's residence under surveillance for about two weeks, but she was no longer visible. Once or twice a day, various maids would come out of the building and return with shopping items. There was no sign of Enver in Berlin. Would he come? It was impossible to confirm. However, one day, a car parked there, Ismail Hakki got out, as well as another person in a fur coat. This incident confused us, but when the new man appeared alone the next day, Hagop followed him and found that he was a doctor, named Wagner.

In the days before the new year, we held consultations with Libarid Nazariants, who worked with Mr. Greenfield as an adviser. Mr. Greenfield was a German-Armenian who ran the Armenian consulate in Berlin. Blond, curly-haired, blue-eyed Nazariants looked more like a pure, northern Slav than an Armenian. He was one of our strong and experienced friends. In his opinion, it was futile to wait for Enver in Berlin.

"There are a thousand and one rumors about Enver," he said. In the past, a Turkish newspaper had written that Enver was on his way to Berlin by plane, when the plane had crashed and he barely escaped death. Enver himself invented and spread such stories in order to cover his tracks. I think such rumors are also circulating here in Turkish circles."

Hagop also did not consider it impossible for Enver to be in Berlin, but for no more than a day or two. That was too little time to get to him.

The meeting became controversial and lasted a long time, but it no longer interested me.

I realized that it was not enough to be in the same city as the criminals. The mission required constant attention and tireless surveillance.

***

At the end of December, I fell ill. My eyes darkened again and I felt dizzy. The last time the sickness had recurred was in Yerevan, three or four years earlier, and I thought it had long gone.

As soon as I felt better, I moved from the "Tiergarten" hotel to an apartment at 51 Augsburger Street, where the secretary of the Armenian consulate, Yervant Apelian, lived. He was a 23 to 25-year-old sharp, young man. It was very difficult to find a room in Berlin at that time. Apelian managed to persuade the hostess to provide me with a room next door.

My 60-year-old landlady, Mrs. Elizabeth Stellbaum, like any German woman, was a meticulous housewife who wanted to keep my room very tidy, even cleaning my shoes. I did not leave any work for her, which at first seemed strange to her, then gradually more pleasant. I explained to her that I was young, she was old, and it was not accepted in our culture for old women to serve young people. She thought that, although this custom was very respectable, she was obliged to do her work, that the conditions of the lease obligated it, and I was paying money for the service. Those mostly face-to-face conversations helped me understand German a little bit.

Apelian was often visited by his friend, Levon Eftian, a cheerful 21-year-old student who lived with his sister and brother-in-law. Within a few days, I befriended them but both were unaware of my mission and thought I had come to study. They were warm-hearted and devoted friends. They were unhappy that I was allocating very little time to learning German. It was intolerable for them and disgraceful for an Armenian student. Not a day went by that they did not raise the issue.

"You cannot go to university this way, my friend," said Apelian.

"Only through love can one learn a language. We need to find a nice teacher for you," joked Eftian.

One evening, suddenly, a very beautiful girl, who taught German, came with him to visit me.

"Do not embarrass me," he said in Armenian, introducing me to the girl. "I said that you had asked her to come because you are sick, and so on."

Surprised, I was forced to confirm this, although I had no desire to expand my circle. A young, beautiful, and especially unpretentious girl, Lola Beilenson had spent her childhood in the Baltic region and knew Russian. I did not understand German and Eftian did not understand Russian, which made general conversation impossible. In these circumstances, the initiative passed to Eftian. He talked about me for a long time. The girl listened and smiled sympathetically. Eventually, a situation was created in which it would have been very rude to refuse. Eftian explained the situation to me, and I agreed to spend two hours a week in language lessons with the girl. My first lessons were so successful that I hoped to overcome my language difficulty in no time.

On New Year's Eve, I was invited to Eftian's sister's, who had a modest tobacco shop on Oranien Street with her husband, Mr. Terzibashian. I met Kevork Kalousdian, another survivor, who owned a grocery store in the same area. I was amazed at how my compatriots, having lost everything and survived death, had been able to regain their position and prosperity within five years. What was more surprising was that the difficulties of life did not suppress their inner moral and intellectual needs. Kalousdian, a former student at an American College, knew as much as a university student, and everyone was fluent in German, as if it were their mother tongue.

The young Mr. and Mrs. Terzibashians spared no effort to make the New Year's gathering perfect. However, it was enough to recall the past for our happy gathering to be covered by a black veil. No, our generation could no longer rejoice on such occasions.

The next evening, I had just returned home from watching Uhland, when Eftian and Apelian entered. I immediately understood from their faces that a new conspiracy had been planned against me. There was a gentle, mischievous smile on Eftian's face, and Apelian looked at me with a searching look.

"You have to go to dance classes with us starting tomorrow," said Eftian, rubbing his hands together with satisfaction.

"What dance classes?"

"European," and embracing Apelian, he danced with him, "Oh, like this ..."

"Are you crazy? Is it a time for dancing?"

"The right time is now; the start of spring, dancing and falling in love."

And he sat in front of me with the indifference of an indolent man.

"Well, how is that going to happen?" I said, meeting the mood.

"First of all, you have to put yourself in order."

"Let the boy first understand the necessity of the following," Apelian intervened, giving special importance to what he was about to say. "The problem is that you can't learn German just by taking lessons; you have not gone beyond what you have learned so far, only *was ist das?* ..."

"Would you like me to lecture in German after just two lessons?"

"You have been here for more than a month," Eftian raised his voice.

"It is necessary to understand the German way of life, to hear the language in a real context, so that your ears get used to it," Apelian said.

"The ear is deaf; it can only learn through the heart."

"That is his responsibility. Let him use all his senses, as long as he learns."

"I am not a dancer."

"How come you are not a dancer, when we have already registered you and paid the money during these difficult times?"

The next evening, 60-70 young people gathered in one of the streets next to Grunewald Park, in the great hall of dance instructor Friedrich's school. The boys were like guard horses, strong, cheerful, and confident. The girls were gorgeous with wavy, braided hair. Together as a group, they were all beautiful, but each, of course, lacked certain things.

We were late. My friends did not have time to introduce me to Mr. Friedrich, which was fine with me, as I was already bored.

But Mr. Friedrich, wearing his starchy shirt, threw his bald head back, shouted something, and pulled his silk handkerchief out of his collar, wiping his sweaty forehead. My friends ran toward the girls, lifted them, and joined the group. Suddenly, Mr. Friedrich made a loud sound like a goose; the piano rumbled and the dancers started to spin ...

I thought, how good it would be if there was a sudden order to dance a "*geond*," for example, even the "beating garlic," or our wonderful "*tadaranis tashdoum*" that Irinsants Zoro used to lead in those wonderful days, waving the red handkerchief at the head of the dance line. I remembered how, despite his old age, he jumped with the flexibility of a monkey, dragging the brides and girls from the field. I envisaged the little children falling out of the line in a commotion and crying, the restrained laughter of the brides, the fiery eyes of the girls. I could hear Zoro's goat-like voice, "The trial is over in my court, the hearts of our Armenian children are filled with hope," immediately followed by various harmonious voices. Oh, those singers still ring in my ears: "Fight, Armenian men, with burning hearts. We start the journey with brave friends." Dear God, how charming all of that had been with its naive simplicity ...

Mr. Friedrich snorted like a goose with a dry throat and the piano changed its tune. I knew it was a "polka." The couples jumped around modestly, turning left and right. Standing in the middle of the hall, the weary Mr. Friedrich led them like a horse trainer in a circus, leaning back and forth. From time to time he ran forward furiously towards those who struggled. The faces of the dancers showed respect and all seriousness; they did not speak. Everyone was interested in a good show and was absorbed in their dance. I just did not understand why everyone was not dancing. A group of men and women were satisfied with just standing, moving their heads and dancing mentally. Apparently, they were in the lower class. And indeed, as soon as the dance was over, my friends appeared and introduced me to a girl who enjoyed dancing with the gentle movement of her head, throwing her thick strand of hair from her left shoulder to her right. With Mr. Friedrich's training and demonstration I began to make some basic movements. I had hardly made a few such turns when suddenly my eyes darkened and I felt dizzy. In order not to fall down, I tried to hold on to my partner's neck. I heard her scream ...

The recurrence of this old ailment worried me. Fortunately, the consequences were not as severe as in Yerevan, and I was able to attend a language class the next day. However, as soon as the lesson began, I regretted being there. I did not understand anything and Miss Beilenson noticed it immediately.

"What happened to you?"

"I'm a little weak."

"No, I noticed a while ago that you are always thinking about something."

"Yes, ma'am," I said, forced to admit the truth.

"Can you tell me what it is?"

"No ..."

She shook her head slightly, dispelling any distractions.

"In that case, tell me about your homeland."

"I have no homeland, Miss," I responded and asked to be dismissed.

Two days later I was able to resume my duties on Uhland street. It was noon when I suddenly noticed my comrade walking down the street from the opposite sidewalk behind two people. I recognized one of the two immediately: Behaeddin Shakir. My heart was pounding. Who was the other?

"It's Dr. Nazim," my comrade whispered when I reached him.

"Where are you coming from?"

"From Azmi's store."

They entered residence number 47. We went to the corner at the end of the street. Less than 15 minutes later, Behaeddin Shakir reappeared and headed up the street.

"Stay in pursuit! I'll wait for Nazim," said my comrade.

I was still weak and tired at that moment and Shakir was moving very fast in the central part of the district where the large Tauentzien street, Kant street and Kurfürstendamm formed the main arteries to Charlottenburg. I almost lost him. I was exhausted when he stopped in front of a magnificent building in Wilhelmstrasse with the flag outside indicating it was the British Embassy. It was not difficult to wait for him during that busy time of day but my head hurt from fatigue. I was wondering what Shakir was plotting and where he would go from there. Suddenly, he came out, looked around like a thief, and left. The accursed man walked at a fast pace through the streets, as if on fire. He seemed to know that he was being pursued. So why not buy a car? He entered the long Jerusalemer street and walked like a demon. I had almost reached the end of the street when suddenly I blacked out and slumped against a wall; the buildings seemed to jump and then it grew dark. I fell ...

I don't know how long I was out. When I woke up, I was surrounded by a crowd. A man was asking for my address.

This time I was in despair. Vahan took me to see Professor Cassirer, a specialist in nervous disorders.

A week passed. Feeling myself a little more energetic, I set myself the task of eliminating the criminals we had already identified: Azmi, Shakir, and Nazim. Having dreamt for years about the main criminal, I now felt that I no longer had the strength to prolong that mission. Anyway, what difference was there between them and Talaat? My comrade, however, rejected it. We held a consultation on the subject and it was decided to leave the solution to the relevant body and continue our reconnaissance.

***

One day, in the second half of February [1921], Hrach announced that a meeting of Ittihad leaders was expected. We all set to work, trying to verify the news, because there was no doubt that Talaat would appear in Berlin or Rome. Two days later, Hrach's information was confirmed: the same news was reported in *Il Lavoro Fascista*. My comrade got an Italian visa the same day to travel to Rome.

The rest of us monitored all the trains departing from Charlottenburg train station, starting from early morning. It was assumed that the Berlin deputies would be leaving from that station because the Ittihadists were based in Charlottenburg. My comrade was ready to leave at any moment; he was supposed to find Talaat in Rome and telegraph me. I had already called Miss Beilenson to tell her that I had to interrupt my classes for a while due to my illness. We had flexed all our muscles. We did not leave any train unchecked, not even freight trains.

One morning,* towards the end of the month, shortly before the departure of the express train, the gloomy Turk who we thought lived in Uhland as a gatekeeper and supervisor, a man we called *mraylatem* (gloomy-face), appeared on the station platform. After five minutes, three Turkish students appeared at the station. It became difficult for Hagop and Hayg to remain there. Almost simultaneously, Behaeddin Shakir appeared with some luxurious travel bags with another person with a light beard, yellowed and folded like a quince, whom I saw for the first time. They waved goodbye to the students and entered a carriage. Barely five minutes before departure, a new man appeared on the platform. He was big, round, well-dressed, and held a cane. I was shaken to the core. He was very similar to Talaat, except for the [missing] thick mustache and fez. His head was half-covered. He quickly approached the people standing on the platform. As he passed, each person straightened up like a soldier. I felt as if someone was pushing me forward. One of the students standing in front took his right hand, kissed it, and said:

"They are already inside, Pasha."

---

* This reference to "morning" instead of "evening" here is a correction Tehlirian made to the Armenian proofs of *Remembrances*. The change was not entered into the Armenian edition of the book. See *Vem Hamahaygagan Hantes*, p. 351.

Hardenberg Street where Talaat and Tehlirian resided.

The "new man" immediately turned to the carriage and knocked on the half-open window with his cane. Who was inside the carriage? I do not know, but I heard someone shout from behind in a full, loud voice.

"*Ermenijesini ounoutmiuyesun* [Don't forget the Armenian]."

The excitement shook me. I went a little further on, behind the people standing in front of the waiting room. Suddenly, my comrade appeared from behind me.

"Did you see? I think it's him ... He is leaving now. Come as soon as you receive my telegram."

The whistle blew and the train left in an instant. The "new man," the students, and "gloomy-face" remained. It had all happened so fast that I had a hard time keeping track of it. The "new man" respectfully said something to those standing near him, and everyone moved to the door, allowing him to walk ahead.

The sudden departure of my comrade caused me great confusion. I couldn't think, but my instinct was to say that the "new man" was Talaat.

I followed him closely. Hagop and Hayg appeared from the corner under the stairs.

"Who is he?"

"I think it's him."

"The main one?"

"Yes!"

"It did not look like him ..."

"They called him Pasha."

"Every dog in exile is now a pasha."

The group was barely twenty steps away from me. They were a step behind the "new man" and only approached him when he spoke. That honor was often bestowed on "gloomy-face." With shoulders as thick as a water-carrier's and a square back, there was no doubt that it was him, but I was not sure about his face ... I did not remember the picture very well.

Suddenly, I found myself in a familiar area. We were walking towards the "Tiergarten" hotel. They stopped at the zoo. Three students said goodbye to them with a respectful Turkish salute. The "new man" and "gloomy-face" passed through various streets and went down Hardenberg street to enter the residence at number 4.

Hagop and Hayg appeared behind me from the opposite sidewalk. We kept that building under surveillance for about an hour, waiting for "gloomy-face," but he did not appear.

That night, I was in a mental turmoil not experienced since the retreat from Yerznga. I was almost certain that the "new man" was Talaat, but my comrades were drowning out my inner thoughts and creating doubts. They were partly right. I wasn't one hundred percent sure.

The city of Berlin was asleep. The silence outside was sometimes interrupted by the noise of a car. The damp cold penetrated my body to the core. I went to bed. "If it is him and we lost him," I worried, dispelling my numbness ... "But where could he even escape to? To another city? Why and how? If he did not go to Rome, it means that his presence is more important here, and if he instructed the others 'not to forget the Armenian,' then he is working on something and has to be somewhere else as a leader. His colleagues could not follow him from place to place. Yes, but couldn't he change his address? Possibly, if he suspects something.

Did we given him reasons to do so? I think not." It was only surprising that "gloomy-face" remained there. Was I thinking clearly or was I delusional? It was as if I were sitting in the hollow on Araul Mountain with my friends around a burning campfire, sparks flying about everyone's faces, and the colors changing from the fire, as Kevork described the Khanasor expedition.

"One thousand five hundred years ago, Commander Vartan [Mamigonian]'s cavalry crossed the slopes of this mountain and camped by the riverbank in the plain below, where the Khanasor expedition began," he said, arms stretching towards the fire.

"Behold, do you see Father Krikor wandering among the armies? Do you hear that? It is a liturgy," he said, staring at the field.

There was a whisper in the field. Voices were heard, sometimes a scream that faded away. My hair stood on end like thorns, my teeth were clenched, my tongue dry and heavy.

"Get up, Father Krikor is coming," said Kevork, standing up and stretching. Suddenly Mourad appeared in front of me.

"Alas, Mr. Mourad, is that you? Where did you come from? You were dead, weren't you?"

"What? Dead? I was asleep."

Others appeared next to him, and behind him.

"And what about Avedis? Isn't he also ..."

"Avedis, too."

"And Arakel?"

"Him, too. Don't you see? The whole world is here ..."

The world was enveloped by a dark and deep abyss that descended slowly into the valleys, into the fields, pregnant with thought, moving in mystery. I could no longer see anything, nothing at all.

"Look this way," I heard Mourad's voice say.

I looked down the mountain, to the distant steppes of the valleys, where, in the darkness, I could make out thousands upon thousands of ash covered troops with countless spear-wielding cavalrymen moving like a wave ...

Then, Mourad shouted, "Get up and saddle the horses! Do you not see that it is light?" No, we did not see the light.

"It's dawn, dawn," said Mourad, turning to Avedis and shouting: "Ride the horses, sound the trumpets so that the inhabitants of all the villages, towns, fields and valleys, men, women and children, up to one thousand five hundred years-old rise up with shovels, spades and sickles, anything they can bring, and join the army ...."

Suddenly, the mountains and valleys shook. Everywhere you looked, there seemed to be dragons that roared and fell silent. Marble masses were moving at dawn. It was the skeletal-looking people that flowed like stagnant rivers, their bones squeaking. Armed with axes, hammers, spades, and shovels, they all ran like a whirlwind. In the distance, up to their waists in the ground, and carrying their tombs, they stared with dull glances. Then, suddenly, bursting with fire from the hollows of their eyes, they jumped out of their graves and ran. Their shrouds blowing in the wind, they moved like chains, swaying. A mob of thousands of skeletons was already on Araul's slopes. The snow-covered bones swayed like waves and climbed higher. The sky was filled with cries of hatred and curses.

"Go forward!" Mourad shouted and jumped on his white horse. He was leading the fighters forward. The lightning from the hooves made the mountain thunder, naked swords blazing. The earth was now roaring and trembling. But in the frenzy, they stood with swords held up to the sky, above the three-beaked vultures flying away from the mountains.

Suddenly, I was left without a horse, with only a bridle and saddle, although I slid further down into the clouds. Below I could already see large rows of gray mountains. I knew those mountains, the gorges of Eomerzade. I cautiously went and sat down. Thousands of generations had lived there, and there was only one skeleton whose soul was slowly swaying like a scorpion climbing up the abyss.

"Who are you?"

"Don't you remember?" he said, digging through the ground at astonishing speed.

No, I did not remember him.

"I'm Simon from Vozm," he said, covering himself with the dirt from the edge of the pit. At that moment, only his skull was left; he looked at me through the darkened cavities of his eyes and laughed silently through his clenched teeth. I was terrified.

"Mr. Simon!" I shouted and awoke to the sound of my own voice.

***

It was dawn. We agreed that Hayg would keep watch on Jemal Azmi's shop, Hagop at Uhland, and I would watch the residence at Hardenberg No. 4. But it was too early. Vahan was at home and in a hurry to get to work on time. I briefly explained to him what was said at our meeting the previous day, asking him to meet Hagop for consultation in the evening.

From there I went to the "Tiergarten" hotel. I thought that if my comrade had taken the room key with him, I would break down the door and take the folder with the pictures. I needed Talaat's picture. I was sure that if I scratched off the facial hair, leaving a small layer under the nose and painted a European hat instead of a fez, I would have the image of yesterday's "new man."

The door was closed. One of the familiar waiters was passing through the corridor. Seeing me, he threw a hand towel on his arm with a swirling motion.

"The gentleman has left."

"Where did he go?"

"Leipzig."

"What a shame. I'd wanted to get my underwear."

"I have the key ..."

At that time, there was a lot going on at the beginning of Hardenberg Street, at the intersection of the wide avenue. One hundred paces away in front of me was residence number 4, which differed from the other houses with its villa-like structure. It had a balcony overlooking the street and an elongated flower garden fenced by iron railings. Shortly afterwards, "gloomy-face" came out with a basket in his hand and went to the shops. So, this fading moon lives here and not in Uhland, I thought. At 10 o'clock, the "new man" appeared on the sidewalk. The same thing happened to me: I could not stand still. He was pulling me like a magnet

184

towards him. He looked up and down carefully for a moment, as if to determine which direction he would go and, shaking his cane carelessly, walked steadily down the street. Crossing the two neighboring streets, he reached the house at 47 Uhland Street. He glanced at the opposite sidewalk where I was passing and entered. It was amazing that we had not noticed him here before.

Hagop had just arrived.

"I could not sleep last night. I was late. What are you doing here?"

"He has arrived."

"Who?"

"Him ..."

"When?"

"Now. Just follow him. Vahan will meet you at 9 o'clock in the evening. We have a meeting. Tell Hayg about it."

I ran to "Tiergarten" to find out whether my comrade had returned on the 9 o'clock train. I came back to Hardenberg street. The "new man" returned home at 11 o'clock. Hagop did not show up. He had probably not seen him come out of Uhland street.

"There were so many people coming and going to Uhland today. I do not know how I missed him," Hagop said in the evening, very depressed.

"Who were they?"

"Except for Dr. Nazim, everyone was a new, unknown person."

"When did Nazim leave?"

"He stayed for barely a quarter of an hour."

"I wish I had followed him."

"How could I know that it would be like this?"

Vahan and Hayg entered. Explaining the evidence that the "new man" was Talaat, I offered to put an end to the issue. The silence was broken by Hagop.

"The facts for taking action are incomplete. It is true that if we take our time, we may miss the opportunity [to get Talaat], but it will be worse if we make a mistake."

"Why?"

(Left to right) Berlin representative of the Armenian Republic Ch. Greenfield and his adviser Libarid Nazariants.

"First, if he is not who we think he is, he will disappear without a trace. Then, if we kill someone else, I do not think we would have done a good thing."

"Do you think that the other person is your cousin?"

"Do not get angry," Vahan intervened, "Let him continue what he is saying."

"What I have to say is simple. The case is going well. We must continue and finish the job when we are fully convinced. I think no one is fully convinced yet. I did not have the opportunity to look at his face and compare it with the picture. I cannot take responsibility under these circumstances."

"And what is your opinion?" said Vahan, turning to Hayg.

"I was going to say the same thing. We haven't had time to find out who lives in the Hardenberg house."

"How could we find out?"

"Don't all residents of Berlin have to be registered in their relevant neighborhoods?"

"But isn't it naive to assume that Talaat would be registered under his own name?" I asked.

"Possibly, but at least we may find out with whom that gloomy-faced Turk is living, as well as anyone else living in the same house. After all, everything can strengthen or weaken our assumptions."

"Although Hayg is a poet by temperament, he speaks like a scientist," said Vahan. "This is a serious problem. We are not murderers. In that sense, it is possible to make a fatal mistake. I have no connections in the district, and it is dangerous to contact the police. I think Talaat enjoys the patronage of the police. However, the problem can be solved by approaching the landlord. Let me make an attempt tomorrow. Would that satisfy you?" he said, turning to me.

"It doesn't matter; it's all the same to me."

"That's not the answer. Yes or no?"

"I have nothing against it. Give it a try."

"Who owns that house?"

"How should I know?"

I was confused and felt abandoned. I had a hard night. I woke up in the morning to light footsteps. Taking advantage of the situation, Mrs. Stellbaum had taken my shoes to clean. The kind woman thought I was sick. She persuaded me to stay at home because the weather was very bad; it was snowing and there was a light breeze.

I went to the "Tiergarten." My comrade had not arrived yet.

There was little traffic on Hardenberg Street and it was so cold that I had to keep moving. I wandered around for more than an hour. I was just thinking that the "new man" would not come out in such weather, when he suddenly appeared and looked carefully up and down the street. He set off at a brisk pace, protecting his face and body from the snowy wind blowing towards him. He reached Uhland and entered the building. Hagop was there so I sent him to Hardenberg. The new man's visit lasted just half an hour that day. He returned to the house where Hagop had seen him, crossing the same sidewalk. It was clear to me that the visits took place between 10 and 11 o'clock.

I was with Vahan in the evening. A little earlier, in the café facing Jemal Azmi's shop, I had learned from Hayg that Vahan had managed to see the owner of the Hardenberg residence, and it

187

was a false alarm. The man living there was a Turkish merchant who ran an oriental café. Vahan stated:

"The landlord is an old woman named Gertrude; a talkative, flighty, but pleasant person. She lives in her second house, in the same area, on Fasanen Street. I introduced myself as an agent of a Swiss insurance company and asked to rent the house at Hardenberg No. 4, which, according to what I had heard, would be vacated soon. She said she did not know about it, as such issues were handled by the janitor. But, wanting to be nice, she pulled out a pile of papers and looked for the contract. 'It is a misunderstanding', she said. 'According to the contract, they still have three months.' I got up, apologizing.

"'Sit down, please', said the woman. 'How many rooms do you need?'

"I replied, 'two or three rooms are enough for me, until I find an apartment in this area.'

"'In that case, maybe you will come to an agreement with the tenants. The house is quite spacious. There is a small hall inside the entrance, to the right of which are two large rooms and one small room. There is another small room on the left. One of the other rooms is a living room, the other is a dining room. I have no objection if the space with the two rooms is given to you. I think they will be pleased to share them. They have a whole nine-room residence at their disposal and, as far as I know, very little furniture. Only three people live there. Even our ministers cannot afford such luxury now.'

"I took the opportunity when the woman took a deep breath to ask, 'Who knows what kind of people they are?'

"'No, they are quiet people, decent Turks,' she said. 'One is a bankrupt former merchant who now seems to be running an oriental café, named ... named ... oh dear, I forgot. Big body, fat, like this, and the woman filled her cheeks with air, as if she were a porter. The other one is a doctor, she said, named Rusouhi, but I don't know what type of doctor.'

"'And the third?'

"'Ali Salih Bey's wife. Ah, I remembered. Ali Salih Bey. This is the former merchant. His wife is so beautiful, so charming', she said with a smile. 'When I asked who she was, the doorman said that she was Ali Salih Bey's wife and this stayed in my mind. Oh, how beautiful she is, just like the goddess of the east. But promise me that you will not fall in love', she said, threatening intimately with her index finger. 'Oh, but wait, I don't think you need to talk to him about it. Yes, yes,' she said, looking at the contract, 'the house was rented by the secretary of the Turkish embassy, Zia Bey. Look, he also signed the contract so you have to approach him.'

"'It's useless, Miss,' I said.

"'Why?'

"'It is very clear, Miss. When a Turk has a wife, there is no way he will accept a tenant under his roof. That is against their law.'

"'What do you mean? What is the reason?'

"'The reason ... not to give into temptation.'

"'Wonderful! Don't you think that's a good law?'

"'What can I say? It is both good and bad.'

"'Why?'

"'Well, it's good as long as it keeps Turkish women away from temptation; bad when their eyes wander ...'"

This is how Vahan ended his story. "I could barely free myself from that talkative woman and promised to visit her again. What do you think?"

"My opinion is that Talaat lives there under the name of Ali Salih Bey."

"How ...?"

"Look ..."

"Tell me how you figure that out."

"There is nothing to tell. Zia Bey would not rent a house for bankrupt merchants, and I do not know a more beautiful woman than Talaat's wife."

"How do you know?"

"I have seen her picture."

Vahan looked bewildered ...

***

Early in the morning, I ran to "Tiergarten." My comrade appeared.

(Top left) Talaat Pasha and German Foreign Ministaer Dr. Richard Von Kühlmann, 1915.
(Top right) President of the Turkish Parliament, Khalil Bey, in Berlin.
(Left) Turkish Minister of War, Enver Pasha.

"Finally!"

"Is he here?" he exclaimed.

"Yes!"

"Do you know the place?"

"Of course!"

"Thank God."

I told him everything in detail, starting from the station until the last moment. He listened carefully

"What time is it?"

"A quarter past nine."

"Let's go. Let's not be late."

"We still have time. Hand me one of Talaat's pictures."

He took the envelope of pictures from the shelf, rummaged through it, and pulled out the one of Istanbul Police Chief Bedri. He then asked:

"Doesn't that 'gloomy-faced' man look like this picture?"

"No, we do not have a picture of him. Give me a picture of Talaat," I said, taking out my pen.

"It is interesting when you say, Rusouhi," he said, handing me a picture of Talaat, "I have neither heard nor read such a name. Hey, what are you doing?"

"I have to scrape off the facial hair."

Suddenly, there was a knock at the door. I hid the picture in my lap. It was the janitor who brought a letter from someone and stated that it had arrived two days earlier. It was a coded message from Paris. The note was about the issue we were dealing with and the message was revealed so slowly that it left me breathless. The first words were, "We learned from a European friend that Talaat ..."

The information was finally clarified. Talaat was in Geneva. At the beginning of February he had had a meeting with a British diplomat there.

I was stunned by this coded message.

"When was it written?"

"Ten days ago."

"It's been a long time since then."

"Yes, that's the problem."

"When was it received here?"

"The janitor was right, two days ago."

Confused, we both went out buried deep in our thoughts. It was too late; Hagop was neither in Uhland, nor in Hardenberg. I showed my comrade the residence of the so-called Ali Salih Bey. We parted with the intention of meeting that evening.

When I got home, I closed the door and started scratching off Talaat's mustache in the picture. I was as impatient as a treasure-hunter who had not succeeded in finding treasure. Suddenly, there was a knock at my door. It was Eftian.

"Brother, where are you?!" he shouted, opening his arms widely. "Get dressed, let's go."

"Where?"

"My sister has invited you to dinner."

"I'm not well today, Levon."

"Impossible. I cannot go home without you."

"Another time."

"Oh, get up, I'm telling you. Today is my birthday."

"Was there no other day to be born?" I said, covering my bitterness with a joke.

"Quick, Apelian and Kalousdian have probably already left, and Karekin will come too."

"Who is Karekin?"

"Karekin from Moush. Don't you know him? He knows you."

Like a dream, I remembered the road from Erzeroum to Yerznga and our coachman Karekin.

"What is he doing here?"

"What should he do? Thinking and talking day and night about the massacres. He has gone crazy."

When we got there, the Terzibashians and Karekin were sitting in the dining room. The lady of the house complained that I had forgotten them.

"Hey!" Karekin exclaimed, embracing me like a bear in his powerful arms.

At that moment, the tragic past needed to be forgotten. He had been all over the world and now worked as a blacksmith in a carpentry workshop in the suburbs of Berlin. Apparently, at that moment, he had been talking about the tragic events. He asked a few questions about Hovnan and Sahag and then turned to the hosts.

"Let me tell my brother, I ran away in the early morning ..."

"What about your mother, your sister?" asked Mrs. Christine, curiously.

"My mother and sisters were among those deported from the Moush plain with their children. I later found out what they had been through ..."

And Karekin recounted the Golgotha of his relatives in detail, pouring out all kinds of curses on Talaat. I waited with a furious, nervous impatience for the end of the story, which reminded me of the fate of my relatives.

"All three of my sisters were kidnapped before they reached the Euphrates. The children remained with my mother. Sourig died in the evening. My mother, seeing that she could not carry the children, kept them hidden in the wheat fields. They spent the night there with other people who were hiding. In the morning, they noticed them and set the fields alight. Those who escaped were driven to the stables of Shekhlan, where the others were gathered. They were told that Talaat would spare their lives if they converted to Islam."

"Let these old stories be, for the love of God," I said, turning to Karekin.

He seemed hurt by my words. He turned to me in a dry tone and said, "Why? Have they touched a nerve in you?"

"We have heard so much that there is no desire left to hear more. Repeating 'Talaat, Talaat' will not end our pain."

"Then what do you want? Shall we erect a monument to the dog?"

"We, who believed in him after the Adana massacre, are the culprits, not Talaat."

"Sir! What are you saying? Woe to the soul of your father, Talaat!" he shouted, slamming his fist on the table.

"Shut up you disrespectful person!" shouted Eftian.

"Hey! He can't be called an Armenian. He is defending Talaat."

There was such commotion that I cursed myself for coming. Kalousdian and Apelian entered the room and remained at the threshold of the door. Karekin, who had completely lost himself, jumped up and snatched his hat from Eftian's hand, shouting, "I will not sit at the table with such an Armenian. Mrs. Christine, I'm sorry."

I was trembling and on the verge of tears, affected by that senseless, unexpected incident.

"He's crazy, don't pay any attention," Kalousdian said.

Eftian, Apelian, and Terzibashian's efforts were not enough to change the mood. As soon as dinner was over, I apologized to the lady of the house and left.

When I got home, I started scratching out Talaat's mustache in the picture. The resemblance to Ali Salih Bey shocked me. When I sketched a European hat with a pencil on him, there were no differences left.

I took the picture and ran to "Tiergarten." My comrade had just returned from the cafeteria and was reading the newspapers. I exclaimed, excitedly, "It's him, believe me! If you remember from the station."

He looked at the picture.

"Now I have no doubt. Although the coded message caused a little confusion, I now understand."

"How?"

"I found out from Hagop that today, Ali Salih Bey visited Uhland at exactly ten o'clock. You said that he had not been there before appearing at the station."

"Yes!"

"It means that he was in Geneva at that time, where he met with a British diplomat. The coded message also confirms this conclusion."

"So?"

"We must finish the job, but first we must see him once more."

"Tomorrow ..."

"Yes, but you have to be very careful. Berlin is restless again. A slight coincidence can spoil everything. Following him in the streets is complicated. There should have been a room available in this area by now."

"That would have been very good, but now, when the job is certain ..."

"The difficult part begins now. It is no longer useful for you to be there. Hagop should be replaced by Hayg at Uhland. Seeing the same person can arouse suspicion. Whatever, the comrades will come now and we will talk."

"Consultations, again?"

"Yes, it is necessary to make a final decision."

Hagop, Hayg, and Vahan spoke one after another. The discussion now was about ending the surveillance and moving on to action. It all seemed like a surprise to my comrades. It was easier to determine where we stood during the initial work, but now it was much harder to express our opinions. According to Vahan, the facts were obvious but insufficient to take action. It was not possible to say what else was needed for certainty. Hayg thought that it was necessary to wait for an opportunity to see Ali Salih Bey's wife and confirm the identity of her husband based on her picture. Hagop was almost certain it was Talaat we were tracking, but considering it a matter of conscience, he did not want to take final responsibility.

In the end, it was decided to find a room in the area of Hardenberg No. 4, both to continue the hunt and to complete the mission successfully. Although this was not the outcome I had expected, I remained silent.

It was the evening of Sunday, March 2nd and Hagop went to work, immediately. He was diligent, open-minded, and conscientious, as well as irreplaceable in any organizational work. Our meeting had ended scarcely two or three hours earlier and we wanted to go out for dinner when Hagop came in, breathless, and stated that he had rented a room at number 37, across Hardenberg No. 4, looking out onto the street. The room would be available in three days and I could move in on March 5th.

***

I was free in the morning. My comrade would watch over Hardenberg and Hagop would watch over Azmi's shop. Instead of him, Hayg would now be in Uhland and meet my comrade at noon. But how would I spend my time before that? I cleaned and tidied my room, and, contrary to Mrs. Stellbaum's grumbling, I cleaned the hallway too. Apelian returned home from work earlier than usual, announcing the bad news. A civil war had broken out in Armenia. The Turks were still in Alexandropol, and there had been executions in the Kars region, which was under Turkish control. There had also been new massacres in the Jajour region.

The day's emptiness was filled with the day's other failure. Ali Salih Bey did not appear again and my comrade had not seen him. Of the Uhland visitors, Hayg only identified Behaeddin Shakir. What did his return from Rome and Talaat's absence mean? We considered all possibilities and assumptions, and the only thing left was the suspicion that the targets had discovered that they were being followed. In such a case, it remained puzzling that Hayg had seen Shakir. Anyway, it was necessary not to be seen in the Hardenberg area for a day or two. This precaution was already needed as soon as I moved to the new apartment.

The following evening, I went to Apelian and asked him to tell Mrs. Stellbaum that I had to move to a new apartment. I told him to tell her that my illness was getting worse. Other than general weaknesses and dizziness, there were now signs of blindness. The previous day, I had been with Professor Cassirer again and he had said that everything was the result of severe nerve damage. The gas lamp was very harmful to me. I could not read a single line at night. Now, I had to rent a room with electric lighting. I paid that month's rent to Mrs. Stellbaum. I wanted her to know that I was satisfied with her in every way and would have stayed were it not for my physical condition. I asked him to inform her of these developments as it was difficult for me to do so. The following evening, I went to my new apartment with Hagop, promising to visit Mrs. Stellbaum again.

My new landlady, a young widow named Mrs. Dittmann, was similarly organized and tidy. Everything was clean and tasteful. She had a maid and the apartment was peaceful, giving the impression of a monastery. The entrance was from the courtyard, through a special iron door, typical for modest buildings, which opened and closed with a screw-shaped bolt. The room was airy. The large, wide window was covered with a luxurious lace curtain. There was a table-like shelf by the bed, a desk, armchair, cupboard, chairs, etc. Directly opposite, on the other side of the wide street, was the residence of Ali Salih Bey. The thick curtains barely separated at the central opening and created a wedge-shaped slit. There was a lot going on in the street at that moment. Workers were returning home and almost everyone was trying not to waste time. Some were reading newspapers while walking, some were eating ...

I could not sleep at night. I had mixed feelings. On the one hand, I was overwhelmed by the fact that I had located my target and was only 25 meters away from the monster. On the other hand, I was concerned whether I would succeed.

Early in the morning, I tidied up my room and took my place at the desk with my German textbook in front of me, just for the sake of it. It was a clear spring day, with the sun shining on the windows of the building opposite. There was a knock at my door and the maid came in with tea, bread, and cheese. Half an hour later, Ali Salih Bey appeared on the sidewalk. So soon! It was a surprise. It was not even 9 o'clock. He, as usual, looked up and down the street. He had a folder under his arm. I immediately took my weapon and went out. When I got to the entrance, he was almost in front of me. He was going in the opposite direction across the sidewalk towards the beginning of Hardenberg street. This was unusual, too. I immediately pulled the door but it did not open. I tried hard but the same thing happened. I realized that I had to turn the bolt first. It did not move. I was losing my mind as I pulled and pushed the door. Nothing. I felt complete despair. I ran to the maid for help as the door was not actually locked. The maid arrived but the door would still not open.

It took more than ten minutes to turn the bolt with incredible effort to get out. But where was he? There was not a trace of the target.

Confused, I looked around for a moment and headed in the direction of the zoo. It was pointless, so I stopped. Suddenly, I thought that he might have gone to Uhland using the parallel streets. I arrived at Uhland and waited for more than half an hour. No one went in or out. Another half hour passed. My brain stopped working. Had I missed him?

Could the criminal have entered Azmi's shop? I crossed the square and entered the store. I saw the other monster for the first time, a step away.[*] He did not even move his head; he was reading a newspaper. I had a strong urge to fire a bullet straight into his forehead. His son emerged from the back corridor, which was covered in carpets. I bought a pack of cigarettes and left.

It was noon. I did not know what to do. There were a lot of policemen everywhere. I walked around and I came to the restaurant. My comrade, sitting in his usual place, was looking through the newspapers. I informed him of my doubts: what if the prey had run away?

During the previous five or six days, he had not left the house before 10:00 am. He went to Uhland and returned home at 11:00 am. He had come out that day before 9:00 am with a folder under his arm. He could, of course, have gone somewhere else, such as the British Embassy. Anything could have happened.

I returned home. A handyman had repaired the bolt on the door.

---

[*] The "other monster," Jemal Azmi, was a CUP activist and governor of Trabizon during World War One. He was responsible for the mass murder of Armenians in that province. He was assassinated in Berlin, 1922.

CHAPTER EIGHT

The Monster Fell on the Sidewalk

I was already sitting at my desk at daybreak. I had tidied up my room so that nobody would need to come in. I had my textbook open and was watching the opposite building across the 25 meter-wide street. It was still early. Workers, craftsmen, and businessmen were rushing to work. Sometimes, noisy trucks passed by.

I was trying to see inside the building opposite through the narrow opening of the curtains on my window, but it was in vain. There was a knock on my door and the maid came in with some tea. Mrs. Dittmann appeared behind her and I looked flustered, as if I had been caught committing a serious misdemeanor. She tried to appear younger and more pleasant than she could possibly ever be. I did not understand anything of the brief conversation we had. I guessed from the hand movements that it had something to do with the broken bolt on the door, which had been repaired and fixed. She gave me a key, for which I had nothing to pay.

"*Danke schön*," I said, to keep matters short.

The hours passed. 10, 11 o'clock ... No one emerged from the building across the street. In the afternoon, I received some belated news from my comrade. A coded letter had been received from Paris. It relayed a message from Constantinople that Talaat lived in Berlin, at 4 Hardenberg Street, under the name of Ali Salih Bey. This was very important news.

I sat motionless in my room for hours watching the opposite building. No light was turned on.

I got out of bed in the morning and felt so broken, as if I had been walking all night. Flu, aches, fever; it was unpleasant. I was looking forward to 10-11 o'clock. Nobody and nothing. It was even doubtful whether anyone resided there.

In the afternoon, my comrade, sitting by the window overlooking Azmi's shop, was reading the news section of the newspaper.

When he heard me grumble, he responded, "If it was an easy task, it would have been finished in these three years. It would have been over by now."

"I suggest we send Vahan to the landlord."

"Why?"

"To find out whether anyone resides in that house."

"The only safe way to check is through surveillance."

During the night, a light flickered in the front room like a candle and then went out.

The next day, as usual, I kept watch until 11 o'clock. Now there was no doubt in my mind that Talaat had escaped. There was also no trace of "gloomy-face," as Rusouhi was called. At noon, I suggested we restart the surveillance at Uhland.

I had a terrible night, overwhelmed by nightmares. I woke up exhausted. After 10 o'clock in the morning, the walls of my room seemed to be suffocating me. Why was it so crucial to have that miserable bolt on the entrance door?

My comrade was in high spirits in the afternoon. Hagop had been able to identify Behaeddin Shakir among several visitors to Uhland.

"Since he is here, it means that Talaat will also appear soon."

"And why are you not assuming that Shakir might also leave?"

"If that were the case, he would have left already. If Talaat had escaped, Shakir would have thought about saving his own skin."

His response was logical, so I turned around and went home again.

That night I saw my mother in a dream. I was leaving Yerznga for the Balkans. The young women were preparing my provisions for the road in the smoke and ashes of the baking house. My mother was motionless on her knees near the clay oven (*tonir*). The little ones were around me with fresh pieces of bread in their hands. Countless flies covered Markar's mouth and head because there was honey on his bread. It was dusk outside. The larks fluttered their wings. When they had filled my shoulder bag, I took it and bid them farewell ...

Then, my mother stood up and came out with me. We walked in silence. Her company was discomfiting. I wished we had already parted so that I would not think about her anymore.

"Mother, how far are you going?" I asked.

"To Sourp Nishan, my son. I have vowed to take you there."

We reached St. Nishan. My mother touched my face, shoulders, and hands like a blind person and murmured, "One by one, you all grow up, take on wings, and fly off, while I stay here."

I told her to go home and continued on my way.

The sun, a fire-like disk, appeared over the horizon from St. Nishan. Suddenly, I heard my mother's broken voice calling from behind me. Looking back, I saw that she was still standing there. I turned to her and asked:

"What's the matter, mother?"

"Are you leaving?" she asked in a barely audible voice.

"Of course. Didn't I tell you to go back?"

Then, she began to walk home silently. After a few steps, she shook her head and increased her pace.

"Mother!" I shouted, but she no longer looked back. She kept on walking, then ran, and suddenly disappeared.

It was morning. I could not calm my nerves and cried like a child.

Later, around 11 o'clock, a car stopped on the sidewalk in front of the building. My heart was pounding. The gloomy-faced Rusouhi and a young woman in a black coat got out of the car. While Rusouhi paid the driver, the woman daintily went up the five or six wide steps and entered the house. I took a deep breath. There was no doubt that she was Talaat's wife. I froze looking out of my window for about two hours. There was no more movement. It was imperative to tell my comrade about this positive surprise.

When he heard this important news, he let me know that he had received a coded letter from the United States by air mail. The comrades, affirming the information from Constantinople, were asking us to finish the Talaat business by all possible means.

Appropriate measures had been taken to punish the other perpetrators and we were not to be concerned about them. The coded letter was in response to our request of early February.

On the morning of March 13th, Talaat's wife appeared on the sidewalk and moved slowly up the street. I knew from Constantinople that she was a capable person and interested in politics. She had been involved in her husband's affairs when he was a simple telegraphic official, then Minister of the Interior, and then Grand Vizier. It was said that she had great influence on him. She was known as a publicist and was no stranger in the narrow circle of Ittihadists. She would sometimes appear on the streets of Constantinople without a veil. Nevertheless, I found it unpleasant to follow her. It was most disagreeable to follow a woman.

She reached the zoo and went inside. It was spring. The green plants and trees that had just emerged from the snow looked as if they had been nicely washed and cleaned. I found the precise rows of marigolds and perfectly regular bushes more interesting than pleasing. She walked confidently to the fountains, where water shot up and descended like rain, forming a fine mist over the mossy ground. Suddenly, my heart was filled with endless longing for our homeland, to see the turbulent Euphrates entering its gorges through steep mountains that kissed the clouds, roaring like thousands of tigers, bubbling with rage, and eventually gushing and flowing on its way.

The lady arrived and stopped there like many others. Gertrude Golt was right. She was beautiful with her pale face, large eyes, thick black hair, and a small mouth. She was sleek and graceful like an Armenian woman. It was evident that she was just admiring the beauty of her surroundings. Yet, it was with her knowledge and on her husband's orders, that tens of thousands like her were sentenced to starvation in the deserts or to wither away in Turkish harems. Here she was, still able to enjoy the benefits of nature in peace.

I returned home.

The next afternoon, I learned from Hagop that Uhland had seemed like a place of pilgrimage. So many people had come and gone. They included Behaeddin Shakir, Dr. Nazim, Ismail Hakki,

Dr. Rusouhi, even Jemal Azmi and six or seven others. Of course, Talaat would appear too.

I went home again and came face to face with Mrs. Dittman in the hallway. She was more than kind but I had still been unable to establish with her the simple, neighborly relationship that I had had with Mrs. Stehllbaum. Dittman always confused me, and the more she wanted to communicate, the harder it was for me to understand what she was saying. Yes, my health is good, so is my work. I did not know why she always assumed that something bad had happened to me. She smiled as I entered my room.

That evening, Rusouhi emerged from the building with a basket. He soon returned and the front door of the building did not open again. As soon as it got dark, a candle was lit in the front hall, but it suddenly disappeared and reappeared in the room to the left of the balcony. It did not last long there either, and the building was once again shrouded in darkness.

I got up earlier than usual the next morning. The sun was shining on the window of the building opposite. I was about to finish my tea and wanted to bring the armchair to the window when I suddenly saw Talaat on the balcony of the building in front of me. I was stunned. Was it him? Yes!

He took a step or two forward, carefully examining the sidewalk, up and down. He then hung his head as if under the weight of his thoughts. Evidently, life was not easy after the crimes committed in the desert. In any case, even though five or six years had passed, fear was inseparable from him. He carried two public death sentences on his broad shoulders: one from the Constantinople Military Tribunal and another one from the Armenian Revolutionary Federation. The first was probably of moral significance for him: instead of honoring his great "patriotic" mission, his own people in his native country had sentenced him to death as an ordinary criminal. But time could heal this "misunderstanding" as future generations would appreciate the work he had done. However, there was also the ARF's verdict. He had failed to kill all the leaders of that organization, but who remained of those he knew? There was, in fact, one person: Garegin Pasdermadjian. Did he not remember their last conversation in Constantinople?

Talaat lifted his thick wrist, rubbed his forehead, and went inside. I looked at the clock; it was 10 o'clock, his usual time to go to Uhland. I picked up my pistol, ready to leave. Suddenly, he appeared at the door and began to descend like an elephant. By the time I got out onto the street, he was already on the opposite side, walking towards Uhland Street. Cold judgment told me that this time it would be impossible to get rid of me, but the excitement had also created a storm inside my head.

"Catch up! Run! Cross to the other sidewalk, and [shoot] sideways into his back! His waist! His head! Quick! Cross the street!"

I stepped onto the street to catch up with him, but suddenly a thought held me back. I was now questioning something that had been clear in my mind a thousand times over. Was it really him?

"Cross the street! Cross! Cross! Straight to the forehead! Quick! Quick! Quick! Run!!"

I caught up with him on the opposite sidewalk and then quickly continued ahead of him. Then, almost running, I crossed the street onto the opposite sidewalk, where he was. I started to walk towards him. There was around 20-30 meters between us. We were getting closer and closer, as he walked casually, carelessly swinging his cane. There was very little distance between us, when an amazing calm pervaded my whole being. As we drew level with each other, Talaat looked at me directly and we made eye-contact ... Without realizing it, something made me murmur, "Hey Talaat." He heard me and his whole body stirred. His own name had terrified him. There was the shiver of death glimmering in his eyes. He knew what was coming ... He tried to turn around to avoid his fate, but I pulled out my pistol and shot him in the head in an instant ...[*]

For a split moment it seemed that Talaat had only been shaken from the shot as his powerful body tensed up; but then he fell on his face like a sawn oak tree crashing with an enormous rumble. A

---

[*] This paragraph is taken from Tehlirian's own handwritten edit on the Armenian language proofs of *Remembrances*. His revised wording was not included in the Armenian publication of his memoir. See *Vem Hamahaygagan Hantes*, p. 351.

woman screamed and fell to the ground. A man ran towards her. I had never thought it would be that easy to slay the beast. For a second, I had the urge to fire all the bullets into his back but, instead of firing, I threw my pistol away. Heavy, dark-colored blood started to immediately form a pool around Talaat's head. It was as if crude oil was spilling out of his shattered skull.

"He killed a man," I heard a voice say.

I looked around and noticed people standing on all sides, staring.

"Grab him! He killed a man!" someone shouted, moving his hands toward me like a net.

But the pool of blood seemed to have mesmerized me.

"Hold him, hold him!" shouted others.

I went past them and nobody tried to stop me. However, when the shouts behind me multiplied, my petrified nerves suddenly gave way, and I threw myself into the neighboring street. I did not know what to do. People chased me, making a terrible noise, while I ran away. Someone coming from ahead caught me.

Could I have avoided it? Probably, if I had thought about it and planned in advance. The crowd immediately surrounded me. I did not understand what they wanted from me. They shouted, waved their fists, and attacked me, though I had nothing to do with them. Someone pulled at me, others started beating me mercilessly. Someone hit me over the head with an object. My eyes darkened and I knelt to avoid falling. Blood was dripping down my face. Many hands and feet landed on me.

"What do you want? I am an Armenian, he is a Turk. What do you care about it?" I shouted in helpless fury.

Suddenly, the crowd gave way and a policeman helped me up.

"They are Armenians, they are Turks," said the crowd, calming down.

My head was bleeding. Other police officers arrived. The crowd retreated. They took me to Hardenberg Street. The monster was lying in the same position on the sidewalk. The police and crowd surrounded him at a distance.

We passed by ....

The furious policemen threw me into a cell at Charlottenburg police station. Then, an official appeared, wrapped my head in bandages, and took me out. I was taken by car to the secret police station. There were a lot of officials and policemen there. One of them took me to a larger cell.

I was filled with an inner satisfaction that I had never felt before. The long-lasting nightmare that had weighed on me like lead had suddenly disappeared. Everything seemed to have changed. My constrained soul was now flying high and wide. Seemingly freed, my thoughts were in all the familiar corners of the world. Lord God, there was so much to think about! I had many thoughts in my head, everything and everywhere, which shone and faded.

I had calmed down by the time I was taken to the chief of the department. I answered questions about my identity, but when he started questioning me, I asked for an Armenian interpreter with the help of my French. They found someone who knew French. I objected, saying that my French was not good enough to answer their questions correctly. Then they took me back to the cell.

It was evening when they took me out again. One of the two policemen took a coil of durable thread from his pocket, the ends of which were tied to a piece of wood that served as a handle. He wrapped the thread around my wrist and held the sticks in his hand. We then left. As a child, I used to play "horse" with my peers in that way. The other policeman joined us with an envelope of papers under his arm. Crossing a number of streets, we stopped in front of a building with a sign saying, "Central Police Station." Passing through several corridors on the second floor, we entered a spacious room. Here, a short, round man was given the envelope in which my pistol appeared. He recorded my name in the register and nodded to the standing officer. I went out with him. There were prisoners who were sweeping and cleaning the corridors. I was in the jail next to the police station. My cell was medium-sized, with a small window and a wooden folding bed that was fixed to the wall. Another piece of furniture was attached to the wall and when I pulled at one end, it opened up as a table. Moving other planks, I had a bench, where I sat down. I noticed a cupboard on the wall to the right. Although I was very tired, I got up and opened it. It contained a plate, a wooden spoon, a saltshaker and two earthenware pots, one of which was full of water, for washing in a clay pot. There was no soap.

It was getting dark in my cell. The electric light hanging from the ceiling was very high and could only be switched on from the outside. The iron door had a round hole, five to six centimeters in diameter, which was closed from the outside with the catch of a movable board. Lying on the bed, I wanted to recall what had happened, but in vain. I felt a chaos of opposing feelings inside me: satisfaction that the operation was over, bitterness that prison was inevitable. I also started feeling the pain of the beating I had received in the morning. My ribs felt crushed, the wound on my head was throbbing, the skin on my knees was grazed, and my body was burning in the heat.

In the evening, I was led to a room on the second floor. A bespectacled official with a goatee beard was sitting in front of the entrance by a desk, where I also saw my gun. Standing next to him was an Asiatic-looking young man who stared at me with burning anger. Another official was flipping through papers under a lamp at another desk to the right. On a corner of a table was some white linen, a European-looking, blood-stained hat, and a cane. The bearded official began to interrogate me. I had a hard time understanding him and after answering one or two questions, I asked for an Armenian interpreter. The investigator seemed stubborn, repeating the same things in different ways, continuing the torrent of questions. He wondered why and how I had killed "Talaat Pasha." How could I answer those questions in German, especially as I had already decided to describe the horrors of the monster and bring the perpetrators to justice? The investigator took my gun and started pointing it at my neck and forehead to find out how I had fired. Not receiving an answer, he put the weapon down and looked at the young Asiatic-looking man.

"Shameless man! How could you kill that lion of a man?" shouted the latter in Turkish.

His question surprised me more than him being a Turk.

"Just as he killed a million innocent people," I replied.

"So, he knows Turkish?" shouted the investigator.

"Better than me," replied the young man.

"So, we can interrogate him with your help. Ask him, please, why he killed Talaat Pasha?"

The young man's voice trembled as he repeated the question in Turkish. I categorically refused to answer any question in Turkish.

The young man approached the other official. The latter wrapped Talaat's hat in several newspapers and handed it to him along with the cane. The young man then left. He was probably a relative or a close friend.

The investigator only now offered me a seat and his attitude changed. I vaguely understood that he was talking about the Armenian massacres. He mentioned Lepsius' name once or twice. I repeated my request to have an Armenian interpreter.

There was a lamp in the cell. In less than a quarter of an hour, it went out and everything was covered in darkness. The prison was so silent that one had to listen carefully to sense that a guard sometimes passed through the corridor. I was preoccupied with thinking about what I would say if I was summoned for questioning the following day through an Armenian interpreter. Sometimes, countless thoughts stirred in my head and I could not sort them out. At other times, I felt like everything was flying out of my head, which was throbbing like an empty barrel ...

It seemed to me that one had to start with the massacre of prominent Armenian public figures, members of parliament, deputies, revolutionaries, editors, teachers, doctors, pharmacists, lawyers, and intellectuals in Constantinople. Talaat was himself once saved by taking shelter with these people during the repression by Sultan Abdul Hamid ...

It seemed to me that it was necessary to first explain the difference between the Hamidian massacres and the deportations. So, what were those differences, I asked myself? The Hamidian massacres lasted four, five, six days, at most a week. Some women and children were able to escape. The wild mob, quenching its thirst for blood, went on to plunder and rob. Many Armenians took advantage of this opportunity and avoided death. The deportations were something else: they were like an ongoing, long-lasting earthquake from which no one could escape.

Whether sleeping or awake, standing or not, it continued day and night, until the last person died. It took as long as necessary to kill the victims by the sword or the axe, by shooting, or through thirst or starvation, beaten or burnt to death, and so on. It had not been possible to understand at first what deportations were all about, but they gradually became apparent, as gendarmes ordered the victims to keep walking. Victims left their birthplaces and looked back to see their homes looking smaller and smaller, the domes of their churches no longer visible, until they were in wide open fields and did not know where they were ...

My head hurt. Oh, how my head hurt! I could not even see anything at a distance. I was in a furnace, as if a muttering numbness pervaded me. Wasn't it right to start with Talaat's direct orders? Recall, for example, the Sirkeji, Selimiye, Sara-Bournou, Sinjan Keoy, Ayash, Kalejik, Chankiri and other incidents and deportations. But how should one describe those events and who would believe the truth of what I said? In the best-case scenario, the bearded investigator could ask:

"Very well. How come nobody in Turkey shouted, 'Enough is enough and end the slaughter?'"

"Of course, there were some among the subordinates who were stunned upon reading Talaat's order. For example, Governor Mazhar, wrapped in a nightgown, shouted, 'Oh, I am sorry! How can I issue an order to kill innocent people? No, Eshraf does not accept! I am sorry!'"

But then, you have Arif from Selanik, red faced, pulling a piece of paper out of his pocket, pointing to it, and shouting:

"In that case, I am the governor. Where is hoja Kara Mehmed from the village of Kala?"

"Effendi!" can be heard from the crowd in the darkness, as moonlight falls on his turban, and a cabbage-like shadow is cast on the ground.

"The 1,200 Armenians of Engiuri and 350 of Stanos villages, stand together," Arif shouts. And the cabbage-like shadow begins to move. The cries of the victims reach as far as Kaplu Bel, where the Cretan Zeki hastily ties their arms ..."

"Believe me, I am telling you the truth like the shining sun. Captain Fishiloghlou Refik escaped from the scene of the massacre, and Hasan and Khourshid Chavush went mad and began beheading the corpses. So everywhere, from Sari-Kishla and Adana-Aleppo via Konia, to Diyarbekir and the mountains of Amanos, the ends of Ayran up to Osmaniye, Hassan Beyli, Islahiye, to Ourfa ... No, no, listen! First let me describe the heroic battle of Ourfa. Those captured, 18 to 25-year-old intellectuals, artisans, patriotic young people, each one worthier than the other, dedicated, self-sacrificing, enthusiastic young people. Only one of them weakened at the last moment."

"For the love of God, kill me with a bullet, so that we are finished sooner," he said.

"Take off their clothes so as not to damage them, then pierce their bodies," ordered Commander Halo.

And if the police investigator says, "Tell me your story in a more general way."

"General?"

"Yes, yes, in general. For example, how did massacres start in cities, in general?"

"In cities in general?"

"Yes!"

"In general, in cities, there was a three-day period given prior to deportation to the massacre sites." Every man was free to take or not to take his wife and children with him."

"What do you mean, to take or not to take?"

"Just like that."

"What if they refused to go to the massacre sites?"

"Those who disobeyed faced the death penalty."

"Where were the massacre sites?"

"First of all, the bloody deportation routes: Adabazar - Boursa - Afion Karahisar - Konia - Mersin. Kastamonou - Chankiri - Angora - Sultan Khan -Adana. Samsoun - Marsovan - Amasia - Sivas - Caesarea - Marash - Aintab - Alexandretta. Shabin Karahisar - Yerznga - Ourfa - Aleppo. Trabizon - Papert - Erzeroum - Moush - Bitlis -Ras ul Ayn ..."

"Leave out the deportation routes."

"Then the big slaughterhouses of 40,000 to 165,000 victims at Boghazlian, Iuch Deyirmenler, Kanlu Kechid, Der Zor ..."

"Enough."

"Then there were those who were killed in separate groups with axes; those killed under the blows of shovels, clubs, and hatchets; those drowned in rivers or the sea; those thrown alive into wells ..."

"Enough."

My God, my God, what was happening to me?

***

As soon as the door opened in the morning, a jail inmate entered, nodded his head amicably, smiled, and took away the bowl of water. He returned shortly afterwards with fresh water, a cup of bitter coffee, hot water, some barley, but no sugar. It was invigorating.

An hour or two later, I was led to another room in the office, where I suddenly came face to face with Kalousdian. He was overwhelmed and hugged me.

"Do not worry at all, the whole community is on its feet to defend you."

Life has a new meaning at such meetings, and I suddenly felt encouraged. He picked up the packets of candy and biscuits he had brought me from the nearby chair but then put them back in confusion.

A friendly and bespectacled man was sitting at his desk.

"Mr. Schultz, a confidential adviser to the Charlottenburg court, is going to question you now. I have been invited as an interpreter," said Kalousdian.

I recalled everything I had thought the previous night, but the investigator started by reviewing my earlier statement.

"No, I am not a Persian citizen," I said, when he reached that point.

"That is what you declared yesterday," said the investigator, as he looked at me in surprise.

"Yes, I came to Berlin with a Persian passport, but I am a Turkish subject from the village of Pakarij in Yerznga."

"Why did you resort to that falsehood?"

"It is not a falsehood. No Armenian can get Turkish identity papers after the massacres."

The investigator shook his head gently.

"Where did you go to school?"

"Yerznga National School."

"Was the certificate of that school sufficient to enter university here?"

"No. I wanted to come as an auditor."

"Do you know German?"

"Yes, as much as one could learn in three months."

"Do you know who Ali Salih Bey is, whom you killed yesterday on the sidewalk at 17 Hardenberg Street?"

"Yes, Talaat Pasha."

"What made you commit that crime?"

"I am not a murderer, but Talaat is. He annihilated our people. I could tell you about the horrors he perpetrated from Constantinople to Der Zor."

Here I should have said everything I had thought the previous night, but the investigator considered it unnecessary.

"Who helped you kill Talaat Pasha?"

"Nobody."

He was surprised and looked at me.

"Even if there were such people, I could not tell you."

It was obvious from his look that he understood my position.

"Which organization ordered you to do it?"

"It was personal."

"What issues did you have concerning Talaat Pasha?"

"Very considerable ones. It was on his orders that my mother, brother and all my relatives were killed along with all other Armenians. From that day on, I only lived in the hope of taking revenge on him."

"How long have you been pursuing that idea?"

"Since 1915, but I started to look for him three years ago."

"How did you find out that Talaat Pasha was in Berlin?"

"Coincidentally. I read it in a newspaper."

"And how did you find Talaat Pasha in Berlin?"

"One day, at the end of February, I suddenly overheard a conversation in Turkish near the zoo. One of three young Turks called a large man who was talking to them, 'my pasha,' and when they parted, the three of them kissed his hand. The latter was very similar to Talaat, whom I knew from pictures printed in newspapers. I followed him to the house at 4 Hardenberg Street. A few days later, I rented a room opposite his house. During the last ten days, I was able to verify that the so-called 'pasha' was Talaat. On March 15th, when he left his house, I shot him."

"So, do you admit that you committed premeditated murder?"

I did not understand the meaning of that question very well. I was rather surprised by the troubled expression on Kalousdian's face while he was translating what I had been saying.

"Of course ..."

"I understand that the idea of revenge may have pushed you into it, but doesn't your conscience torture you after the murder?"

"On the contrary, my heart is filled with satisfaction that, finally, the one million innocent victims have been avenged."

"So, you came to Berlin not to study, but to kill Talaat Pasha?"

"I was dreaming of studying mechanical engineering in Berlin even before the war. But everything was turned upside down ..."

The investigator sat back, playing with the pencil in his hand.

"Do you know that according to law you could face the death penalty?"

"Yes, but after succeeding in my mission, it really does not matter."

"When did you decide to commit the murder?"

"I swore to kill Talaat at my mother's unknown grave. When I got my hands on him, I would definitely kill him."

"Tell us how you killed Talaat Pasha."

"On the morning of March 15th, I suddenly saw Talaat from my window going out into the street. I took my pistol and caught up with him. I hurried down the opposite sidewalk, parallel to him. I walked ahead of him and when he was someway behind me, I crossed to the sidewalk and turned to face and shoot him. When I was a few steps away from him, he suddenly realized what was

Armenian orphaned and refugee girls at Port Said (Egypt), August, 1918.

going on. He looked terrified. He was attempting to turn around and avoid his fate, when I lodged the bullet in his head."

"Do you remember crossing the street near the music school?"

"No ..."

The investigator then paused for quite a long time in order to ascertain where the killing had taken place. From behind or from the front, from the side or from the back, at what distance and so on. I was tired. My head hurt; cold sweat was dripping from my body under the bandages. Kalousdian whispered something to him, and I was released ...

When I returned to my cell, the inmate appeared. He washed the wounds on my head and wrapped them in new bandages. He talked constantly. He knew my name, my surname, and the charges against me. He knew about the massacres and Talaat. He knew almost as much as an investigator. His watery, light-colored eyes always seemed wide open. His face was thin, pale, and expressive. Of course, I did not understand much of what he said, but my mind was clear: he thought I had done very well in killing Talaat, and he, if he were Armenian, would have done the same. But it was not worth being beheaded for killing such a monster. He wanted to let me know, as a friend, that everything depended on the preliminary interrogation. If I said that I had killed Talaat Pasha for personal revenge, I could get fifteen years of hard labor. However, if I said that I had killed him for political reasons, that is, intentionally, I could be executed. The surname of this interesting man was Levine. From what was said, I understood that he had been imprisoned for fraud. Did he want anything from me? I do not know. In any case, I gave him some of the sweets Kalousdian had brought, which he quickly put in his pockets.

A little later, he reappeared with someone else. They placed a large pot next to the door. It was noon. They were distributing food. He filled my bowl and put it on the table. There was everything in that soup except meat or fats. It was all vegetables. Levine whispered that if I wanted, he could bring me a newspaper.

Two or three hours passed.

I heard someone call out my name, "Solomon."

I approached the hole in the door. While I was thinking how to get a newspaper, he quickly slipped a copy of *Morgen Post* under the door. The main headline read in large letters, "Former Great Leader Talaat Pasha Killed in Berlin," with a sub-heading, "Political Revenge by an Armenian Student." I thought what Levine had said about "beheading" and "hard labor" were not so meaningless after all. I understood why Kalousdian had been uneasy with my general answers during the interrogation ...

Schultz continued the interrogation towards evening. This time I tried as much as possible to give a more personal account, which was in any case a large part of my motivation. When it was over, I managed to exchange a few words with Kalousdian. He said that the Turks were working hard to win the case against me. The Armenian community was working hard for the court to release me. They wanted to turn the case into a national issue. Kalousdian did not sign my testimony in the morning as an interpreter in case it prejudiced my case in court. I began to realize that the issue at hand did not only concern me and I had to cooperate with instructions from my friends outside ...

I had just returned to my cell when I heard a voice, "Solomon!"

It was Levine. He slid something under the door. It was a piece of a mirror. I could now see that I had been disfigured. One part of my nose was swollen, there was a wound under an eye, a pierced left cheek, a wound on the right side of my forehead ...

"Solomon!"

Him again.

"What?"

"Was he the Armenian ambassador?"

"Who?"

"The person who was present at the interrogation."

"Yes!"

In the morning I was summoned for questioning again, this time by Manteuffel, an interrogator at the criminal court. He was an elderly, bald man who had lost the warmth in his voice and had a stern expression. I tried my best to give a personal character to my actions, but I could not deny that I had committed the murder intentionally. At the last moment, I learned from Kalousdian that the community had decided to engage prominent Berlin lawyers for the defense.

When I returned to the cell, the door was open. Levine was washing the floor. It was as if he were connected to all the holes and crevices of the jail through a telephone network. He was quickly informed of all developments that took place there. Manteuffel was the man who had impoverished Levine by presenting an obvious accounting error as a forgery. And what forgery! A problem of only 50,000 Marks,[*] when the value of the mark had fallen, and he had not been involved at all! That was how crucial "preliminary interrogations" were. In my case, he thought I had done very well by saying, "I am not the criminal, but Talaat is."

"Wonderful. However, you should not have said it in the preliminary interrogation, but at the end of the trial. This way you appear as the aggressor. 'I am not the criminal, but Talaat is!' Do you understand what you said? The bare facts are that you killed

---

[*]   Around US$600 today.

him and he died. Who will prove that he was a murderer when only recently he had been honored here ...?"

The gloomy guard now appeared at the door and Levine quickly finished his work and left.

***

Five days later I was transferred to the central prison. It was unpleasant because I had adapted to the conditions of my life and had a friend like Levine. He was actually sadder than I was in this regard.

The central prison covered a very large area, with many buildings, yards, and sections in between. In the criminal section, the cells were arranged in two rows in a large hallway. In the center of the hall, an official near a desk took detailed notes concerning my clothes and possessions, even my handkerchief. He gave me a ticket and sent me to the first floor. There was an exceptionally clean shower room with all the necessities. As I came out of the shower, I saw that my clothes had been replaced with prison clothes. I got dressed and went back to the official who gave me a new ticket and handed me over to a guard.

My new prison cell was spacious and bright. The same kind of folding bed, table, bench, rack, etc., as in the former prison. But the cleanliness was exceptional. The supervisor explained the rules and responsibilities. In the morning, as soon as the first bell rang, I had to get out of bed, wash, and have the water bowl ready. The second bell, a quarter of an hour later, meant that I was to receive water, immediately scrub the cell, collect the garbage, and put it near the door. The third bell, after a quarter of an hour, meant that the garbage had to be placed into the garbage cart. Then, a quarter of an hour later, the bell meant that the daily ration of bread was being distributed. Later, the bell would signal the distribution of coffee. Then exercise, lunch, coffee again, dinner, and finally, bedtime. The prospect of such a life was frightening ...

"Now, I am ringing the evening coffee bell," said the guard ...

It was the same food as in the previous jail. However, there was one difference that was especially noticeable here: the regime was strict, the discipline was rigid. At night, life froze in this huge prison-world.

The following day was Sunday and the prison chaplain visited me after coffee in the morning.

Apparently, this was a regular practice for murderers in prison. The pale-faced priest, with his slender, slightly curved, chubby hands and ugly face, knew French, which was easier for me to understand. He began his preaching by letting me know that he was aware of the suffering of the Armenian people from the works of Dr. Lepsius and understood the reasons for my actions.

"However," he said, "our Lord Jesus Christ commands us to drink the cup of bitterness to the last drop to receive the glory of heaven."

Everyone in life has to fulfill their responsibilities and I patiently listened to his sermon seasoned with examples of the earthly life of our Lord Jesus Christ, his infinite forgiveness, and cosmic goodness. The priest had no words of condemnation for my actions. He was well acquainted with human weaknesses. But vengeance, even the feeling for it, was against the spirit of the Gospel. As a Christian, I should have known that. It was clear that I had been tempted to commit a crime.

"But the Lord is merciful and kind. It is enough for you to follow the path of repentance, so that you can live a more unburdened life in prison ..."

Realizing that it was difficult for me to understand German and that my French was incomplete, he promised to send me the Holy Bible in Armenian and left satisfied with his visit.

Later, when I was sitting, not knowing how to kill time, the door opened, and the guard handed me a single volume of the Old and New Testaments in Armenian. My eye fell on John's revelations, where it said:

"And I saw a beast coming out of the sea, having seven heads and ten horns. And there were ten crowns upon his horns, and on his heads were names of blasphemies. And the beast which I saw was like unto a leopard, and his feet were as the feet of a bear, and his mouth as the mouth of a lion; and the dragon gave him his power, and his throne, and great power. And one of his heads was as it were wounded unto death; and the wound of his death was healed, and the whole earth was amazed after the beast. And they

worshiped the dragon which gave power unto the beast; who is
like unto the beast, and who can do war with him? And he was
given a mouth speaking great things and blasphemies, to do his
will for forty-two months. And he opened his mouth in
blasphemy against God, to blaspheme his name, and his
tabernacle, and the inhabitants of heaven. And it was given unto
him to make war with the saints, and to overcome them; and
power was given him over all nations, and peoples, and tongues,
and nations. And all the inhabitants of the earth shall worship
him, whose names are not written in the book of the Lamb
slaughtered from the beginning of the world. He that hath ears, let
him hear. Whoever is taken captive will be taken captive. Whoever
kills with a sword, he must be killed with a sword. Here is the
patience and faith of the saints ...”

“And I saw another beast coming up out of the earth, having
two horns like a lamb, and speaking as a dragon,” it continued,
“and the first beast had all power before him, and compelled the
earth and its inhabitants to worship the first beast, whose wound
of death was healed. And he did great signs, and even sent down
fire from heaven upon earth. And he caused the inhabitants of the
earth to murmur with signs which he had given them to do before
the beast; and he spoke to the inhabitants, that they should make
an image of the beast that was wounded with the sword and was
healed. And it was given unto him to give life unto the image of
the beast, that the image of the beast should speak, and that
whosoever would not worship the image of the beast should kill
him. And he commanded all things, both small and great, and the
poor and needy, and the free and the servants, to take the mark on
their right hand or on their forehead. And that no one can buy or
sell, but only he who has the mark or the name of the beast or the
number of his name. Wisdom is here. Whoever thinks, let him
count the number of the beast, for it is the number of a man, and
his number is six hundred and sixty-six ...”

I remembered that the great Russian writer Tolstoy, in his work
War and Peace, had carried out an experiment in this regard:
designating the first nine letters of the French alphabet, that is, A-
K, as 1, 2, 3, 4, 5, 6, 7, 8, 9 and then the letters K to Z as multiples
of ten, 10, 20, 30, etc. He then calculated the sum of the letters that

Soghomon Tehlirian, 1921.

made up "L'empereur Napoleon" as 666. But, at that time, he did not know that that man would literally become a beast to man in the future …

I already knew that the Armenian massacres had lasted forty-two full months. From May 1915 to October 1918, that is, from the first deportation order to the Mudros Armistice. And I was distracted by the thought that the beast John was referring to was Talaat himself, when suddenly the door opened. I was summoned to a meeting. Three prisoners were waiting in line in the reception room. I waited for half an hour until my turn came. A monk was sitting in an armchair in the waiting room. Seeing me, he got up, crossed himself in a solemn, measured manner, and then looked at me and said in his nasal voice:

"In the name of our Lord Jesus Christ, I bless you for killing the beast and avenging us all. I will leave for Rome soon, but I will return quickly for your confession and on this basis ask the Pope to give you his blessings for your patriotic deed …"

The prison official intervened so that we would not speak in a language he did not understand. The Armenian priest presented me with a Jerusalem cross and left. The visit was such a surprise that it seemed as if the Prophet Jonah himself had visited me. Stunned by the mental anguish and confusion of the day, I returned to my cell, the Jerusalem cross in my hand …

The bells of the prison chapel were ringing. The sound was like the ringing of bells at Sourp Nshan of Yerznga! While one peal rang here, the other seemed to continue forever. Here, the bells rang as if we were having a wedding and were incomprehensible. Going in, I picked up Testaments.

The door opened again. This time we were taken into the church. The prisoners came out of the basements and stood in a row facing the back of the next person's neck, so that the newcomers could neither see nor talk to those already standing in the row or lined up behind them. Climbing the few steps of the staircase, we entered an amphitheater-shaped hall, which had a curtain that was more reminiscent of a theater than a church. The structure of the benches was astonishing. Although they were arranged in rows, each bench was a separate cage from which we could see neither below nor above, neither left nor right. We could only look directly at the stage. Wooden boards descended above our heads and similar structures separated us to our left and right. The boards under our feet were so long that they covered the head of the person sitting below.

There were books on small shelves at either side of the benches. I took the book on my right. It was a Gospel for Catholics. I put it back and took the book on my left. It was a Gospel for Protestants. I put it back, waiting for what came next.

Suddenly, the curtains opened, and the pale-faced priest appeared. He crossed himself facing us and began to pray. Then, at the end of the prayer, he gradually began to hum and then actually sang, and the hall was filled with countless voices. From the depths of the unknown, the prisoners sang both softly and fiercely, as protest and plea. It was wonderful. It seemed as if it was not people who were singing, but the hall.

When the hum had passed, the priest gave a sermon. I did not understand anything. I only knew that he was talking about "Loving one another." But how could we love each other if we could not see each other's faces?

CHAPTER NINE

The Trial

After a new interrogation by the criminal court, I was allowed to see my legal representatives. One day, at the end of the month, I was surprised to see Hagop Zorian, who had come as an interpreter with my first defense attorney [Adolf] von Gordon. During the last interrogation, there was an issue as to who had rented the residence at 37 on Hardenberg street for me. Kalousdian knew about it, as for Hagop [who had actually rented it], I thought he had already left Berlin.

"Don't worry, it does not matter. I really wanted to see you," he said.

Von Gordon, a tall and stocky man, came to collect my signature regarding my legal defense and get acquainted with my case. He had acquaintances and friends in the prison offices, and it took him a long time to get to work.

"I had just arrived on Uhland," said Hagop, "when Behaeddin Shakir appeared. Barely a quarter of an hour had passed when I suddenly saw 'gloomy-face' running hastily towards the meeting point. I immediately realized that something had happened. Within seconds, Shakir and 'gloomy-face' rushed out, almost running towards Hardenberg. I followed them faster than before and understood everything before reaching 17 Hardenberg Street, where the body was lying on the ground. There was a large crowd. I do not know what happened to 'gloomy-face.' I was standing next to Shakir. For an instant, he seemed broken-hearted and then approached the corpse with unsteady steps. A policeman stopped him. Shakir, as if waking up from slumber, looked around and automatically brought his hand to his pocket. At that moment, an elderly official signaled him to come over and take a look. Shakir, with a trembling hand, raised the cloth thrown on the corpse and confirmed that the victim was Talaat. The bullet had entered under his ear, passed through his brain, and exited from the forehead. Shakir covered Talaat's body, regained his composure, and withdrew in a quiet and slow manner. The elder officer, who had given him permission to see the body, approached and shook his hand.

"'This is a very painful event. I am so confused and shocked that I do not know what to do. Please accept my condolences, Doctor.'

"Apparently, he had been in Turkey during the great war and was well acquainted with Turkish political circles in Berlin.

"'It is not enough to express pain,' said Shakir. 'Talaat Pasha was everything to us. All our hopes are buried with him. The Pasha was always ready to pay his debts; it can be said that he carried that account in his pocket. Of course, the perpetrator is an Armenian, isn't he?'

"'Yes, a young Armenian man was arrested in a very bad condition. The people wanted to lynch him.'

"'But what are you doing here, Dr. [Ernst] Jaeckh?' Shakir suddenly asked him.

"'It is not a coincidence. I received an order from the Ministry of Foreign Affairs to check the identity of the deceased, so I drove here.'

"'Very well, but why is the corpse lying on the ground like this, in front of this crowd? Who will remove the body? Does the Prosecutor General's Office need to give permission?' asked Shakir. This so-called Jaeckh was apparently unable to answer that question. He thought for a moment, then scratched his neck, and spoke to the policeman guarding the body. He then turned around and said:

"'There is no need to get an order from the Prosecutor General's Office. The municipality has already been informed to come and move the corpse, but their vehicle has not arrived yet. Unfortunately, all the undertakers' vehicles are busy today. But one of them will probably be released soon and come to transport the body.' Behaeddin Shakir was astonished and after thinking for a while, continued:

Turkish Executioners of the Armenian Nation.

This photograph was taken four months before the armistice (1918) at Apraham Pasha's farm in Beoyiukdere. Turkish ministers went to feast there every Friday after the Selamlik ceremony. Enver personally confiscated this farm.

The CUP Camarilla of Murderers

1. Talaat, Minister of Interior, then Grand Vizier, the real head of the Ittihad. He was assassinated in Berlin, 1921.

2. Enver, Minister of War and Generalissimo, killed in Turkestan, 1922.

3. Said Halim, Grand Vizier and tool of the CUP, assassinated in Rome, 1922.

4. Jemal, Minister of Navy and Commander of the Army in Palestine, assassinated in Tiflis, 1922.

5. Dr. Siuleyman Nouman, an Ittihad bootlicker.

6. Ahmed, Enver's father.

7. Hiuseyin Jahid, Ittihad executive member and editor of *Tanin*.

8. Mejid, prince consort, friend of Talaat and Enver.

9. Ismayil Hakki, plunderer of war supplies and state treasury.

10. Hiuseyin Hilmi, former Grand Vizier and Ottoman ambassador to Vienna.

11. Rahmi, Governor of Smyrna. He saved the Armenians under his rule.

12. Unknown.

13. Midhad Shiukri, General Secretary of Ittihad Committee.

14. Selaeddin, prince consort, a close friend and informer to Talaat about palace affairs. [not identified on photograph]

Hardenberg Street, outside house number 17,
where the cross marks the spot Talaat fell.

"'So, the corpse of the prime minister of a country which remained loyal to Germany till the last minute of the Great War is shown such respect that it remains on the streets for hours?'

"Jaeckh, was obviously moved and replied:

"'Because there are no free undertaker's vehicles in the city hall, they will be very late to arrive. If you want to cover the cost, we can arrange an ordinary car.'

"It was as if lightning had struck Shakir on his head. What does this mean? Did he really say that a corpse is left on the street for hours because there was no vehicle available to pick it up? Shakir looked at Jaeckh with his mouth open and suddenly hastened off. A little further away, on the sidewalk, someone was drawing on the ground with a cane, while answering the crowd's questions and pointing in different directions.

"'The Turk had gotten there, the Armenian came like this and suddenly fired. Boom! The Turk fell on his face. The Armenian remained for a while. I shouted: He killed a man! Catch him!'

"'I shouted: he killed a man, but no one moved. At that time, the Armenian went there, then fled. We caught him on Fasanen street and almost killed him, thinking that he [Talaat] was General Kapp. The poor thing looked very similar to him, but after consideration, he turned out to be a Turk.'"

Hagop was so preoccupied with his story that he did not notice von Gordon entering.

"Please don't get up," said von Gordon.

I told him about my past, present, and everything related to the case. He made extensive notes and asked additional questions. During breaks, Hagop recounted the events.

I asked him not to visit me in the prison anymore and returned to my cell.

***

Four days later, I was called to see the second defense attorney, [Johannes] Werthauer. It was a pleasant surprise to see Vahan Zakarian with him. He had come instead of Hagop as an interpreter.

Dr. Werthauer was a handsome man, above-average height, sympathetic, and sad-faced. He had other kinds of questions. First of all, he asked about the massacres, and how I knew about them. He then asked about my childhood, birthplace, parents, feelings, and sentiments. He even asked about my dreams and experiences in the days prior to the shooting. They were things that had more to do with my person rather than my deed. He did not take notes. He had only one sheet of paper in his folder. The paper had information about me, and he sometimes looked at it and continued his gentle and patient conversation. He had another client to see and gladly allowed Vahan to stay with me for a little while.

"Yes, yes, wait, I'm not done yet," said the attorney.

Naturally, our conversation then turned to the incident. Vahan had been present at Talaat's funeral.

"The body remained unburied for five days," he said. "They wanted to transport him to Constantinople, but the government there refused." It could not have been done any other way because the European press everywhere was still dealing with this [Armenian] issue: exposing events and condemning the mass murderers.

"The Armenian communities are elated everywhere: all newspapers dedicate pages to the incident, but the Turks are not idle. They are trying to win the lawsuit in every possible way. They managed to bribe some writers who published pro-Turkish articles in newspapers. The day before the funeral, they flooded Berlin with obituaries in which they maligned Armenians. We had to publish a leaflet, in the name of the community, in which we presented the case as the just revenge of the Armenian people.

"They brought many wreaths on the day of the funeral. At 10 o'clock in the morning, a crowd had already gathered in front of Hardenberg No. 4. Foreign hats were noticeable, such as fezzes, wraps, and fur hats. Turks in green uniforms maintained discipline. Photographers and cameramen rushed there. A religious ceremony was held at Talaat's residence. The 'muezzin' of the Turkish Embassy, Shoukri Effendi, recited the Muslim call to prayer, 'Allah Ekber,' followed by the prayer of death, after which the ceremony of the judgment of the deceased was performed.

"'Here rests Mehmed Talaat Pasha, one of the most virtuous servants of Allah. Is there anyone among you who says otherwise?' shouted Shoukri Effendi.

"'No!' exclaimed the mourners unanimously.

"The clergyman started the funeral ceremony. The women were crying. The coffin was taken out at 11:30. It was a picturesque procession of the East moving solemnly through the crowded streets of Berlin. Police officers were clearing the way. The coffin was followed by a carriage loaded with wreaths. Then came 100-150 Muslim students from different places and ethnic backgrounds, Arab, Egyptian, Indian, Persian ... They walked steadily, all bearing the symbol of '*Ittihad ve Terakki.*' The corpse was followed by the clergyman in a purple dress, with a white veil, gold ribbons on his forehead, and his chest decorated with splendid medals. There were many wreaths and new ones kept arriving until the last minute. Among them were the wreaths of the German Foreign Ministry and the German-Turkish Union, representatives of various Turkish consulates, Afghans and other organizations. Former Maritime Minister Mahmout Moukhtar Pasha, Gebert, von Zimmermann, Kühlmann, General Seeckt, General Kress Kressenstein, heads of various ministries, the head of Deutsche Bank, Kuerner, the aristocrat Oppenheim, and others. The government expressed its condolences through von Schulenburg. At noon, the funeral procession arrived at the cemetery. Behaeddin Shakir could hardly utter his farewell to the deceased. The words were choking in his throat. He was surrounded by Muslims of all the Eastern nations as if he were the representative of the entire East.

"'We are ready to continue his mission. His work is our work.'

"The burial became a political demonstration. Emir Shakip Arslan spoke on behalf of the Arabs of Beirut, and Idris Bey from Kazan spoke on behalf of the Tatars of Russia. The poet Abdulkader also spoke. Then a Turk with a miserable face spoke, raising his fist and inviting those present to take an oath to avenge for the victim. Many took the oath. An Indian in a white hat, Dr. Pillay, spoke on behalf of all the oppressed people. Mirza Hassan, a lecturer at the Oriental Seminary in Berlin, quoted the Persian philosopher Saadi in his obituary, 'Humanity is one body.

When one of the parts hurts, the whole body feels pain.' Speaking on behalf of the Germans, Günther, the former director of Anatolian Railways, said, 'Now that a great man cannot be appreciated by his contemporaries, history will glorify him with its pen. We Germans bear the stamp of his sublime character in our hearts.' The president of the German-Turkish Union, Ekog, laid a wreath, with a ribbon on the coffin that read, 'To the great politician and loyal friend.'

"Dr. Ekog wished for Talaat's soul to live forever in German-Turkish relations."

***

All the interrogations ended in May. At the end of the month, I was examined by several neurologists. The trial began on June 2nd, 1921.

It was only on that day that I realized the enormous size of the prison with its adjoining buildings, warehouses, and workshops. I was endlessly led from yard to yard, through heavy and glum buildings, as laborer and artisan-prisoners were let in and out through the doors.

The Third District Court of Berlin was located next to the prison. Without seeing any streets, we reached the building and entered through a door in a long corridor on the left. There was much commotion in different parts of the spacious building. Uniformed officers were running around at a light jog. Officials were exiting and entering with folders under their arms. Civilians were standing in front of doors: they were coming to court to do official work. The entrance to the center in this part of the building was under supervision. I entered accompanied by guards and found myself in a magnificent hall. The high ceiling rested on six slightly arched columns. Below, the courtroom was divided into galleries with a semicircular courtyard in the center, surrounded by three low-risen structures of fine wooden ornaments. Entering through the back door, I took a seat in the defendant's special section with one of the guards.

It was 9 o'clock in the morning. At the center of the arched pillars, near the floor, was a huge chandelier with ribbon-shaped ornaments which were sparkling in the rays of the blazing sun

The murderer of a million Armenians, Talaat Pasha.

penetrating inside. At the furthest end of the courtroom, I was separated from the hall at a height of three or four steps. To the left, behind a separate table, sat the court secretary. In the center, at the same level, was a three or four-meter-tall table-like structure, in front of which sat the Presiding Judge of the court, Dr. Lemberg, with two assistant judges. At the other end of the building was Dr. Gollnick, the prosecutor. Below me, on the left, behind a long table, sat the three defense attorneys, the interpreter Vahan Zakarian and Kalousdian, as well as medical experts. In front of them, in a special section of the hall, near the tables, sat the twelve jurors. Little by little, back and forth, the witnesses took their seats. In the front row, I saw Mrs. Talaat, dressed in black, staring at me. Sitting to her left was Miss Leola Beilenson; to her right were Mrs. Stellbaum, Mrs. Dittmann, then the Terzibashians, Eftian, Apelian, and a few strangers. To the front, towards the center, were correspondents. From the center of the hall to the front, over a large area, were amphitheater-like benches for the public, which were completely occupied. In the parallel sections, some of those present remained on their feet, extending towards the center in the direction of the attorneys and jurors. Apart from the Germans, there were quite a number of Turks and Armenians.

The deep silence in the hall was interrupted by Dr. Lemberg, who opened the court. My defense attorney von Gordon requested that Dr. Lepsius and Liman von Sanders were included in the group of witnesses as well-informed experts on the Armenian issue.

Although the prosecutor pointed out that the incident took place not in Armenia but in Berlin, he did not object to the proposal. The aforementioned entered through the front door. In a few words, the judge reminded the witnesses of their responsibilities and divided them into two groups. Reading aloud the names of the 19 witnesses to be heard during the first session, he asked them all to leave the hall and wait to be invited inside.

The usual questions about my identity began: my childhood, my parents, my education, Yerznga, the massacres. Then, the judge paused for a long time. Finally, after completing those preliminary questions, he moved on to the period related to the case.

"When were you in Yerznga after the massacres?"

"At the end of 1916, shortly after the Russian occupation."

"Whom did you find there of your relatives?"

"No one. Everyone was killed. Only my brother's ten-year-old daughter [Armenouhi] was found with the Kurds."

"Was she the only one left out of 17 people?"

"Yes!"

"Did you visit your home?"

"Yes!"

"What did you see there?"

"Part of the house was destroyed, doors and windows were broken and looted, and the other part was occupied by Russian soldiers. I was very upset to find our house in ruins. I passed through the vast garden, which had been destroyed and uprooted, with the trees cut down. Everything was deserted. Deep in the garden, I collapsed to the ground."

"Did you lose consciousness?"

"Yes!"

"How long did it last?"

"I do not know."

"What did you do when you woke up?"

"I went to the neighbors who had converted to Islam, the only Armenian survivors in the city."

"So, you found only one [Armenian] family from the former population of the city, and they had converted to Islam?"

"Yes!"

"When the Russians captured Yerznga, did they reconvert to Christianity again?"

"Of course."

"So, they were the only ones left of the population of Yerznga?"

"Yes, and a few individuals, only twenty people."

"How long did you stay in Yerznga?"

"A few months."

"Where did you go then?"

"Tbilisi."

"When did you leave Tbilisi?"

"Autumn, 1918."

"Where did you go?"

"To the North Caucasus."

"What were you doing there?"

"I was sick."

"What illness did you have?"

"A nervous breakdown and then, typhus."

"How many times were those nervous breakdowns repeated after seeing your paternal house again?"

"Several times. I do not remember exactly."

"When did you leave the Caucasus?"

"At the beginning of 1919."

"Where did you go?"

"Constantinople."

"For what purpose?"

"To find traces of my relatives."

"There was a coup in Constantinople at that time. How long did you stay there?"

"About a year."

"Where did you go afterwards?"

"Paris."

"While in Constantinople or Paris, did you talk to deportees about the events [of 1915]?"

"Rarely, and only with my close friends."

"Who was considered the perpetrator of the atrocities?"

"I learned about them from newspapers in Constantinople."

"Earlier, did you know who was the perpetrator of the massacres?"

"No."

"When did you come to the conclusion that Talaat Pasha was the main culprit?"

"When I was in Constantinople, from newspapers."

"Did you know at that time where Talaat Pasha was?"

"No."

My defense attorney von Gordon intervened.

"I would like to ask the defendant whether he had read in newspapers that Talaat Pasha had been sentenced to death by a military court in Constantinople for the atrocities."

"I read about it when I was still in Constantinople and when Kemal, one of the prominent perpetrators of the massacres, was hanged. I knew from newspapers that Talaat and Enver Pasha were also sentenced to death."

"How many Armenians were there in Yerznga?"

"About twenty thousand."

"Was all of this population deported and did you see only one family and a few individuals on your return to Yerznga?"

"Yes!"

"I would like to know whether the defendant knows that in 1908 the Armenians, together with the Young Turks, particularly Talaat and Enver Pasha, brought about a revolution and put their national hopes in them; and that they were terribly disappointed to see the Young Turks treating Armenians worse than Sultan Abdul Hamid had done," said my third defense attorney, Niemeyer.

"I knew that Armenians collaborated with the Young Turks and that they were very disappointed when the Adana massacres took place, in which 40,000 Armenians were killed."

***

Following the suggestion of the judge, the secretary read the opening charge.

"Soghomon Tehlirian, a student of mechanical engineering, born on April 2, 1897 in Pakarij, a Turkish citizen and Protestant, who resides in the Charlottenburg area, Hardenberg street 37, near Mrs. Dittmann, has been jailed since March 16th, 1921, and is accused of the deliberate and predetermined killing of Talaat Pasha, the former Turkish Grand Vizier, on March 15th, 1921, in Charlottenburg. This crime will be considered according to Article 211 of the Penal Code. He will remain in custody on these grounds. Berlin, April 16th, 1921, Third State Court, Sentence Room 6.

"If you had to say 'yes' or 'no' to this accusation, what would you say?" asked the judge.

"No."

"Please ask him why he doesn't consider himself guilty," requested defense attorney von Gordon from the judge.

"I do not consider myself guilty because my conscience is clear."

"Why is your conscience clear?" asked the judge.

"I've killed a man, but I am not a murderer."

"You say that your conscience is clear, but ask yourself a question: Did you want to kill Talaat Pasha?"

"I do not understand that question. I have already killed him."

"I mean, did you have a plan to kill him?"

"No."

"When did you go to Geneva from Paris?"

"At the end of 1920."

"And Berlin?"

"At the beginning of December."

"Did you live at 51 Augsburger Street in January?"

"In December."

"Did you change your apartment later?"

"Yes!"

"When?"

"About a week or two before the incident."

"What was the reason for that change?"

"I had decided to kill Talaat."

"Weren't you preparing for the incident by doing so?"

"At that time, killing Talaat was a strong inner need for me."

"So, did you want to live near him?"

"Yes!"

"Tell me, please, is it true that before the incident, you checked whether Talaat was in Berlin?"

"Yes, I had seen him about five weeks earlier."

"Where?"

"When I heard a conversation in Turkish near the zoo, where someone was called 'Pasha.' When I looked behind me, I saw that it was Talaat Pasha. I followed him. At the beginning of Hardenberg Street, the three companions said goodbye and kissed his hand, and Talaat Pasha entered the house with someone else."

"So, it's not definite that you knew about Talaat Pasha being in Berlin before that, is it?"

"No."

"Why did you call on Professor Cassirer at that time?"

"I was sick. I was nervous and dizzy."

"When was the nervous breakdown during which a bank official picked you up and took you home from Jerusalemer Street?"

"I do not remember."

"Were you still living on Augsburger Street at that time?"

"Yes!"

"Who were your acquaintances?"

"Terzibashian, Eftian, Kalousdian, Apelian."

"Since January, apart from taking lessons from Beilenson, what have you done?"

"I have visited my acquaintances."

"I think you also took dance classes."

"Yes, once."

"Is it true that you had a nervous breakdown during the lesson?"

"Yes."

"How were you with your previous landlady, Mrs. Stellbaum?"

"Very good."

"Were you satisfied with Mrs. Dittmann?"

"Yes!"

"What was the reason for the killing?"

"I was walking in my room when I saw Talaat Pasha on the balcony of his house. I was deeply shocked. He was the one who killed my mother, my brother, my relatives, and thousands of my compatriots. I saw him coming out, took my gun, ran after him, and shot him."

"When you came out, did you see Talaat on the opposite sidewalk?"

"Yes!"

"Did you approach him and cross Hardenberg Street?"

"I ran across the street until I reached and passed him. Then, I crossed the street and approached him."

"Did you look at his face? Did you talk to him?"

"I did not talk to him. I leveled with him on the sidewalk and shot him."

"Did you target his head?"

"I was right next to him."

"What happened next?"

"All I know is that Talaat Pasha fell to the ground. Blood flowed from his head and a crowd of people gathered around."

"Didn't you notice that Talaat was accompanied by a woman?"

"No."

"Didn't you see Mrs. Talaat?"

"No."

"What did you do after the killing?"

"I don't remember."

"Don't you remember that you ran away?"

"I did not intend to run away. The crowd forced me to run when they attacked me."

"What did you think about your endeavor?"

"I felt heartfelt satisfaction."

"And today?"

"I am still very satisfied with what happened."

"Don't you remember what you said to the crowd during the beating to justify yourself?" asked Mr. Niemeyer.

"I said that I am Armenian and he is a Turk. It has nothing to do with you."

"I would like to know how the defendant recognized that person to be Talaat. Had he seen him before or did he recognize him through his pictures?" asked the prosecutor.

"I hadn't seen him before. I recognized him from pictures published in newspapers."

"What other nationalities lived in Yerznga besides Armenians?"

"Twenty to thirty thousand Turks."

***

After that, Judge Lemberg interrogated the witnesses.

A Charlottenburg merchant, Essen, related how I leveled with Talaat and fired.

"A woman passed by a little ahead and fainted. First, I lifted the woman, thinking that she was injured. Then, I ran after the defendant and arrested him on Fasanen Street. Naturally, a crowd gathered. People were beating the defendant mercilessly. One of them was constantly hitting him on the head with a key, others were shouting, screaming ...”

From the examination of the witness, it was revealed that the unconscious woman was a passer-by and not Talaat's wife, as the newspapers wrote. Mrs. Talaat was informed at the request of the judge that her testimony was no longer needed and she could leave.

The next five witnesses repeated the same thing from different angles. Charlottenburg Police Chief Knaus, who was the first to interrogate me, tried to prove that the murder was premeditated. Then, my first landlady, Mrs. Stellbaum, was called. It seemed like a long time had passed and I realized how much I had missed her. For a short time, that foreign woman became like a relative to me. She looked at me with her elderly eyes and said:

“Yes, the defendant lived with me. I can testify well about him. He was very decent and modest. I do not have a maid and I do the housework myself, but he did what he could not to burden me. He didn't let me clean his shoes. He was very modest and honorable in every way.”

“Did he get sick when he was at your house?” the judge asked.

“He was very nervous. He could not sleep.”

“Did you know that he was visiting a doctor?”

“Yes, Professor Cassirer.”

“Weren't you surprised that he suddenly moved?”

“How not! In response to my question, he said the doctor had told him that gas light was harmful to him and that he needed sunlight. I believed him because he was very nervous.”

The expert witness, Dr. Liepmann, interrogated her at length about my mental state.

My other landlady, Mrs. Dittman, testified about me in the same way. Regarding the incident, she said:

“On the morning of March 15th, the day of the incident, my maid informed me that the gentleman was crying in his room. I said, ‘Leave him alone, maybe one of his relatives has died.’ He left a little later.”

“Did you have any doubts?” the judge asked.

"Not at all, until my maid came home and said, 'Mr. is killed,' and I replied, 'Are you crazy?' Then I learned that he had killed someone."

"Was the defendant calm as normal that day?"

"One day, one of his acquaintances came and said that he was ill and needed a sunny room," said Mrs. Dittmann, intending to tell a long story ...

"Didn't you notice anything when he was with you?"

"No."

"Was he studying?"

"Yes, he came out very rarely."

"Did he have any visitors?"

"Not at all."

"Have you ever seen him nervous?"

"He was shy. He could not look at my face, he was confused."

"Was he intimidated?"

"He seemed terrified."

"Like being persecuted by heavy thoughts?"

"Yes!"

"Did you noticed whether he suffered from any ailments?"

"No, but he said he was sick, nervous."

"Defendant," said the judge, "Who went to Mrs. Dittman to rent an apartment for you?"

"The president of the Union of Armenian Students."

"Is he here?"

"No ..."

"Did the defendant look upset or depressed?" Liepmann asked Dittmann.

"He was hesitant, at least in my opinion. The young man was very hesitant," she said with a smile, turning her gaze to Liepmann.

"Did you see the gun when the defendant was with you, Mrs. Stellbaum?" the judge asked my former landlady.

"No."

"Did the defendant have a lot of possessions?"

"No, he only had one chest that was always open."

"Defendant," the judge turned to me, "Where did you keep the gun?"

"In my chest."

"Did you keep it in the chest when you were at Mrs. Stellbaum's house as well?"

"Yes, it was in my chest."

"I have not seen it," murmured Mrs. Stellbaum.

"It is surprising that you often looked at the trunk and did not see the gun."

"I cannot say that I have looked at the trunk that often," said Mrs. Stellbaum with restrained anger ...

It was the turn of my young teacher, Leola Beilenson.

"Did you give the defendant language lessons?"

"Yes."

"What can you say about his manners and behavior?"

"He took classes from January 18th. At first, he studied very well, but in the end, he was distracted."

"Did he tell you that he was ill and went to the doctor?"

"At the end he said that he was seeing Professor Cassirer, he was taking medicine, and it was difficult for him to work. During one lesson, I noticed that he could not even read what he had written. It was obvious that he was ill and I told him afterwards that it was pointless to continue the lessons. After that, the lessons were interrupted."

"When was that?"

"Approximately in the second half of February."

"Did he come again later?"

"Once he came and said that he felt poorly. He seemed to be in a state of mental anguish, very sad."

"Did he talk about his tragedy?"

"Only once, when I asked about his homeland during the lesson. He said that he no longer had a homeland and that all his relatives had been killed. The anguish was so obvious in his answer that I no longer wanted to ask."

"Is it possible that the classes were interrupted at the beginning of March?"

Talaat's funeral in Berlin.

"Maybe."

"Maybe shortly before March 5th, after changing the apartment?"

"He did not come from his new apartment anymore."

"Perhaps there was a real reason that he had to change his apartment and interrupt his classes?"

"I don't know. In March, about a week before the incident, he informed me over the phone that he had changed his apartment and that he wanted to resume classes once he felt better."

"Defendant, why did you interrupt the lessons?"

"My health was not well."

"Weren't you bored when you were with Mrs. Dittmann?"

"Why should I be bored?"

"Because you no longer had lessons."

"The lessons did not give me special pleasure ..."

As far as I could understand, the problem was hovering around the question of "premeditation" that was a grey area concerning mental health. Yervant Apelian was called. Due to the line of questioning, he told the court about my dizziness during the dance class, my visit to the doctor, my life, and my condition. Regarding the last point, the judge asked.

"Did he ever talk to you about the reason behind the loss of his relatives?"

"No."

"Did he ever mention Talaat being in Berlin?"

"No."

"Did he inform you in advance about his intention to move to Mrs. Dittmann's?"

"No, but one day he asked me to tell Mrs. Stellbaum that he wanted to leave the apartment because the doctor had said the gas lamp was harming him."

"So, he justified his move by his health condition?"

"Yes."

"Did he tell you that he found an apartment on Hardenberg Street?"

"No, I did not know where he was."

"Shortly before he moved, did you notice any change in his manners and behavior?"

"No."

"Hadn't he talked to you about killing Talaat?"

"No."

"But haven't you been together often?"

"After that [the assassination], I was surprised about it too."

"Did you know that Talaat Pasha lived on Hardenberg Street?"

"No."

"Didn't he talk to you about Talaat?"

"No."

The judge sat back.

"When you Armenians talk about the massacres, what do you mostly focus on?" asked my attorney von Gordon.

"The atrocities that we faced."

"Didn't the defendant tell you that he had lost his relatives during the massacre?"

"Yes, once. But we did not talk about it at all."

"That's very surprising," interrupted Liepmann.

"One day, I had Lepsius' book, *Deutschland und Armenien*, in my hand. I translated a few lines. Suddenly, he took the book from my hand and said, 'Let us not open old wounds.'"

"So he avoided remembering those events?"

"It seems so ..."

The interrogation of Eftian and Terzibashian also did not reveal anything. But here was Schultz, a confidential adviser at the Charlottenburg court who interrogated me on March 16th, and he began to argue that the crime was predetermined.

"I still remember the defendant's answers quite clearly," he said. "He confessed without difficulty that he had killed Talaat knowingly and intentionally." And when I asked him the reason, he said that Talaat was the man by whose order his relatives and compatriots were killed in Armenia. That's why he decided to take revenge for his relatives and came to Berlin for that purpose. He acquired the gun in his homeland. He tried to find the traces of Talaat and, after finding him, rented a room right opposite his residence to watch and observe him. One day, noticing that Talaat was leaving, he picked up his gun and approached him. To avoid any mistakes, he went in front of him, satisfying himself that the passer-by was actually Talaat, and killed him.

Meanwhile, the drowsy prosecutor took notes and asked further questions. The interest in the audience was sharpened. My attorneys tried to prove Schultz's testimony worthless. The struggle started. First, Kalousdian, the translator, delivered a significant blow to the testimony. He said that I was not able to give evidence that day because I had been beaten, smacked about, and exhausted. Schultz confirmed that I had indeed been tortured but he argued that I gave the impression of being completely calm. The judge wanted to find out whether my answers had been led by the line of questioning. My defense attorney, Niemeyer, questioned the translation of my statements and asked whether Kalousdian hadn't related his own personal impressions. He reminded Schulz that the translator had brought me candies, and when Schulz had shouted his objections to giving sweets to a murderer, the translator had responded, "What murderer! For us, he is a great man." Von Gordon grabbed Kalousdian's testimony to draw attention to the intrusion of personal dispositions in the translations provided. For his part, Kalousdian said that he had been so skeptical of the accuracy of my answers that he refused to sign the interrogation. The judge clarified these circumstances, which made my initial statements worthless ...

***

After a half-hour break at noon, the trial resumed with the interrogation of Mrs. Christine Terzibashian. Counselor von Gordon asked the judge to question the witness about the massacres.

"Where did you live during the war?" the judge asked the witness.

"I was in Garin [Erzeroum]."

"Is that your homeland?"

"Yes!"

"Were there deportations in Garin?"

"In July 1915, the inhabitants were gathered and informed that they had to leave the city."

"Were there any announcements in the city that Armenians were obliged to emigrate?"

"First, they informed the rich families of the city through the police. Then, they informed everyone else that the city would be evacuated because it was in a dangerous military area. The rich people of the city found out about it eight days earlier, and the rest of us only one day before the deportations. Then, it turned out that what had been announced was a hoax and only the Armenians would be exiled."

"Were people taken away from the city at once?"

"Four times."

"In four groups?"

"Four groups in eight days."

"Did those who were left behind know what happened to the previous groups?"

"No."

"Was there a certain destination?"

"First, we had to go to Yerznga."

"What group were you in?"

"The second."

"Describe. How many people were deported, how far did you proceed, and what happened?"

"Our family consisted of 21 people. Only three of them survived."

"How big was the group?"

"500 families."

"How did your relatives die?"

"Our family consisted of 21 people. We rented three ox carts and put whatever we could in them. We took food and money with us. We thought we were going to Yerznga: my father, mother, two brothers, the eldest 30 years old, three boys, the youngest six months old, my sister and her husband, six sons, the eldest 22 years old. I saw with my own eyes the loss of everyone. Only three members survived ..."

The woman's voice trembled. She took her trembling hand to her chest and stood up.

"I swear that they were deported by orders from Constantinople."

"In what way?"

"When we left the city, the police gathered in front of the gates of Garin fortress and checked for weapons: knives, umbrellas, and so on. We reached Papert [Baiburt]. As we passed in front of this city, we saw corpses here and there."

"Were the corpses from the previous groups of Garin?"

"No, from Papert. Then we reached Yerznga. They promised to provide us lodgings, but they did not even allow us to drink water."

"How did the massacre, during which your relatives were killed, take place?"

"When we came a long way, they separated 500 young men from the group."

"One of them was one of my brothers who managed to escape and come to us. We dressed him in women's clothes. The other young men were slaughtered ..."

The judge's eyebrows rose in surprise. His eyes widened.

"What happened to the selected men?" he asked.

"They were killed and thrown into the water."

"How do you know?"

"I saw it with my own eyes."

"Did you see them being thrown into the water?"

"Yes, they were thrown into the river, and the current carried all of them away."

The judge gulped.

"What happened to those who were left behind?"

"We cried and cried, but we were pushed forward with bayonets."

"By whom?"

"Thirty policemen and a detachment of soldiers."

"What happened to your relatives?"

"Everything was emptied from the carts. We carried whatever we could on our backs and reached Malatia. But they did not allow us to enter the city and drove us to the mountains. Here, the remaining men were separated from the women. Everyone was axed to death, only ten meters away from us ..."

This was all very unusual for the judge, and he had a hard time conducting the interrogation.

"Men and women?"

"No, only the men were killed. When it got dark, the police came and abducted the beautiful women and girls. Those who protested were bayoneted, their legs were cut, even the ribs of pregnant women were broken ..."

There was great commotion in the hall. Mrs. Christine [Terzibashian] looked up and yelled in a trembling voice:

"I confirm this under oath ..."

The stunned judge contained himself.

"How were you saved?"

"They killed my brother. When my mother saw that, she collapsed and died. Then a Turk wanted to take me as his woman. I resisted and my son was killed ..."

"How were you saved?" yelled the judge, with a clear desire to stop the nightmare.

"I noticed some smoke at a distance [and went there]. I saw my brother's wife who had just gone into labor. They drove us to Samsek. The woman stayed there ..."

"How many were left?"

"Approximately 600 people."

"And from your family?"

"My father, my two brothers, and I."

"So you remained in Samsek?" he asked coldly.

"Yes! My father got sick there, and they took him away. Although my brother managed to bring him back, he died in the evening ..."

"And your two brothers?"

"They are alive ..."

Looking back, the judge took a deep breath.

"Is this all reality or imagination?"

"The reality is much worse than what I have related."

"Did you stay in Samsek?"

Adolph Von Gordon.

"No, they drove us to Sarouch [Sourouch] ..."

"Well," interrupted the judge, who regretted his question, "Who was responsible for that catastrophe?"

"Everything was done by the order of Enver Pasha. The soldiers made us kneel and pray for his prosperity for sparing our lives ..."

Those words caused new consternation and emotional outrage in the public gallery, thus interrupting the woman. Defense attorney Niemeyer now continued.

"It is clear from the apparent commotion that what the witness said seems unbelievable. But we have thousands of such reports at our disposal. However, in order not to cast the slightest doubt on the credibility of the witness, I will now ask that the two well-informed experts, Professor Dr. Lepsius and the honorable Liman von Sanders, are questioned about the Turkish police and military during that time."

Dr. Johannes Lepsius was in his sixties, with a beautiful forehead, shortsighted blue eyes, a childish mouth, a greyish short beard, and plump, stern cheeks. The memory of his efforts and appeals [on behalf of Armenians] was still very fresh, and the gratitude of the Armenians to the German patriot was very great. During the massacres, he published, *Bericht über die Lage des Armenischen Volkes in der Türkei* [1916], which became the first major publication about the atrocities. German censorship spared no effort to limit the distribution of this book and did everything in its power to ensure that public opinion about the Turks in the German press was not "stained." During the entire duration of the war, the German press had no right to mention a single word about the events [concerning Armenians]. Under these conditions, the persecuted Armenophile, Dr. Lepsius, spent his days abroad on charity and relief work. He then published the above title in a completed form, *Der Todesgang des Armenischen Volkes*. He thus did great service towards telling the truth by publicizing, immediately after the armistice, many documents the German Foreign Ministry possessed on the deportations and massacres [of Armenians]. Now, he began his testimony, turning his blue eyes, through his sharp glasses, on the judge.

"The general deportation was decided by the Committee of the Young Turks headed by Talaat and Enver Pashas, who implemented the decision with the help of the Young Turks.

"The deportation of April 1915 affected all Armenians in Turkey, with very few exceptions that I will mention later. Before the war, there were only 1,850,000 Armenians in Turkey. There is no exact census of Turkey. This number is determined by the available statistical information, which corresponds with the census of the Armenian Patriarchate. Before the war, the Armenian population was spread in European Turkey (Constantinople, Adrianople, Rodosto) and Asiatic Turkey (Anatolia, Cilicia, Northern Assyria, Mesopotamia). The majority of Armenians lived in Eastern Anatolia, on the Armenian

Dr. Johannes Lepsius.

Highlands, in the ancient homeland of the Armenian nation, in six vilayets [provinces]: Garin, Van, Paghesh, Diyarbekir, Sepasdia and Kharpert. In western Anatolia, facing Constantinople, on the southern shores of the Marmara, also lived a large fragment of the Armenian nation. In southern Anatolia was Cilicia, with the Taurus plains, and the northern Assyrian countries bordering the Gulf of Alexandretta, part of the ancient Armenian homeland."

Lepsius lowered his glasses and wiped them while blinking his tired eyes.

"The entire Armenian population of Anatolia was deported by order of the highest rank to the northern and eastern edges of the Mesopotamian desert: Der Zor, Raqqa, Meskene, Ras-ul-Ain, all the way to Mosul. Approximately 1,400,000 Armenians were displaced," he said, as he put on his glasses again, and raised his voice.

"What does this mean? The decree signed by Talaat stated, 'The purpose of deportation is annihilation.' And according to this decree, the task was implemented. Ten percent of the population deported from the eastern provinces to the south arrived in the resettlement zone. The remaining 90% were killed along the way. The women and girls were kidnapped by the police and Kurds, while others died of starvation and exhaustion. Thousands of Armenians, driven from Western Anatolia, Cilicia, and northern Syria, gradually gathered in concentration camps of thousands at the edges of the desert. These were then largely annihilated by systematic famines and massacres. When the concentration camps were filled with new arrivals and there was no room left, they were led into the desert in groups and slaughtered. The Turks say they adopted the idea of concentration camps from the British, who concentrated the Boers in South Africa. It was officially announced that the deportations were precautionary measures, but individual men of authority openly announced that the purpose of deportations was to exterminate the Armenian people. My words are derived from documents I published after gathering them from the records of the [German] Imperial Embassy and the Ministry of Foreign Affairs, in particular the reports of German consuls and the German ambassadors to Constantinople."

Lepsius took out his handkerchief, wiped his forehead, and continued with his thoughts:

"You heard here an account of the suffering of Mrs. Terzibashian during the deportation. Hundreds of such detailed reports, all bearing the imprint of personal experiences, have been published, mostly in German, but also in American and British publications. The realities are undeniable. The methods everywhere are similar to those related by Mrs. Terzibashian. Otherwise, the question should be, how is it possible to kill millions of people in such a short time? This was possible by the most brutal means, as was proven at the trial of Talaat Pasha and his comrades by a Military Tribunal in Constantinople. The tribunal consisted of an army commander, three generals, and a captain. The first of the five counts in the indictment concerned the massacre of Armenians. On July 6th, 1919, the military tribunal sentenced all the main culprits of the massacres to death: Talaat, Enver, Jemal, and Dr. Nazim. The execution of the order to annihilate the Armenians was passed from Constantinople to provincial, sub-provincial, and district governors, that is, to regional administrators. Officials who did not want to obey the instructions were discharged from their posts. For example, the governor of Aleppo, Jelal Pasha, refused to carry out deportation orders in his province.[*] Talaat dismissed and transferred him to Konia. Jelal Pasha took surviving Armenians there under his patronage. As a result, he was expelled from this province as well and was left without an official position. And yet, he proved to be one of the worthy and righteous governors of Turkey. Another governor, Reshid Bey, in Diyarbekir, ordered the murder of two kaimakams who refused to carry out the deportations.[†] Violence was used against the disobedient Turkish population, officials, and the military. A commander of the 3rd Army announced that whoever came to the aid of Armenians would be killed in their home and their property would be set on fire. If any officials helped Armenians, they were to be discharged of their position immediately and brought before a military court."

The court and the members of the public seemed to be frozen in the face of these unheard-of revelations. Lepsius continued:

"Out of the initial 1,850,000 Armenians, 1,400,000 were deported. So, 450,000 people were still left; of these, 200,000, who were spared from exile, were mainly the populations of Constantinople, Smyrna, and Aleppo. The German consul Rössler, who was accused of being an organizer of massacres in the conspiratorial press, played a major role in the liberation of the Armenians of Aleppo. In Smyrna, General Liman von Sanders prevented the deportation of Armenians. Von der Goltz, a field marshal, did the same. When he came to Baghdad, he learned that the Armenians of Baghdad had been exiled to Mosul and that they would be deported to the Euphrates with the Armenians of Mosul, that is, to death ... He warned the governor of Mosul that he was banning the deportation. And when the governor received a new order to organize the deportation, von der Goltz resigned. Enver Pasha was forced to give in to von der Goltz but added a note on

---

[*] The reference here is to Mehmed Jelal Bey.
[†] This reference is to the governor of Diyarbekir, Dr. Mehmed Reshid Bey, who ordered the murder of two kaimakams, Huseyin Nesimi Bey (Lije) and Sabit Bey (Beshiri or Batman).

Collage showing Tehlirian, German and Turkish officials in a
train compartment, and scenes from the Armenian Genocide.

his written order, "His position as supreme commander does not give him the right to interfere in the internal affairs of the Turkish state." The ambassadors in Constantinople prevented the deportation of Armenians in the capital. Let me make a passing remark here: we often read that the Armenian merchant class oppressed the Turks and the angry Turkish population spontaneously rose up against the Armenians. It has been proven that neither the 1895-96 massacres nor the current ones were the result of spontaneous unrest, but the application of the orders of state officials. Evidently, in trade centers like Constantinople, Smyrna, and Aleppo, the Armenian merchant class was spared death, both in the past and now, partly because they were in a position to save themselves. In contrast, the entire Anatolian [Armenian] peasant class, who made up 80 per cent of Armenians, along with craftsmen, who were mostly Armenians, were deported and destroyed in the desert. The rest of the Armenian population, about 250,000 people, escaped deportation because of the Russian occupation of the border provinces and refuge in the Caucasus. This was the period when the Russians advanced to the western shores of Lake Van. When they retreated, they took Armenians‎ with them, but not because they loved Armenians. Yanushkevich, the head of Nikolai Nikolayevich's officer corps, announced that Russia would settle Kurdish and Cossack communities instead of Armenians in the evacuated regions in order to form a large military zone against the Turks. The goal of the Russians was to achieve an 'Armenia without Armenians.' In any case, the Russian advance saved the lives of some 350,000 Armenians, although the Russian retreat deprived them of their homeland. These deportees still live in a very arid region of the Caucasus, subject to years of famine and distress. One has to ask oneself, how were such events historically possible? I will try to answer this question briefly.

"The Armenian Question did not sprout on its own; it was the product of European diplomacy. The Armenian nation fell victim to political rivalry between Russia and Great Britain. In the chess game between London and St. Petersburg, Armenians were the pawns who were pushed forwards and sometimes sacrificed. Humanitarian outbursts, 'Christian patronage' were excuses."

Lepsius mentioned a number of well-known historical facts; how proposals for Armenian reforms by foreign powers during the reign of Abdul Hamid were preceded and followed by the massacre of Armenians, finally leading to the annihilation of Armenians during the reign of the Young Turks.

Then, returning to the subject of deportations, he described the exile and massacres of Armenian intellectuals with great emotion.

"Talaat's personal friend, Vartkes, an Armenian member of parliament, had not yet been arrested," he said. "Vartkes went to Talaat to find out why he was being persecuted [and Talaat responded]: 'In our difficult days, you held us by our throats and raised the issue of Armenian reforms. Now, we must take advantage of our favorable situation and disperse your nation in such a way that you will not think of reforms for the next 50 years.' Vartkes commented, 'So, you want to continue the work of Abdul Hamid.' Talaat answered, 'Yes.' That threat was carried out accordingly. The trial of the Constantinople Military Tribunal, according to a report in *Journal Officiel*, revealed that the exile of Armenians was decided by the committee of the Young Turks, and that Talaat Pasha, the soul of the committee and its most influential member, had ordered the extermination. One could submit a written report on this issue based on German and Turkish documents. The point of my testimony is to clarify that political intrigues of states pushed matters so far, that, first Abdul Hamid, and later, the Young Turks, were so suspicious of Armenians, that they concluded that there was nothing left to do but exterminate them ..."

CHAPTER TEN

The Prosecutor Demands the Death Penalty

Lepsius' testimony left an overwhelming impression not only on the uninformed public, but also on the lawyers and judges. Von Gordon confessed that he did not have such a complete view of the horrific events. The public expressed its emotions in whispers. Prosecutor Gollnick rubbed his head as he leaned on papers in front of him. The jurors were still immersed in their incomplete notes. For a moment, the judge did not know what to say or do. Defense Counselor Werthauer took the opportunity to ask Dr. Lepsius a few questions.

"Why did the political games of Great Britain and Russia contribute to the annihilation of Armenians?"

"Because they instilled the fear in Turks that they [Great Britain and Russia] wanted to create an independent Armenia, and that possibility endangered the existence of Asiatic Turkey," Lepsius replied.

"We used to think that the mutual hatred of Armenians and Turks was hundreds of years old, because the former are Christian, and the latter, Muslim."

"The dream of creating a Pan-Turkish, Pan-Islamic state, with no place for Christians, were the idea of the Committee [of Union and Progress] and Enver Pasha."

"So, did they decided to annihilate Armenians, so that they [Armenians] would not gain independence like the Balkan peoples?"

"Yes, as Count Metternich, who was the German ambassador to Constantinople in 1918, wrote in his dispatch of July 30th, stating, 'The Armenian issue is over. The Young Turk pack is looking forward to the moment when Greece turns against Turkey. The Greeks constitute the civilized element of Turkey.

They must also be destroyed, just like the Armenians.' This is what Count Metternich wrote."

The judge then proceeded to the testimony of another well-informed witness of developments in Turkey, Otto Liman von Sanders. Tall, with a round face, the handsome Sanders, despite knocking on the doors of his 70s, still kept his freshness. Starting in 1913, he was the head of the military mission Emperor Wilhelm sent to Constantinople. He reorganized the Turkish army and led the conscription drive in August 1914, three months before Turkey entered the war.

"I would like to add a few words to what Dr. Lepsius said from a military point of view," said von Sanders. "In my opinion, everything that happened in Armenia called the 'Armenian massacre,' should be divided into two parts. First, the deportation order of the Young Turks. We can hold the Turkish government fully responsible for this order and only partially responsible for the consequences. Second, the battles that took place in Armenia, when Armenians turned to self-defense. They did not want to be disarmed by the Turkish government and joined forces with the Russians to fight the Turks. Naturally, those battles opened the door to massacres. I think these two elements should be differentiated. The Turkish government ordered deportations based on reports by high-ranking military and political officials that the military found it necessary to empty eastern Anatolia of Armenians."

This is what Enver had told Lespius in response to the great philanthropist's request to at least save the lives of Armenians living by the sea.

"Since mistaken and inaccurate things have been said against Germans," the commander continued, "I would like to emphasize here that the colonels and commanders-in-chief on the Caucasian front consisted of Turks. I have already said that these military and political officials reported to Constantinople about the situation. Because of these circumstances, the deportations were put into the worst hands. One should add that the Turkish police [gendarmes] were very good before the war. It was a 85,000 strong, select force. But they were drafted into the army and, instead, an auxiliary police force was formed, which did not consist of good elements. It included bandits and vagrants. They were the least disciplined. These were the circumstances that should be considered when discussing the unrest that took place during the displacement of Armenians. It was not the Turkish soldiers who instigated the atrocities, but a random police force which was created of necessity. It should also be noted that conditions during that period were so poor that not only Armenians but also many Turkish soldiers died of malnutrition, disease, and a lack of organization. Thousands of young soldiers died in my army during the invasion of Gallipoli. I think these things should be taken into consideration" said the commander. Then, after a pause, he continued, "Finally, we cannot ignore the fact that the forces accompanying Armenians [on deportations] were partly influenced by the idea of 'holy war,' and since Armenians were Christians, it was thought a good thing to be strict with them. The lower officials might have made this sentiment worse. Anyhow, the Kurds, who were the enemies of the Armenians, always attacked and massacred them ..."

The commander pulled a silk handkerchief out of his pocket, wiped his wide forehead, and tried to loosen his collar with his fingers. He then continued:

"As far as I know, the German government did everything possible to alleviate the suffering of Armenians at that time, as much as they could. But it was difficult. I am especially aware of the fact that Ambassador Metternich made strong appeals to the Turkish government about its anti-Armenian rhetoric. There were many suspicions concerning our involvement, but I can say that no German officer took part in the measures taken against Armenians. On the contrary, we intervened where we could. I must stress that I never received any order signed by Talaat about Armenians. The orders I received were signed by Enver and they were minor, sometimes completely meaningless. For example, I once received an order to expel all Jews and Armenians from the officer corps. Of course, the order was not carried out, because I needed them as translators. I often received such meaningless orders."

Soghomon Tehlirian Trial. In the distance of the courtroom, the judge with two assistants. To the right, the general prosecutor. To the left, standing, the accused, Soghomon Tehlirian. In front of him, near the table, the defense attorney.

It seemed that the commander had finished his speech, and the judge even made a confirming motion, when, suddenly, Sanders recalled something important.

"In February 1916, when I received word from [Bavarian] Deputy Wilmar that the vali [governor] wanted to deport the Armenians and Jews of Adrianople, I went to Constantinople and, through my efforts, the deportation was stopped with the intervention of Count Metternich and Ambassador [Marquis Johann von] Pallavicini. Another time in Smyrna, when the vali had taken 600 Armenians out of bed at night, stuffed them in wagons, and wanted to deport them, I threatened to use armed force against his policemen if they harmed any Armenian. The vali was forced to withdraw his order. This fact is related in Dr. Lepsius' book. This is almost all that I know. I would like to emphasize that I have not been to Armenia, I have not been close to the Armenians, and the Turks have not asked me for advice on the measures taken against Armenians. On the contrary, everything was hidden from us, so that we would have no idea about internal political developments. The biggest slander of the foreign press is the allegation that we had a role in those orders. On the contrary, in accordance with our duty, we intervened where we could. There were scattered Armenians living under my jurisdiction, and the incidents I just mentioned are the only ones that involved me. I do not know to what extent Talaat was involved in the anti-Armenian orders. As far as I know, the main order for the deportation of Armenians was on May 20th, 1915. In any case, it was the result of the Committee's mentality, which then received ministerial approval. The operation, as I said, was in the hands of the governors and their subordinate officials, and most of all, the terrible police. In any case, I have to say that, during the five years I was in Turkey, I did not see a decree signed by Talaat against Armenians, nor can I testify that such a decree was issued ...

***

After Sanders' testimony, a situation arose in which it seemed that I was not the one to be judged, but Talaat and him [Sanders]. His testimony was irrelevant, devoid of inner conviction, formal and heartless and, most importantly, inaccurate, so that it had no effect on the proceedings. Not only the court, but also the intelligent public understood that an entire nation could not be destroyed by "military necessity" and it was not right to blame "lower officials" for the crimes of "higher officials." The slaughter could have been stopped if the deportations had really been implemented incorrectly. It is meaningless to express reservations about that decision and point to "bad" implementation or fictitious political developments, in which, anyhow, thousands of women and children had no part.

My lawyers were clearly disappointed with their decision to invite this expert. Von Gordon expressed that disappointment very carefully.

"Your Excellency, did you say, although not in a positive way, but you implied, that the officials responsible for the atrocities were the subordinates?"

"For the cruelty but not deportations," replied the commander.

"The honorable Liman von Sanders has disturbed our conscience," von Gordon told the judge. "He said that Talaat Pasha was not responsible for the unrest, but for the disorderly bodies entrusted with the execution of deportation orders." That is the exact opposite of the common understanding among Armenians, and in particular, what Dr. Lepsius believes. I consider it my duty to present here five telegrams received from the vice-governor's office in Aleppo ..."

Von Gordon made a nervous gesture towards the judge, stood up, and said:

"I would like to read two of these telegrams here. Professor Lepsius has examined them ..."

"It would be anticipating [or getting ahead of] the evidence, if you read those telegrams now," the judge interrupted him.

"But I must disclose their content," von Gordon said excitedly, and continued without permission. "The telegrams confirm that Talaat personally gave the order to destroy all Armenians, including children. It was previously ordered to only spare children who would not remember their parents. Then, in March 1916, the order was revoked, as children were considered to be harmful to Turkey. The accuracy of these telegrams can be attested to by the man of letters, Aram Andonian, who received them from the office of the vice-governor of Aleppo after the British occupation and provided them to the Armenian delegation."

But von Gordon was not concerned with exposing the bitter realities, but the need to protect me.

"Personally, I consider it possible, even probable, that the jurors believe the defendant, that he had been convinced, with firm conviction and not without good reason, to the depths of his heart, that Talaat was the instigator and man responsible for the horrendous atrocities against Armenians. If there is such conviction among the jury, then I can forego reading the telegrams."

This was how he introduced the moral foundations of the defense.

"Please reject that offer," Prosecutor Gollnick intervened sternly. "The honorable judge has allowed a great deal of discussion about Talaat's personality. No one doubts that the defendant was convinced of Talaat's guilt concerning the atrocities. This clearly explains his motive. However, it is impossible for this court to pass judgment on Talaat's [actual] guilt. In such a case, we would have to make a historic decision, for which we would need different materials to consider."

In general, although von Gordon was satisfied, the tension did not subside quickly. Defense attorney Niemeyer pointed out that Talaat was a senior government official, the Grand Vizier, and the representative of the state, who was responsible for everything. It was impossible to think otherwise ...

The judge then turned to the reports of medical experts who had examined me separately in prison. One of them, Dr. Robert Störmer, the privy medical counselor to the court, was a 60-year-old dry, straight-talking man, who diagnosed my fainting spells as epileptic fits caused by psychological reasons linked to a nervous disorder. This illness, he argued, instead of alleviating my condition, actually aggravated it.

Soghomon Tehlirian's defense attorneys
Dr. Werthauer (left) and Prof. Niemayer (right).

"One of the characteristics [of this disorder] is mental perseverance and tenacity of will, which is usually very rare," he said. Logical perception and detailed planning before action are hallmarks of this illness. In any case, such patients, regardless of any obstacles, carry out what they have in mind. This is why the defendant did not shy away from the difficulties of finding his hated enemy and pondering how he could carry out his plan in the most expedient way. When the watch from his room is over, he takes the weapon and runs out. He carefully examines the clothing [of his target] and strikes at the spot between the hat and the coat. In this I see the implementation of a very well-prepared plan."

Störmer did not deny that the "horrific events" in Armenia had a profound effect on my psyche, but they did not affect my ability to freely decide and act, for which I was responsible in accordance with the law.

Prof. Liepmann presented another point of view.

"From the very beginning, I must say, the defendant has been a man of rare sincerity and has not given false impressions about himself," he said. "He is still very reserved. There is a kind of resignation in him, as he made it clear; whatever happens, let it be so. He is no longer interested in life. All this did not come from him, he had to constantly dig and pull it out. It is quite clear that we are not dealing with a madman here, and his action did not take place in a state of mental darkness. The problem here is mental turmoil and an 'overwhelming thought.'"

Liepmann explained that that thought was created by a sensitive temperament exposed to severe psychological trauma. The overpowering idea is embedded in this kind of character and gradually dominates them, always present, always acting and oppressing the person to submit to its authority.

And then, he explained how I succumbed to that idea.

"The reason for this overwhelming thought is the internal need for revenge born as a result of the murder of his mother, relatives, compatriots. Once under the control of this thought, and against his will and desire, he could not get rid of its oppressive influence."

On that basis, Liepmann considered that I was not in full control of my mental faculties at the time of the murder. He summed up his report by calling it "emotional epilepsy."

Professor Cassirer, whom I had seen before the incident, came up with new facts to confirm Liepmann's view. The same view was held by two other medical experts, Bruno Haake and Professor Edmund Forster. The last two were even willing to consider that I had committed the murder out of complete lack of free will ...

The day passed. The continuation of the trial was postponed for the next day. After my contacts with the outside world, my desire for freedom intensified as if I were in prison for the first time. I was trying to recall, to compare the pros and cons of the day, and to draw conclusions about the probable outcome of the trial. The hope of survival was getting stronger in me. Lepsius' report, in particular, was a source of great moral satisfaction. He clarified everything that I was thinking of saying during my first interrogation, about three months earlier ...

I saw my mother in my dream that night. It was as if I were passing through a boundless desert, and on all sides in the endless desert, piles of sand dunes were scattered like petrified waves of the sea. And I followed human footprints, which sometimes appeared and sometimes disappeared. Suddenly I saw my mother in rags, lying on the ground in the sand, staring at me. I rushed forward to pick her up.

"No, my son, I'm dead, it's no use, go home," she said wearily. "But do you see what they have done to me? Not even a handful of soil on me. It is very cold at night, I am cold, especially my sides."

"Wait, mother, I'll cover you well."

"Yes, cover me, my child, cover ..."

And I carefully covered her bare feet with sand, her almost bare ribs and chest, and when I got to her head, she said:

"No, my son, let my head be open, so that I can breathe ... now it is good. Thank you very much. Now, go home ..."

***

The trial resumed in the morning in front of a larger crowd. More people were left standing today. The upper floor was occupied by judicial and other officials, as well as notables.

At the beginning of the session, Dr. Lemberg announced that the factual part of the trial had been exhausted and he formulated the following three questions for the jurors to consider:

"1- Is defendant Soghomon Tehlirian guilty of deliberately killing Talaat Pasha on March 15th, 1921 in Charlottenburg?" He clarified that the question referred to unintentional murder. The next question was formulated as follows:

"2 - Did the defendant commit the murder intentionally?" This question should have been answered if the first one had been answered in the affirmative.

Finally, if the first question was answered in the affirmative and the second in the negative, it was necessary to specify:

"3 - Are there any mitigating factors?"

He then added, "The matter now belongs to Prosecutor Gollnick."

"O jurors!" Gollnick began, "It is not the legal side of the present criminal case that gives exceptional significance to this case" and explained the intense interest, "which is noticeable not only in the courtroom, but also in our country and even abroad.

The reason is different. The case covers the psychological aspects of the World War. It touches on the brutal, bloody events in faraway Asia Minor, and we seem to hear again the thunder of the general war. Another reason for the significance of the incident is the identity of the victim. An anonymous hand rose from the masses and brought down a man who had held the destiny of his country during difficult days in the struggle of nations, a man who had been the ally of the German nation, and a man who was highly honored and exalted."

He cleared his throat with a light cough and continued, leaning forward a little:

"First, the following question must be clarified: 'Was the incident intentional or unintentional?' When I ask myself about it, another question naturally arises: 'What were the reasons for the defendant to take that measure?' There is no doubt that we are dealing with a political assassination. The motive of the defendant was political hatred, political malice. Here you have heard many things that happened in distant places. There is no doubt that terrible things have happened, terrible things have happened to the Armenian people, and there is no doubt that terrible things have happened to the defendant's family. Fate has hit him hard to the core, as all his relatives have been put to death. And so was the idea of revenge born. There is no doubt that the defendant saw Talaat as the perpetrator of the fate that befell him, his family, and many of his compatriots. Talaat was seen not only as the Minister of Interior, who bears formal responsibility for everything that happened during his tenure, but also as the actual and moral perpetrator of the crimes mentioned.

"Gentlemen," cried Gollnick, raising his voice, "the determination of these motives is enough to judge Tehlirian's action from a punitive-legal point of view. But the interrogation of witnesses also extended to the question of whether Talaat Pasha was really the actual and moral perpetrator of the crimes. In my opinion, in order to judge the act from a criminal-legal point of view, it does not matter whether he was, or was not, the perpetrator. Nevertheless, I have to address these issues as they became the subject of the interrogation of witnesses. It is beyond doubt and confirmed by the testimony of witnesses that

Armenians and their friends are convinced that Talaat Pasha organized the Armenian horrors. However, gentlemen, this is a biased view, and it would have been easy to bring here a range of witnesses who would have come up with a completely different view of what happened. I have spoken with many Germans who were in Turkey and witnessed the events very closely. They have a completely different understanding. They said that it was an irrefutable fact that the Constantinople government had decided to exterminate the Armenians, perhaps because state and military concerns about self-defense had prompted the deportation order, which, in any case, had extreme consequences.

The judge interrupted this complicated assurance, asking him not to dwell on issues that were not the subject of the interrogation of witnesses.

"I can use that right, as much as there is a difference in the views of the experts. In my opinion, the information provided by Dr. Lepsius, as interesting as it is, has the weakness of giving events a very systematic and planned nature. It is not difficult to see that Dr. Lepsius came to this conclusion not on the spot, from personal experience, at the time of the events, but from information he had received later. That is why I think I have the right to give more weight to the justifications of General Liman von Sanders, who had a high official position at the time, was well aware of the events, and mentioned the differences between the Constantinople government's deportation orders and the manner in which those orders were carried out. The government of Constantinople had information that the Armenians were planning to betray [their country], that they were conspiring with the allied states against the Turks, and that they had decided to attack the Turks from behind at an opportune moment in the war in order to claim their independence. The Constantinople government, concerned for the well-being of the state and military, found it necessary to deport Armenians. As for the manner of deportations, one must keep in mind, gentlemen, that Asia Minor is not a country that has the special conditions enjoyed by civilized peoples ..."

Here Gollnick thought for a moment that he might have offended the memory of the defendant with an unpleasant remark, and added:

"I want to be careful in my expressions. I have in mind those conditions which we enjoyed before the war. Traditions are brutal and bloodthirsty in Asia Minor. One of the experts already said that there was a 'holy war' declared, and when the people of another race and religion saw how the Turks expelled Armenians everywhere to concentrate them elsewhere, that naturally became a signal to attack the Armenians. And thus, the ugliest instincts of human nature came to the fore: plunder, murder, and so on. The expert also pointed out that the gendarmes who were called to duty were no longer the former elite soldiers, but vagabonds gathered without proper examination, who later carried out the known murders on their own initiative.

Gollnick at the time was like other naive Europeans who are easily persuaded by whimsical and convenient interpretations of what happens in distant, unfamiliar countries, as they are influenced by "reasonable" explanations. In any case, he continued:

"On these grounds, I must say that the interrogation of witnesses does not entitle me to say that 'it has been proven that Talaat Pasha is the person who is personally and morally responsible for the horrors committed.' Similarly, I cannot be distracted by documents that were offered for presentation here. As a prosecutor, I know how, for example, during the turmoil of the revolution in our country, such documents were published with the signatures of important people; documents, which, as it later turned out, were forged. Finally, I cannot be pushed into a misunderstanding by the verdict, which was mentioned here, against Talaat Pasha in Constantinople. I do not know how much the objective truth is clarified there. It may be so, but it is well known that after the overthrow of any former political regime, former accomplices are considered criminals. And the change that took place in Turkey in those days was more than brutal. The government of the Young Turks, a friend of Central European states, was removed and replaced by another, which was forced to fall into line with the enemies of those states, the allied countries.

Therefore, we cannot understand whether the objective truth was established during that trial.

"Let me go back to the killing," Gollnick continued, looking at his notes. "It is clear to me that the defendant was convinced that the main perpetrator of the massacres was Talaat. Gentlemen, this is undoubtedly not a dishonest reason, given the scale of the crimes. It is a motivation that can and will be understood humanely if there are people capable of loving and hating. And when there is a question whether the defendant acted with premeditation, it turns out that he did. If you look at how the defendant, after seeing his paternal home in ruins in Yerznga, travels across Europe to Berlin, it turns out that he is imbued with the raging, cold-blooded idea of revenge. He seems to be pulled magnetically to the door of the house where the victim lives. Thus, the statement he made during his first interrogation is completely true. He said, 'Seeing the ruins of my parents' house, I adopted the idea of revenge, which I decided to carry out. That's when I bought the gun.' Then, we see how the defendant, with some planning and consideration, turns to the implementation of his plan. We see how he leaves his former apartment, how he is able to reason with his health condition, how he manages to find a new apartment across Talaat Pasha's residence, how he watches and checks when Talaat Pasha leaves the house, how he runs after him with a gun on March 15th, and then, how he gets ahead of him to check his identity. Then, passing by him, he deals the deadly blow from behind. The aim was so well taken that death was instantaneous."

Gollnick was prophetically right in this case.

"Gentlemen," he said, looking at the jurors, "we see that the defendant was acting in a cold-blooded manner and planning everything. After the murder, he threw the gun away, and tried to escape. And when he was caught and beaten, he shouted, 'Neither the victim nor I are Germans. You Germans have no reason to worry.' Gentlemen, considering all these circumstances, everyone will conclude that the murder was committed in a premeditated, ruthless, and deliberate manner. This is also the defendant's temperament; he is not a hotheaded or impetuous person. On the contrary, he is a reserved, calm, and melancholic person. He is not

Yugoslavia, 1921. *(First row, left to right)* Soghomon's maternal uncle's daughter, and brother Misak's daughter Armenouhi. *(Second row, seated)* Uncle Oskian, Soghomon's father Khachadour, paternal uncle Asadour. *(Third row, standing)* Mihran Der Ghazarian (Armenouhi's husband), paternal uncle's son, Nerses, brother Setrag and Soghomon.

one who gives himself to entertainment and laughter, or erupts in anger, but someone who mulls over things, and pursues his thoughts and ideas. I think we can say that the main facts of premeditated murder have been objectively verified. But that is not enough to punish the defendant. It is necessary to examine whether there are any circumstances that make the act unpunishable. And this is where Article 51 of the criminal code comes in, according to which, there is no punishable act if a culprit has carried out an act without awareness of what they were doing, or suffered from mental illness that precluded the exercise of free will at the time of such an act. The question now is whether these circumstances apply to the case of the defendant. It is self-evident that if all the experts say the same thing, the court will naturally follow their point of view. Unfortunately, we do not have such a unanimous opinion of experts here, so the court is forced to decide for itself whether the provisions of Article 51 are applicable in this case or not. It is therefore necessary to examine the personality of the defendant, as he showed himself during the trial. I think he left such an impression that one could say that he is perfectly normal mentally, his answers are confident, and always to the point.

"His personality is revealed to us in the course of his life, as far as we know, since he lived like other young people. He visits his relatives and compatriots, takes language and dance lessons, and his landlords describe him as a calm and decent man. Thus, we see that he is in a fairly normal state, apart from the moments of epilepsy. That is why I think it is necessary to join the opinion of those experts who reject the application of Article 51."

Dr. Gollnick thought for a moment before concluding. Apparently, it was not so easy for him to reconcile the human dimension with the provisions of the law and added:

"Gentlemen, our basic law does not recognize mitigating circumstances in the case of premeditated murder, and I can understand that it will seem harsh to some if I have to demand that the defendant be found guilty of premeditated murder. But, gentlemen, we must not only consider the defendant, but also the victim. It should be considered that a man in his best years was deprived of his life, whose widow and relatives mourn his death, and who, at least among his compatriots and co-religionists, enjoyed the reputation of a great patriot and honorable person. And finally, gentlemen, the great range of factors which were presented here in favor of the defendant, in accordance with our basic law, will certainly be taken into account by the highest institution that grants pardons. Therefore, Mr. Jurors, I propose to give a positive answer to the questions presented to you, to find the defendant guilty of premeditated murder."

It was not possible to defend Talaat's case any better ...

CHAPTER ELEVEN

No, He is Not Guilty

Prior to this period, I never realized my motivation to kill Talaat with such clarity. I was never concerned in the slightest about defending myself, let alone what was now happening in court.

Von Gordon spoke first on behalf of the defense.

"Gentlemen Jurors, Mr. Prosecutor mentioned that, even if you found the defendant, Tehlirian, guilty, and thus gave grounds for him to be sentenced to death, the evil would not be great because the President of the Republic would either mitigate the sentence or pardon him.

"This is not a permissible way to influence you. If you find the defendant guilty, he will be sentenced to death, and none of us knows what decision the German president will take regarding a pardon. Here, we only have to decide what is right and not show the path to pardon. I would welcome the Chief Prosecutor as a defense lawyer, but he does not speak in defense of Tehlirian when he makes such comments, but on behalf of Talaat Pasha, based on, unfortunately, facts reported to him by others.

"Gentlemen, I consciously avoid that type of defense. I have a whole arsenal of telegrams, and there is a witness sitting there who can confirm their authenticity. I submitted to read those telegrams here but withdrew them because it is enough for us to know that Tehlirian, as in the case of all of his compatriots, was convinced that Talaat was responsible for all of the horrors that took place, as I am sure you do too. The simple and indisputable fact is that 1,400,000 out of 1,800,000 Armenians were deported and one million of them were killed. I would like to ask everyone to consider whether such a massacre could have been possible without systematic leadership and planning. Was the Turkish government really powerless to take measures against this drawn-out catastrophe? Can you believe that?"

Von Gordon then brought his hands together for a moment and looked at the jurors under oath, as if waiting for answers to his questions. He then added with a slight pain in his voice:

"A few days ago, a crude booklet, entitled, *The Secret of Talaat Pasha's Assassination*, was published here by some opponents. One can presume that a large state is hiding behind the venture. 'The young Armenian,' the booklet states, 'who undertook to kill Talaat Pasha, is an instrument of barbaric fanaticism, a characteristic of his race. His touching story of how Turks dragged his parents away naturally only aims at arousing the sympathies of judges.'

"Needless to say, there is no secret concerning the killing, and if the author of that booklet was here yesterday and heard Mrs. Terzibashian's account, they probably would have left with a desperate need to withdraw their words. We wanted to bring more evidence in this respect. We have with us two sisters from a German relief organization who were in Yerznga during the deportations and reported what they saw to our Ministry of Foreign Affairs.[*] However, I decided not to question them because Mrs. Terzibashian's testimony was enough. I do not intend to recall those horrible scenes here. I will only say that the defendant was under the spell of those horrors when he returned to Yerznga during the Russian advance, hoping that someone from his large family might have survived. He came and saw his homeland half-destroyed. There was still much to remember about his loved ones, with whom he had lived and spent his childhood. Yes, there was so much that reminded him of his once-existent hearth. When he saw his orphaned and desolate house, and imagined the horrible scenes of the massacres, this healthy, vigorous man fainted and collapsed to the ground. What had he seen in Yerznga? Of 20,000 Armenians, there only remained one Islamized family and several individuals. Only twenty people, out of twenty thousand Armenians."

Von Gordon spoke, picking his words carefully, one by one. Then, suddenly, he exploded: "Gentlemen, these are impressions

---

[*] The reference here is probably to Thora Wedel-Jarlsberg and Eva Elvers.

that one cannot forget until one's death ... yet, it is interesting that our client, according to testimonies, remained very reserved and reticent to talk about them. Indeed, those who have such infinitely deep experiences do not speak of them with pleasure. Tehlirian hardly spoke about those events. 'I have no homeland, my relatives have been killed,' he told his teacher when asked in his class. 'Let go, for the love of your God, let us not open the old wounds,' he said to his friend Apelian while reading Dr. Lepsius' book.

"Gentlemen, you do not see here the man who clings to those bloody events, but one who tries to avoid them. And then, suddenly, there is a twist. He accidentally meets people who speak Turkish, and the one they call 'Pasha' happens to be Talaat. It is not difficult to imagine the shock he experiences. We know the rest.

"This is the man in question, and I, in turn, want to legally answer the question of how his actions should be judged. First of all, was it a premeditated act? In the eighth volume of its rulings, the Supreme Court points out the differences between our current penal code and the former Prussian one. Under the previous code, planning an act up to 14 days prior to its implementation constituted premeditation. Today, that law has changed: the Supreme Court affirms that the moment of perpetration of a crime is of paramount importance. What matters, then, is not when a decision was made, but whether it was premeditated at the time of the enactment; in this case, whether Tehlirian was free at that moment from a storm of passion, emotion, and visions. I do not want to answer that question, which, in my opinion, can be seen in what happened.

"We heard the opinion of several experts about the mental state of the defendant. Mr. Störmer, our experienced forensic pathologist but not a psychiatrist, has come to the conclusion that we are dealing with a case of physical epilepsy which, although impacts on the expression of free will, does not destroy free will. Mr. Lipmann very subtly clarified that epilepsy is not a physical state here, but the result of formidable mental duress related to the events that had taken place and the destruction of the defendant's paternal home, rendering him ill. Thus, according to Lipmann,

Tehlirian is psychologically ill, with minimal responsibility for his actions. Professor Cassirer fundamentally shared the same opinion and agreed with him.

"At the beginning of his speech, Mr. Forster, a prominent psychiatrist and professor, joined Professor Cassirer and Professor Lipmann in his conclusion. Then, based on new psychological experiments, he came to the conclusion that serious illness played a major part in the present case. 'Anyhow, I have reasonable doubts about that,' he said. Returning to the issue at hand, and proceeding from Professor Forster's doubts, I have to point out to the court that the law accepts no doubts. According to the law, it must be fully established that a given person was responsible for his actions. Even the slightest doubt, even in this case, renders the defendant completely irresponsible. Regarding the verdict, it is not enough to argue that there were no circumstances that could have undermined free will; it is necessary to prove otherwise, that is, 'This person is responsible.'

"A decision of the Supreme Court literally states, 'Free will does not apply when, as a result of a mental disorder, certain thoughts, or feelings, or external influences overpower the will so strongly that the patient's decision, through natural consideration, becomes impossible.' So, when the totality of mental factors are considered, and the whole self is the impulse behind an action, only in such a case can the responsibility for an action be attributed to the 'I' as a whole. 'If one is under the influence of an overwhelming idea, which overshadows other factors, and leads to an action, then, it is not the "I," but a sick part of such a person that performs a given action,' says the law. Departing from such premises, one must now ask: can you confidently assert that the moment the defendant saw Talaat Pasha, took his weapon, and rushed out to attack him ... he was perfectly in control of all his mental powers to make a decision of his own free will? Two of the experts say, 'No, it is impossible to say that he was responsible,' while the others are confused."

Von Gordon then turned to the jurors and said, "Gentlemen, I think these explanations are enough for you to be able to determine your position. I know some people may say that it is unfortunate that someone hosted on German soil was killed. In our time, when there are struggles everywhere, when Armenians and Turks are still fighting, it is necessary to come to terms with what happened. Everyone has an understanding that during Talaat's government a sea of blood was spilled and at least one million men, women, children, old and young, perished. If one more drop of blood was added to it on Hardenberg Street, we should understand that we live in terrible times. I have no intention of making a final pronouncement here about Talaat the man, but I have one thing to say: he, along with many of his friends, was willing to exterminate the Armenian people in order to create a large, purely Turkish state. Of course, he used measures that are intolerable for us Europeans, but when it is said that life in Asia is not valued and such horrors are understandable, one should not forget that it is in Asia that Buddhists live, who treat man and even animals with special care. However, I do not want to hold the person now buried in the ground responsible. He deserves what two genius Frenchmen, Gustave Le Bon and Henri Barbusse, have said about the horrors of the Great War: 'Behind certain figures are spirits, demons, who rule over them. They are just instruments of right or wrong ideas and stimuli that are thrown in front of people back and forth like chess pieces. They think they have free will, but in reality, they work under other pressures.' No matter the horrors of what happened, we should not be so timid as to wrap everything around the necks of unfortunate individuals. It will be even more horrible if the German court casually accepts the injustice of condemning the defendant in the same manner, given the unparalleled fate suffered by him.

***

Von Gordon seemed to be bargaining. He wanted to save me by any means possible. His formal interpretation of the law, however, was not the same interpretation he had argued at the beginning of his speech.

Dr. Werthauer's defense was based on other premises. His voice, at first, sounded soft and smooth, with a refreshing inner strength that seemed to sway the audience. However, little by little, a dominant theme developed in that voice, whose main thrust concerned real justice.

"O jurors," he said, "in the form given to you, you have to provide an answer concerning the killing [of Talaat]. You will have to respond 'yes' or 'no.' That is the issue we are examining here. I am sure you will respond negatively to the question whether the killing was premeditated, and I will not speak about it. I will only talk about whether you will answer 'yes' or 'no' to the question regarding the killing. The [judge's] questionnaire already gives us a definite 'no' because it does not ask, 'Did the defendant kill Talaat Pasha?' but 'Is the defendant guilty of killing Talaat Pasha?' Everyone feels that the defendant will be released. The unfortunate thing is that you may be wondering, since the defendant has killed a man, does not the law require that we convict him? I must say that this conclusion is wrong from the point of view of the same law. According to our German law, you must acquit the defendant. What everyone feels here in this room for the present case is coincidentally the same as required by law. The defense has no intention of tarnishing the reputation of German law, represented by you and us, with an unjust verdict. The whole world is watching us, and your decision will be a verdict that may have legal significance even thousands of years later.

"Our penal code has general and specific sections. An article in the latter states: 'A person who kills another person intentionally, etc., is considered guilty of murder,' but the general part [of the penal code] refers to each individual case separately. Article 51 instructs that in some cases there can be no punishment, even if a crime has been committed according to other parts of the law, i.e., theft, murder, etc.

"This is the article that deals with the mental and psychological state of a perpetrator. The subject of self-defense, which means resisting an attack, is covered two articles later. The third part of the same article states that, even if the necessity of forced self-defense does not exist, a given person, overwhelmed with fear and panic, may still act in forced self-defense and remain free from punishment.

"Regarding the first issue, the ruling of the Supreme Court maintains that diminished responsibility negates the basis of punishment of an accused person for an alleged crime. If there is a case for diminished responsibility, the defendant cannot be subject to a ruling under Article 51. It is not enough to say that there is no basis to accept diminished responsibility. It has to be actually established that there were no negative circumstances that could have impacted on the defendant at the time of committing a crime. If there are any doubts in this regard, then the defendant has to be acquitted. This is the point that Dr. von Gordon explained earlier about the loss of free will and the complete Self. I would like to add one more thing. There is an old saying, for thousands of years, of 'one's head spinning.' In such cases, one's free consciousness is disturbed. In such states, one does what one would not normally do under any other circumstances. Let me recall one decision of the Supreme Court. An argumentative individual goes to church. The priest preaches on a subject that is completely contrary to that person's opinion. He listens more and more attentively. He becomes furious and then forgets himself to such an extent that he shouts out loud, 'Shut up! You are lying!' That person is taken to court for disrupting the church service. However, he is released without charges because he was influenced by what the priest had said, his consciousness had been disturbed at the moment he shouted, and he was no longer the master of his will."

Dr. Werthauer seemed to only notice the jurors and his words seemed to focus on one of them.

"Now, everything that was said about the defendant at the moment of the killing can be stated in a few points. Objectively, if you want to judge the will, disposition, and state of mind of the defendant at the moment he carried out his actions, you have to consider that he is a man from the more hot-blooded southern nations and not the more cold-blooded northern ones. Also, keep in mind that, as Mr. Prosecutor said, he comes from a much more bloody background. It is well known that wherever the Turks have set foot, they have carried their bloody flag with them. In 1683, we saw them at the gates of Vienna. Had they reached there, there would not have been much left of Germany.

"There is some bloody tradition among those southern nations, not only Turks, but also Armenians. The fact that Armenians and Turks are officially at war [today] is objectively connected with this. Wherever these two nations meet, they act as enemies and consider it their right to come face to face as warriors. When the defendant said to those who beat him immediately after the incident, 'I am Armenian, he's a Turk, this doesn't concern you,' he should have added, 'Besides, we face each other and live with war and vengeful mentality.' Then you also heard here that Talaat was sentenced to death. Verdicts are either accepted or denied. If we do not recognize other court's judgment, we cannot demand that others recognize our judgment. Talaat was sentenced to death by a military tribunal. I am not at all a friend of military or war tribunals. But wherever there are wars and military tribunals, there are undoubtedly decent judges who make the right decisions. I have no doubt that the high-ranking and educated judges, who carefully examined and tried the criminals of Constantinople, also gave a correct and fair verdict," he concluded.

The prosecutor shrugged his shoulders in displeasure and wrote down some notes. Dr. Werthauer continued:

"It is inadmissible to say that the verdict was made under the pressure of British naval cannons. I have never heard British judges using that approach to influence court proceedings. You can say whatever you want about Great Britain, but British justice has set an example for all times and countries. It would be correct to investigate the reasons for the sentence meted out and you will see that the Armenian massacres, together with four other charges, were determined accordingly and the convicted defendants were sentenced to death. The death penalty in the case of one of the convicts, who was in Constantinople, was carried out. I personally oppose the death penalty as well as murder. However, after that death sentence was passed, Talaat was forced to flee abroad and hide under a false name so that his sentence would not be carried out. I have no doubts about the fairness of that decision. I find it very clear that Talaat was guilty of wrongdoing and that verdict had an impact on every Armenian. Every just and thoughtful person should have thought, 'That man is sentenced to death, he must have committed those crimes, therefore he deserves the death penalty,'" he concluded.

"Finally, everything related to forced self-defense must be considered. These people, Enver and Talaat, lived in Germany under false names. It was said that they were the 'guests' of Germany. I will resolutely reject this. I do not believe that the German government allowed such criminals who fled their homeland to hide here as 'guests' under false names. Talaat, of course, would soon follow Enver from here to conspire against the Armenian people again. If someone, as the liberator of his people, killed him, he was certainly guided by the horrors perpetrated by this man, the enemy of the Armenian people: a man who would massacre Armenian women and children again if he were to leave Germany. In a broad sense, there is repressed and forced self-defense in the act of the accused."

It seemed that I was the only one who understood him and felt the pain of his words.

"Jurors under oath, I would not want to talk about politics in the courtroom if the prosecutor had not said a number of things in favor of Talaat. He said that 'Germany's ally' had been killed. That is not true. Talaat and the Committee were allies of the Prussian and German military governments. These people have never been allies of the German people. It is true that they overthrew the old Turkish government and remained in power for about ten years at the cost of human blood. It is true that the former German government was their ally but I can never and under no circumstances accept that Talaat and his friends are allies of the German people. Talaat could have been an honest man, but he was a member of a militant regime. One of them, who was not wearing a military uniform, yet was giving orders and brutally defending the flag of violence. The order to expel an entire nation is the most monstrous thing and can only be the product of a warmonger's brain. If, as stated here, the Young Turks Committee was convinced that the good gendarmes had been removed and only the opportunists remained, then they had no right to issue a deportation order. And if the deportations were handed over to them anyway, then they are responsible for the consequences. If the Armenians had even allied with other peoples and betrayed them, the Young Turks still knew that there were thousands of women and children who had no idea of the case, and therefore the first condition of the deportation order would have been a strict order to care for women, children, and men who had nothing to do with the 'traitors.' If I were not opposed to the death penalty, I would in any case justifiably consider it for a person who gave such an order out of 'military necessity' without taking responsibility for its consequences on the innocent. I just consider everything that is said about this 'military necessity' to be nonsense. If this or that number of people remained in separate mountain villages, it would have nothing to do with 'military necessity.'"

He then turned to the judge, held his breath, and said, gravely:

"Armenia has always aroused the appetite of oppressive nations. The people of the Armenian highlands have always been the prey of such nations. For more than 500 years, Armenia has been divided into three parts. From time immemorial, foreign tribes, one after another, have passed over Armenia like a storm. The tribes that devastated Asia, Hungary, and reached the Rhine; people like Attila [the Hun], who still remain in our memory, devastated Armenia in the most brutal way, destroying its people. It was this long-suffering artisan and farming people that the Young Turk government attacked. When we say Young Turk, we really mean the old Turk, and the old Turk is the same as the strong man, the warmonger. When the war broke out, the Young Turks' Committee thought that they could now annihilate the Armenians, because none of the great powers of the world could forbid them from doing so. This was also not the only basis of what they did. There was also religious hatred and bigotry; they wanted to massacre Christians and they hoped that citing the Qur'an would make it easier to implement the ancient Turkish ideas of forceful coercion. The Young Turks took the opportunity to exterminate the only Christian people on their far away borders. They did not dare to do that to the Armenians living in Constantinople but in distant places, with telegrams addressed to the governors, copies of which are in our hands, ordering extermination to the last man. Behold, we have before us the murder of a nation whose responsibility falls on the Young Turks Committee, and in particular, on their most influential minister, Talaat."

Casablanca, February, 1951. *(Right to left)* Soghomon; His wife, Anahid; Daughter-in-law, Alis; Sons Zaven and Shahen.

Werthauer now spoke as if the court were condemning Talaat, and he was conveying his concluding words.

"Gentleman Jurors, on the morning of March 15th, 1921, the millennial torment of his people echoed in the defendant's soul, as well as the wholesale massacres of 1915. I recall the case of Wilhelm Tell. Gessler mocks and insults the people, condemns them to slavery, and forces Tell to shoot an apple on his own son's head. Which one of the world's avowed judges would have condemned Tell if he had killed the governor with his arrow? Is there anything more human than what has been made clear, here, before our own eyes?"

He paused for a moment, as if to see whether anyone would oppose him.

"He is the avenger of one million people, an entire nation, as he faced the man responsible for the murder of that nation. He came forth as the spirit of justice against brutal force. He came as the representative of humanity against inhumanity, the representative of bright justice against dark injustice. He acted in protest against the collective oppression of the oppressed. He came in the name of one million victims, against one who, along with others, is guilty of this crime. He acted as a representative for his parents, sisters, brothers, and finally, his brother's two-and-a-half-year-old son. The Armenian nation of a thousand years, down to the youngest child, stands with him. He carries the flag of justice, humanity, and vengeance. It was with these thoughts that he threw himself against someone who had desecrated the honor of his family, ordered the destruction of all goodness, and ordered the extermination of an entire nation. Now, you sworn jurors, decide what happened at the time of the murder in his soul and mind. Just remember that all humanity is watching you ... the eyes of justice."

Werthauer dissipated all of the self-justification that had been circulated in the courtroom and outside to explain and justify the massacres by the Ittihadists. Given those arguments, the trial was increasingly becoming an illegal exercise, devoid of any moral basis.

***

Dr. Niemeyer, a professor of law at the University of Kiel, tried to explain that side of the case. He dwelled on the inner meaning of the letter of the law: the law alone, by its formal nature, cannot express justice. There is almost no understanding of a legal principle, law or article, that a person cannot defend on some logical grounds. But, there cannot be justice without an understanding of the spirit of law. There is a necessity for logic when looking at law and legal texts in terms of approaches, explanations, preparation, and instruction. But these cannot be the ultimate guide for the administration of justice. This is the point of trial by jury, which allows for the merits of a given case to be considered at the jury's own discretion, regardless of the formal rules of laws, as well as an understanding of the provisions of the law.

"The calling of jurisprudence is to understand such connections and give meaning to the dead letter of the law," he said.

"It corresponds to the meaning of life, the meaning of the state, society, human coexistence. The article of law on the basis of which you, the jurors, will give your verdict, states, 'Whoever intentionally kills a person, if he committed the killing intentionally, should be punished with death.' So, if you answer 'yes' to the question you have been given, Soghomon Tehlirian's head will fall under the ax of the executioner. But suppose, under different circumstances, someone files a lawsuit against the official executioner himself, accusing him of premeditated murder. After all, 'whoever intentionally kills a person, if he committed the murder with intent, will be punished with death.' In that case, gentlemen, you must also say 'yes.'

"Here in Berlin, 40 years ago, a law professor argued in this manner. However, in the present case, a small matter has been overlooked in the law. Many articles in the Penal Code do not explicitly state that punishment depends on lawlessness and the awareness of lawlessness. Add a few words to the recently mentioned law as follows: 'Whoever kills a person illegally ...' in that case, it is correct and in line with the realization that punishment always requires illegality. Along with this, there has to be an awareness of unlawfulness.

"In Tehlirian, that consciousness is relative and has a national characteristic. During an assessment of his awareness of what is illegal, we have to start from the premise that for Easterners, among whom Armenians should be counted even if they converted to Christianity as early as 300 AD, law, religion, and morality are the same thing.

"We heard how, during the honorable judge's questioning, when the defendant was asked whether he considered himself guilty or not, he answered 'no,' and when the honorable judge asked, 'Why do you not consider yourself guilty?' the defendant answered, 'My conscious is clear.' That is very understandable. For him, moral and legal concepts are synonymous. He cannot comprehend that what is morally right can be legally wrong. 'I killed a man, but I am not a murderer,' he said. He cannot conceive that something that is morally correct could condemn him to a death penalty. I am absolutely convinced that the defendant's clear conscience is as solid as a rock, that he has acted in accordance with the law, the real law, which is all that matters to him.

"One also has to consider the defendant's relationship to his people. Armenians are like a big family. They were once a great state. They lived in the Turkish state as a long-suffering people. In

1830, when the Greeks were liberated, then the Egyptians in the 1840s, and even later, the Danube river nations, the Bulgarians, the Romanians, the Serbs, the Montenegrins, and the Albanians, the Armenians remained patient and calm because they hoped for reforms to address their issues as well, that their lives and property would be secured, that they would have the opportunity to participate, to some extent, in their internal governance. Such was the mood with Article 61 of the Treaty of Berlin in 1878. However, there were no changes, and their condition got worse."

"In 1896, I visited Constantinople twice, and what I heard from eyewitnesses about the Armenian massacres of 1895-96 made a terrible impression on me. Then came the Sassoun massacre, the Adana massacre, and finally the 1915 deportation and general massacres. Then, on March 15th, 1921, we all know what happened. Whether we like it or not, we have to accept that this trial is not like any other trial. This trial extends outside the narrow confines of this hall and forces us to turn our gaze into the distance, connect with and try to understand other people, other conditions, and to be fair to them. We are obliged to give the verdict of the Second District Court and the Court of Jurors in such a way that reflects the essence of right, the aspirations of humanity, and the interconnectedness of this case.

"If you want to give matters such due consideration, I do not think you will condemn Soghomon Tehlirian to death. Regarding this trial, I would like you to ask yourselves what the outcome of the verdict will be: not politically or otherwise, but what will be the outcome of the verdict in terms of supreme justice and the values we hold most dear, making life bearable and dignified."

After Niemeyer's words, a real duel started between the prosecutor and my lawyers. The prosecutor was no longer addressing the dictates of the law, but the moral basis of the trial, to which all three of my defense lawyers alluded. His remarks in this respect were entirely directed against Werthauer.

"The second defense attorney," the prosecutor stated, "seems to want to divide humanity into two parts: the warmongers, from whose hearts the devil has taken away their sense of justice, humanity, and compassion, and the rest, who hold those high qualities in their souls. You know, of course, the great poet

Foreground, sitting on either side, Sebouh (left) and
Armen Garo (right). Sitting above them, Soghomon
Tehlirian. Photo taken in the United States.

Heinrich Heine. He rebelled at every opportunity against the
principles of life under the influence of Christianity and glorified
the cheerfulness of classical Greece. One of the famous critics of
the poet has said about him, 'As he got older, he saw nothing in
the world but only small Nazarenes and wealthy Greeks.' The
same thing reminds me of the division presented by the second
attorney into warmongers and non-warmongers. He can keep that
perspective, and I will resolutely present another one.

"He did not like the fact that I described the slain man as a loyal
ally of the German people. I must repeat that the Turkish people
fought shoulder to shoulder with the German people and can
definitely be described as the latter's ally. I do not consider it
honorable to deny someone's past, to some extent, no matter what
the political perspective of that individual. I must protest most
strongly that the defense attorney described the two defenders of

this Turkish policy, Enver and Talaat Pashas, in insulting terms, as criminals who had fled their homeland."

"According to Article 190 of the Penal Code," Werthauer responded, "news or controversy about a punishable act is proven when a perpetrator is legally convicted. Talaat, Enver, and Jemal pashas, as well as Dr. Nazim were convicted on June 10th, 1335, according to the Turkish calendar, by a Turkish military tribunal of eminent judges. They were convicted of committing a heinous crime of killing Armenians and killing the innocent. This verdict is legal, and it is wrong and contrary to German law to say that I commit the crime of insulting these people by calling those who are legally convicted of the most heinous crimes, criminals. It is not known to me whether those criminals who fled their homeland and lived here under false names have enjoyed such a defense of warmongers. The prosecutor also said that the Turkish people, as loyal comrade-in-arms, stood side by side with the German people. That, of course, is true, and no one has argued otherwise. But the Turkish people are not responsible for the war, just as the German people are not responsible. Talaat and Enver Pasha are not being discussed here because they declared war, but because they carried out deportations, as a result of which horrible crimes were committed against the Armenian people, crimes the likes of which are unparalleled in human history. I personally do not understand how politics can be brought into this issue. In the utter depravity of it all, all politics is irrelevant, and I cannot understand how one can even utter a word in favor of the deportation orders. Is it not true that even the German people were unjustly accused of having played their part in those events? Only the unconditional rejection of all those principles, the condemnation of such criminal orders, can ensure us the respect to which we are entitled," he concluded.

"When I later said that the warmongers were the defenders of the use of force, I did not say anything new, and I am surprised that the prosecutor accepted that as something new to him. Anyone who, like the German people, has suffered from the depraved actions of warmongers, must hate and strive to eradicate them. Warmongers are not the people: they have no homeland, no nation, no human feeling. They have only a sense of force, the purpose of which is to oppress others. The court must judge fairly and mete justice. We, the defense attorneys are not begging for mercy here; we just want the criminal law to be applied and the case for punishment in this trial is a negative one.

"This is because, at the moment when the defendant went down the street and aimed his gun at his victim, he did not act with free will; he was not the only one who went down the street: history, the millions killed, were inside him. It could be said that he was carrying in front of him the flag of honor of his whole nation, the flag of all the tortured, defiled, abandoned families."

He glared at the prosecutor's chair and turned to the jurors:

"How often have you had to judge a husband who, returning home, sees his wife's infidelity and kills her? Who would think of condemning such a person? And here? Were not all the virgins of an entire nation dishonored? The example of Heinrich Heine, which the prosecutor invoked, did not impress me at all, because I am less of a poet than Mr. Prosecutor."

The commotion in the hall interrupted him for a moment.

"The consideration of our government, the government that had allied with Talaat and Enver Pasha, had no bearing on me at all, because no one asked me or the German people about our opinions prior to concluding that alliance. The only thing that concerns me is that you do not take a wrong step, thinking that if the defendant killed someone, then he is guilty. After all, what the prosecutor wants is an answer to the following question: 'Did the defendant kill?' What we want you to ask yourself is, 'Is the defendant guilty of having killed?' We kindly ask you to listen to us regarding this matter."

The debate was over.

The judge gave the necessary instructions to the jurors under oath, explaining to them how to approach each question, and by what majority of votes they should reach their final decision. The jury then isolated itself for consultation.

My impressions of the day were so many, and the moral atmosphere around the case was so heartwarming, that any punishment would have seemed a minor issue. The jury meeting lasted for about an hour, during which I wandered in all the places where I had acquaintances, friends, and relatives. Life itself probably consists of such moments ...

The jurors appeared. One of them read in a trembling voice, holding the paper very close to his eyes:

"I testify with honor and good conscience, regarding the jury's decision, whether the defendant Soghomon Tehlirian is guilty of killing a man, Talaat Pasha, on March 15th, 1921, in Charlottenburg.

"No. Otto Reinecke, head of the Jury."

Suddenly the hall shook with thunderous applause. The judge signed the decision, asking the secretary to do the same and read, "The defendant is released, innocent of all charges."

A new, longer applause interrupted him.

"The imprisonment order against the defendant has been revoked."

German society seemed to want to make up for their mistake against me on March 15th. The judges left, but the applause and shouts of joy continued. In a moment, my compatriots and defense attorneys appeared before me. They reached out to congratulate me. I did not know what to do until my guard reminded me to go to prison. The journey was short and the release formalities took a little longer. When I found myself on the street, the crowd was still there. The enthusiasm of the public appeared more like a demonstration. In the commotion, someone took me in his arms and began to kiss me, sobbing. It was Karekin from Moush. Eftian, Apelian, Kalousdian, Zakarian pushed me towards a car with policemen standing by. As I entered the car, I saw Mrs. Stellbaum, Dittmann, and Miss Beilenson waving their handkerchiefs.

We were accompanied by more than ten cars on either side of a wide avenue. My compatriots led me to a place where the entire Armenian community had gathered ...

END

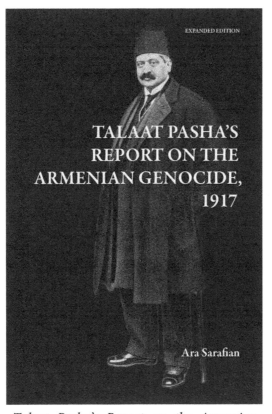

Talaat Pasha's Report on the Armenian Genocide, 1917 [expanded edition], comp, ed and intro by Ara Sarafian, (London: Gomidas Institute, 2022), ISBN 978-1-909382-72-5. Based on Ottoman statistical surveys and reports, Talaat Pasha's private papers detailed around 1,200,000 Armenians 'missing' in the Ottoman Empire circa. 1917. This work presents Talaat's core understanding of the Armenian Genocide as early as 1917.

Child Survivors of the Armenian Genocide.

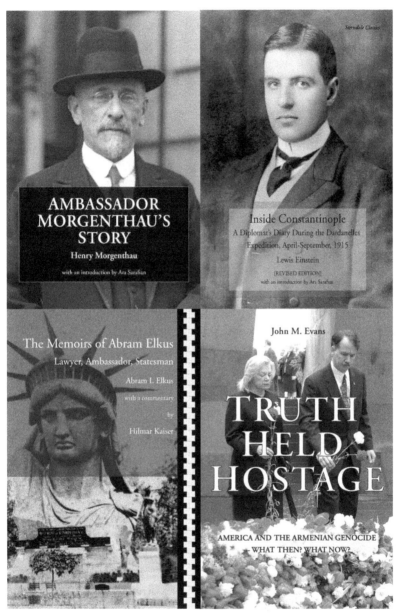

The United States and the Armenian Genocide.

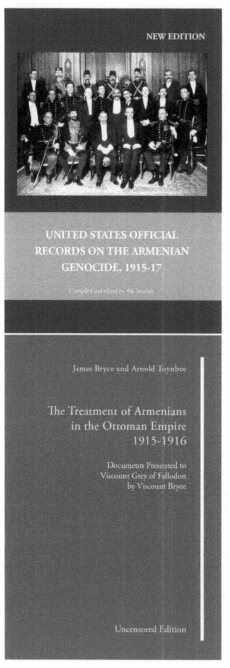

NEW EDITION

UNITED STATES OFFICIAL
RECORDS ON THE ARMENIAN
GENOCIDE, 1915-17

Compiled and edited by Ara Sarafian

James Bryce and Arnold Toynbee

The Treatment of Armenians
in the Ottoman Empire
1915-1916

Documents Presented to
Viscount Grey of Fallodon
by Viscount Bryce

Uncensored Edition

Two seminal works on the Armenian Genocide.

A systematic collection of United States consular and diplomatic reports on the Armenian Genocide, *United States Official Records on the Armenian Genocide, 1915-17.* These are among the core records that informed Henry Morgenthau, the American ambassador in Constantinople, and the United States government in Washington DC about the mass extermination of Ottoman Armenians in 1915.

The critical "uncensored edition" of the 1916 British Parliamentary Blue Book, *The Treatment of Armenians in the Ottoman Empire, 1915-1916,* was the first systematic thesis of the Armenian Genocide. It was published in 1916 and was largely based on United States consular records from the Ottoman Empire. This annotated edition is a seminal work in its own right.

Both titles published have been published by the Gomidas Institute.

Gomidas Institute
42 Blythe Rd.
London W14 0HA
England

Email: *info@gomidas.org*
Web: *www.gomidas.org*

Milton Keynes UK
Ingram Content Group UK Ltd.
UKHW022020210324
439825UK00001B/103